Auditing: A Systematic Approach

Auditing: A Systematic Approach

Edited by
Hugo Romero

www.willfordpress.com

Published by Willford Press,
118-35 Queens Blvd., Suite 400,
Forest Hills, NY 11375, USA

ISBN: 978-1-68285-819-6

Cataloging-in-Publication Data

Auditing : a systematic approach / edited by Hugo Romero.
p. cm.
Includes bibliographical references and index.
ISBN 978-1-68285-819-6
1. Auditing. 2. Accounting. 3. Financial statements. I. Romero, Hugo.
HF5667 .A83 2020
657.45--dc23

For information on all Willford Press publications
visit our website at www.willfordpress.com

Contents

Preface

This book has been an outcome of determined endeavour from a group of educationists in the field. The primary objective was to involve a broad spectrum of professionals from diverse cultural background involved in the field for developing new researches. The book not only targets students but also scholars pursuing higher research for further enhancement of the theoretical and practical applications of the subject.

A systematic and independent examination of statutory records, books, accounts documents and vouchers of an organization is known as auditing. It aims to see how far the financial statements as well as the non-financial disclosures present a fair view of the firm. It also attempts to ensure that the books of accounts are properly maintained as per the law. Different types of auditing include information technology auditing, performance auditing, quality auditing, project auditing, energy auditing, forensic auditing and operation auditing. It is done commonly in areas such as internal controls, quality management, project management, water management, and energy conservation. Different approaches, evaluations, methodologies and advanced studies on auditing have been included in this book. It also outlines the processes and applications of auditing in detail. Those in search of information to further their knowledge will be greatly assisted by this book.

It was an honour to edit such a profound book and also a challenging task to compile and examine all the relevant data for accuracy and originality. I wish to acknowledge the efforts of the contributors for submitting such brilliant and diverse chapters in the field and for endlessly working for the completion of the book. Last, but not the least; I thank my family for being a constant source of support in all my research endeavours.

Editor

An investigation of compliance with International Financial Reporting Standards by listed companies in Turkey

Volkan Demir [a] and Oğuzhan Bahadir [a,1]

[a] *Galatasaray University, Istanbul, Turkey*

Abstract: This study investigates the extent of compliance with international financial reporting standards (IFRSs) by listed companies in Turkey. Based on a sample of 168 companies we investigate the extent to which companies comply with IFRS disclosure requirements in their year - 2011 financial statements. Compliance levels range from 64 percent to 92 percent, with an average of 79 percent. The results unveil a considerable extent of non-compliance. The overall level of compliance with IFRSs disclosures is positively related to firms being audited by Big 4 auditing firms. Compliance is also negatively associated with the level of leverage. Other company characteristics, such as profitability, company size and age are determined to be statistically insignificant in explaining the level of disclosure compliance with IFRSs. The findings add to the growing concerns regarding the lack of effective monitoring in the Turkish capital market.

Keywords: IFRS implementation, IFRS compliance, disclosure checklist, company characteristics, Turkey

1. Introduction

Globalization of financial markets has accelerated the demand for more understandable and internationally comparable financial reporting. International Accounting Standards Board (IASB) was formed to develop a single set of high

---

[1] *Corresponding author:* Galatasaray University, Çırağan Caddesi, No: 36, Beşiktaş, İstanbul, Turkey; Email address: obahadir@gsu.edu.tr

quality, understandable and enforceable global accounting standards that require transparent and comparable information in general purpose financial statements. IFRSs (International Financial Financial Reporting Standards) which were issued by IASB aim to increase the consistency, transparency and comparability of financial statements. Numerous developed and developing countries have been accepted IFRSs (Demir *et al.*, 2013: 74). A major milestone towards IFRS adoption was the decision of European Commission to adopt IFRS for listed companies. In 2002, European Union approved a regulation requiring all European Union listed companies to comply with IFRSs beginning in 2005. As a result of these developments, the desired goal of internationally comparable financial reporting was almost achieved. However, companies' compiance level with IFRSs requirements is still in question.

In recent years, the issue of compliance with IFRSs has received a great deal of attention from many researchers. The extent to which companies comply with IFRSs disclosure requirements, as well as the association between the level of disclosure and company characteristics (namely; company size, leverage, profitability, company age, and audit firm size) are examined in many researches. However, the results obtained from these researches are inconsistent. For example, Dumontier and Raffournier (1998), Naser (1998), Ali *et al.* (2004), Akhtaruddin (2005), Alsaeed (2006), Al-Shammari *et al.* (2008), Hossain and Hammami (2009), Al-Shammari (2011) and Juhmani (2012) found a positive influence of company size on the level of compliance with IFRSs while Street and Bryant (2000) and Glaum and Street (2003) reported insignificant association.

This paper investigates the disclosure practices of listed companies in Turkey to see how they comply with mandatory rules established by IASB. In addition, it examines the association between company characteristics and the extent of disclosure. This study contributes to the literature by extending international accounting compliance studies in developing economies and by providing insights to compliance level of listed companies with IFRS disclosure requirements in Turkey, a code-law country with a very different cultural and institutional framework from that of common law countries.

Using a self-constructed disclosure compliance checklist, the extent of 168 listed companies' compliance with relevant IFRSs at the end of 2011 is measured. Data was collected manually from annual reports of companies which are available at web site of Istanbul Stock Exchange. The results reported that the mean level of disclosure compliance with IFRSs was 79 percent. The level of compliance was lower than that observed in developed countries such as Australia (0.94; Tower *et al.*, 1999), and Germany (0.81; Glaum & Street, 2003). This suggests that incentives for compliance are less in Turkey than in developed countries. Compared to developping countries, the level of compliance in Turkey is higher than that observed in Jordan (0.63; Naser, 1998), Bangladesh (0.44; Akhtaruddin, 2005) and Saudi Arabia (0.33; Alsaeed, 2006) but lower than that observed in Gulf Co-Operation Member States (0.82; Al-Shammari *et al.*, 2008), Kuwait (0.82; Al-Shammari, 2011) and Bahrain (0.81; Juhmani, 2012).

The association between the level of disclosure and company characteristics is analyzed using regression analysis. Results show that disclosure compliance varies by leverage and audit firm size. Leverage is negatively associated to the level of disclosure compliance with IFRSs while the level of compliance is associated with having a Big 4 auditor. Other company characteristics, such as profitability, company size and age, are found insignificant in explaining the level of disclosure compliance with IFRSs.

The remainder of the paper is organized as follows. The First section presents the corporate financial reporting environment in Turkey. The Second section reviews relevant literature and includes hypotheses. The Third section describes sample selection, data collection and statistical method. Results are reported in the Fourth section. Conclusions, limitations and suggestions for further research complete the paper.

2. The environment of corporate reporting in Turkey

The need for attracting foreign investments and the application of Turkey for full European membership require Turkey to adopt and implement IFRSs. Turkish Accounting Standards Board [1] (now Public Oversight Accounting and Auditing Standards Authority) was formed to set and issue Turkish Accounting Standards compliant with the international standards, to ensure uniformity, high quality and confidence in the area of financial reporting. Some countries adopt IFRSs as their national GAAP, while some other countries use IFRSs as guidance to develop their own accounting standards. Turkey lies in the second category. All of IFRSs were translated into Turkish and accepted as TFRSs (Turkish Financial Reporting Standards).

An important development in reference to the wider adoption and application of IFRSs in Turkey is the communiqué issued by Turkish Capital Markets Board wich mandates listed companies to present their financial statements in accordance with IFRSs since the fiscal year beginning after 1 January 2005. Furthermore, New Turkish Commercial Legislation which was legalized in 2012 and entered into force in 2013 adopted several accounting and reporting measures aimed at improving the local investment environment. These measures included the mandatory implementation of TFRSs by all companies, whether listed or non-listed, from the year beginning with January 1, 2013. According to the decision of

Public Oversight Accounting and Auditing Standards Authority, all listed companies will prepare and present their financial statements in accordance with TFRSs from the period beginning with January 2013. However, only non-listed companies with total assets of more than 150,000,000 Turkish Liras, total revenues of more than 200,000,000 Turkish liras and number of employees of more than 500 will adopt TFRSs for the year 2013. The Board plans to reduce gradually these criteria and so TFRSs will supersede Turkish GAAP and full transition to IFRSs will be achieved in the near future.

3. Literature review and hypothesis development

There are two accepted global financial reporting languages, the Unites States Generally Accepted Accounting Principles (US GAAP) and the IFRSs. Compliance with disclosure requirements of these global financial reporting languages has been measured in prior research. The majority of studies in the literature focused on the level of compliance with mandatory disclosure requirements and the association between the level of disclosure and corporate characteristics. These characteristics include size, listing status, leverage, profitability, industry, type of auditor, size of the equity market, number of shareholders, degree of economic development and culture. Evidence produced on this research area is mixed.

Malone *et al.* (1993) investigate the extent of financial disclosure of 125 oil and gas firms which are preparing their financial statements in accordance with US GAAP. Using a weighted index of disclosure items, Malone *et al.* (1993) identify a positive association between the level of information disclosure and four corporate characteristics, namely, leverage, listing status, leverage and number of shareholders. However, size, profitability and auditor type are determined to be statistically insignificant.

Dumontier and Raffournier (1998) test the association between the level of disclosure and corporate characteristics on a sample of 133 Swiss listed companies. Univariate analyses show a positive influence of size, internationality, listing status, auditor type and ownership diffusion on voluntary compliance with IFRSs. Inversely, leverage, profitability and capital intensity are found to be insignificant in explaining the level of compliance. They conclude that political costs and pressures from outside markets play a major role in the decision to apply IFRSs for Swiss listed companies.

Naser (1998) empirically examined the effect of specific financial characteristics on the comprehensiveness of disclosure in the annual reports of a sample of 54 companies in Jordan which are preparing and presenting their financial statements in accordance with IFRSs. His findings reveal that disclosure compliance improved after international standards were adopted. The empirical evidence also show that company size, leverage and return on equity are positively related to the comprehensiveness of disclosure of the sample companies. Other corporate characteristics such as industry type, audit firm size and ownership structure, however, are found to be unrelated to the level of compliance with IFRSs.

Street and Bryant (2000) examine the factors associated with the the overall level of disclosure and the level of compliance by analyzing 1998 annual reports of companies claiming to use IFRSs. Their results show that the overall level of disclosure is greater for companies with US listings. This finding supports the idea that there is a significant association between listing status and overall level of disclosure. In addition to listing status, their findings indicate that the accounting policies footnote and the audit opinion provide a better indication of the overall level of disclosure. On the other hand, overall level of disclosure is found to be unrelated to other variables including size and profitability. Following a similar methodology, Street and Gray (2001) examine compliance with IFRSs required disclosures. Like Street and Bryant (2000), Street and Gray (2001) report a significant positive association between the level of compliance with IFRSs and having a US listing.

Glaum and Street (2003) examine compliance with both IFRSs and US GAAP for companies listed on Germany's New Market. Based on a sample of 100 firms that apply IFRSs and 100 that apply US GAAP, they investigate the extent to which companies comply with IFRSs and US GAAP disclosure requirements. Their results show a considerable extent of non-compliance implying lack of effective supervision in the German capital market. Moreover, the average compliance level is significantly lower for companies that apply IFRSs as compared to companies applying US GAAP. The overall level of compliance with IFRSs and US GAAP disclosures is positively related to firms being audited by Big 5 auditing firms and to cross-listings on US exchanges while company size and company age is not significantly related to the level of compliance with IFRSs and US GAAP disclosures.

In other study, Ali *et al.* (2004) examine disclosure compliance of listed companies within the three major countries in South Asia, namely India, Pakistan and Bangladesh and evaluates the corporate attributes which influence the degree of compliance with these standards. Using a scoring system to develop a total compliance index for each sample company, the results indicate significant variation in total disclosure compliance levels across companies and different national accounting standards. Their results also support the idea that compliance levels are positively related to company size, profitability and multinational-company status. However, leverage levels and the quality of external auditors are found to be insignificant in explaining the compliance level.

In order to examine the association between company characteristics and the extent of disclosure, Akhtaruddin (2005) investigates disclosure practices of listed companies in Bangladesh. His results show that many corporate annual reports do not meet the disclosure requirements of IFRSs in Bangladesh. In addition, his analysis does not support the hypothesis that old companies will provide more information than new companies and company status has no effect on disclosure. However, he finds little support for the relationship between size and profitability and the level of disclosure.

The impact of several firm characteristics on the extent of voluntary disclosure is another research area. Alsaeed (2006) developped a disclosure checklist consisting of 20 voluntary items to assess the level of disclosure in the annual reports of non-financial Saudi firms and to empirically investigate the hypothesized impact of several firm characteristics on the extent of voluntary disclosure. His findings report low disclosure level. Further, the study revealed that large firms tend to present more voluntary information than small firms. The remaining firm characteristics (debt, ownership dispersion, company age, profit magrin, return on equity and liquidity) however, were found to be insignificant in explaining the variation of voluntary disclosure.

Al-Shammari *et al.* (2008) investigate the extent of compliance with IFRSs by companies in the Gulf Co-Operation Council (GCC) member states. They find that compliance for both measurement and disclosure increased over the period 1996-2002. Moreover, the level of mandatory compliance increases with a company's size, leverage, and internationality as suggested by the literature. Al-Shammari *et al.* (2008) also report that compliance improved in Kuwait and Oman more so than in the other GCC member states thanks to monitoring and enforcement in these countries beginning in 1999.

In a study examining the extent to which non-US firms comply with IFRS disclosure requirements in their 1999 and 2000 annual reports, Hodgdon *et al.* (2009) find that compliance improves between 1999 and 2000. Their results also reveal that auditor choice is positively related to firm compliance when controlling for unmeasured, firm-specific effects.

Hossain and Hammami (2009) studied the association between firm-specific characteristics and disclosure in Qatar. A total of 44 voluntary items developed to assess the level of disclosure in the annual reports of 25 listed firms. The findings indicate that age, size and complexity are significantly positively associated with the level of disclosure, however, profitability is found to be insignificant in explaining the variation of voluntary disclosure.

In the empirical study that examine the extent of disclosure compliance with IFRSs by 168 companies listed in the Kuwait Stock Exchange for the financial year ending in 2008, Al-Shammari (2011) reports that the mean level of disclosure compliance with IFRSs in Kuwait (0.82) is lower than that observed in developed countries. Moreover, multivariate regression analysis provides evidence that the level of compliance is associated positively with company size, age, internationality, auditor type and negatively with liquidity.

Based on a sample of firms listed in Bahrain Stock Exchange, Juhmani (2012) examines the level of compliance with mandatory IFRSs disclosure requirements and the association between the level of disclosure and corporate characteristics. His findings indicate that the level of compliance is positively and significantly associated with company size and audit firm size while profitability, leverage and company age are found to be insignificant in explaining the level of compliance with IFRSs disclosure.

3.1. Company size

It is commonly argued that because larger companies act to protect their reputation and avoid government intervention (Watts & Zimmerman, 1978; Holthausen & Leftwich, 1983) they are more likely to comply with accounting standards. This argument is supported by agency theory framework (Jensen & Meckling, 1976), which proposes that larger firms having higher agency cost because of a more complex organizational structure use disclosure to reduce informarmation asymmetry between company insiders (managers) and providers of capital (outsiders). On the other hand, larger firms are more likely to be more international that is, to have more foreign investors, foreign sales, or to have foreign stock exchange listings (Al-Shammari et al., 2008). The findings of empirical studies investigating the association between disclosure compliance and listing status, such as Malone et al. (1993), Street and Bryant (2000), Street and Gray (2001) and Glaum and Street (2003), show that companies which are cross-listed have higher levels of compliance. Hence, there is a general agreement that a positive relationship between the size of a firm and its extent of disclosure is to be expected. Studies of the relationship between disclosure compliance with IFRSs and company size are, however, mixed. For instance, Naser (1998), Dumontier and Raffournier (1998), Ali et al. (2004), Alsaeed (2006), Juhmani (2012), Akhtaruddin (2005), Hossain and Hammami (2009), Al-Shammari et al. (2008) and Al-Shammari (2011) report that company size is positively related to IFRS compliance, while Malone et al. (1993), Street and Bryant (2000), Street and Gray (2001) and Glaum and Street (2003) find no significant relationship.

The size variables considered in previous studies include revenue (Hodgdon et al., 2009), total assets (Naser, 1998; Street & Bryant, 2000; Juhmani, 2012), firm value (Glaum & Street, 2003), number of employees, and number of shareholdings.

Consistent with Street and Bryant (2000) and Juhmani (2012), we measure company size using companies' total of assets.

Based on the above discussion, it can be expected that companies with a higher size disclose information to a greater extent than companies with a lower size. Thus, the hypothesis developed for the study is as follows:

H1. *There is a significant positive association between the company size and the extent of mandatory disclosure.*

3.2. Profitability

The influence of profitability on the level of compliance with IFRSs may be based on several arguments. As suggested by signaling theory, since managers of more profitable companies wish to signal their success and strength to outsiders, companies with larger profits are more likely to disclose more information. Moreover, in order to justify their position and compensation package managers of more profitable companies are expected to disclose more information than nonprofitable companies.

With respect to the association between the extent of compliance with IFRSs disclosure requirements and profitability, prior studies show inconsistent findings. For example, Malone *et al.* (1993), Durantier and Raffournier (1998), Street and Bryant (2000), Hossain and Hammami (2009) and Street and Gray (2001) find no association between profitability and the level of voluntary compliance with IFRSs disclosure requirements. Similarily, Glaum and Street (2003), Al-Saeed (2006) and Juhmani (2012) report that profitability is not significantly related to the level of mandatory compliance with IFRSs disclosure requirements. On the other hand, Naser (1998), Ali *et al.* (2004), Akhtaruddin (2005) and Al-Shammari (2011) report a positive relationship.

Researchers of previous studies have used net profit to sales (Akhtarrudin, 2005), earnings growth, dividend growth, return on assets, and return on equity (Juhmani, 2012; Hodgdon *et al.*, 2009; Al-Shammari, 2011; Akhtaruddin, 2005) as proxies for profitability. Consistent with most previous research, we measure profitability using companies' return on equity (ROE), measured as the ratio of the companies' net income to the companies' shareholders' equity.

Based on the arguments, it can be expected that companies with larger profits disclose information to a greater extent than companies with a lower profits. Thus, the hypothesis developed for the study is as follows:

H2. *There is a significant positive association between the firm profitability and the extent of mandatory disclosure.*

3.3. Leverage

It has been suggested that leverage is relevant in explaining variation in the extent of disclosure compliance. According to Jensen and Meckling (1976) the level of information disclosure increases as the leverage of the firm grows. Therefore, companies with higher leverage can be expected to comply with IFRSs to reduce agency costs, to reassure debtholders that their interests are protected (Al-Shammari, 2011). Moeover, companies with higher leverage can be expected to disclose detailed information to enhance their chance of getting funds from financial institutions.

Prior studies report mixed findings regarding the association between leverage and the level of disclosure, some studies some studies have reported a positive association (e. g. Malone *et al.*, 1993; Naser, 1998; Al-Shammari *et al.,* 2008), other studies reported a negative relationship (Juhmani, 2006; Al-Shammari *et al.*, 2011). Hovever, most of the previous research report that leverage is not significantly related to the level of compliance with IFRSs disclosure requirements (e. g. Dumontier & Raffournier, 1998; Ali *et al.*, 2004; Alsaeed, 2006; Juhmani, 2012).

Prior research has used a number of measures of leverage including debt to total assets, total debt and debt to equity ratios. The present study uses the total debt to total assets ratio as the measure of leverage. Based on the above discussion, it can be expected that companies with higher leverage disclose information to a greater extent than companies with lower leverage. Thus, the hypothesis developed for the study is as follows:

H3. *There is a significant positive association between the level of leverage and the extent of mandatory disclosure.*

3.4. Company age

Company age has often been used in previous studies examining disclosure variability. It is generally argued that old firms disclose more information. Several factors support this argument. First, old companies are more likely to have established, well-organised professional staff to deal with the technical aspects of their financial statements. Their accounting systems are more capable to produce detailled information. Therefore, older companies with more established accounting systems are more likely to be able to meet the detailed IFRSs requirements than younger companies with less established and less comprehensive accounting systems (Al-Shammari, 2011). Second, since old firms try to enhance their reputation and image in the market, they are more likely to comply with disclosure requirements of IFRSs (Akhtaruddin, 2005). Third, young firms are not likely to disclose full information about their financial results and position, because this may prove to be harmful if sensitive information is disclosed to the established competitors (Owusu-Ansah, 1998).

Previous research have examined the effect of company age on the level of disclosure compliance with IFRSs. However, empirical results from the research are mixed. For example Glaum and Street (2003), Akhtaruddin (2005), Alsaeed (2006) and Juhmani (2012) have reported no association between company age and the level of information disclosure, while, Hossain and Hammani (2009) and Al-Shammari (2011) reported a positive association between firm age and level of disclosure compliance with IFRSs. The Turkish evidence regarding the influence of firm age on the level of disclosure compliance with IFRSs is tested by the following hypothesis:

H4. *There is a significant positive association between company age and the extent of mandatory disclosure.*

3.5. Audit firm size

The extent of a company's compliance with IFRSs may be associated with audit firm size. Agency theory suggests that large audit firms act as a mechanism to reduce agency costs and exert more of a monitoring role by limiting opportunistic behaviour by managers. Moreover, large audit firms are more likely to associate with clients that disclose a high level of information in their annual reports (Malone *et al.*, 1993). Therefore, companies audited by large audit firms are more likely to comply with IFRSs disclosure requirements compared to those audited by small audit firms. Conventionally, larger audit firms are identified as being one of these Big Four international audit firms, and smaller audit firms are the rest.

The empirical evidence on relationship between information disclosure and size of audit firms has provided mixed results. While Dumontier and Raffournier (1998), Glaum and Street (2003), Hodgdon *et al.* (2009), Al-Shammari (2011) and Juhmani (2012) report a positive association between audit firm size and the level of disclosure, Malone *et al.* (1993), Naser (1998) and Ali *et al.* (2004) identify an insignificant relationship between these two variables:

H5. *There is a significant positive association between audit firm size and the extent of mandatory disclosure.*

4. Methodology

4.1. Sample selection and data collection

The sample used to measure the level of compliance with the mandatory IFRSs disclosure requirements and the association between corporate characteristics and the level of compliance consists of the firms included in Istanbul Stock Exchange national index. These companies fall into 15 industries: agriculture-forestry and fishing, mining, manufacturing, electricity-gas and water, construction and public works, wholesale-retail trade-hotels and restaurants, transportation-telecommunication and storage, financial institutions, education-health-sports and other social services, renting and business activities, technology, professional-scientific and technical activities, administrative-support service activities, real estate activities and miscellaneous. To ensure that no bias was introduced into the analysis by including companies which, because of their activities, were unable to disclose some of the items in the disclosure index, only those non-financial companies with a primary interest in manufacturing activities were included (Ali *et al.*, 2004). The number of companies was thus reduced to 194. However, 26 companies are eliminated because of incomplete data. Therefore, the final sample consists of 168 manufacturing companies listed on Istanbul Stock Exchange national index.

The data for measuring the dependent and independent variables investigated in this study were manually collected from the sampled companies' annual reports that were downloaded from the official website of the Istanbul Stock Exchange. The annual reports of year 2011 were chosen because they are relatively more recent and easier to obtain.

4.2. Disclosure compliance index

In order to select proper items of information that are expected to be disclosed in IFRS based financial statements, we consulted the mandatory disclosure checklist used in prior studies. Furthermore, we considered mandatory disclosure requirements of all IFRSs while constituting the disclosure checklist. Appendix 1 presents the items included in the disclosure index.

Table 1 shows the distribution of 215 items of information included in disclosure compliance index: general presentation items 30%, statement of financial position items 24%, statement of profit or loss and other comprehensive income items 12% and special topics items 34% .

Table 1. Distribution of index items

	No. of Items	%
General presentation	65	30
Statement of financial position	51	24
Statement of profit or loss and other comprehensive income	26	12
Special topics	73	34
	215	100

There are two methods for determining the level of corporate disclosure: weighted and dichotomous approaches (Cooke, 1989). The weighted approach is based on the assumption that all items of information are not equally important and, therefore, researcher allocates arbitrarily weights to each items. Most researchers measuring compliance with IFRSs mandatory disclosure requirements employ the "dichotomous" disclosure index approach (Juhmani, 2012; Al-Shammari, 2011; Hossain & Hammami, 2009; Al-Shammari *et al.*, 2008). This method gives equal weight to the individual items required to be disclosed by all standards. One main problem of dichotomous approach is that a company may be penalized by assigning a score of zero for the absence of an item of information that is not applicable to it. In order to overcome this problem, the relevance of each absent item needs to be investigated and then classified as non-disclosure for a relevant item of reporting and non-applicable otherwise (Akhtaruddin, 2005). Following the prior researches, our study adopts "dichotomous" disclosure index approach in which we assigned a value of one if the company discloses an item of information and zero otherwise, when a disclosure is deemed irrelevant for a specific company, then the item is ignored in the computation of the index for that company.

Disclosure compliance index thus arrived at for a company is additive as follows:

Where, d = one if the item d_1 is disclosed; zero, if the item d_2 is not disclosed;
        n = number of items.

4.3. The independent variables

Five company characteristics were examined for their association with the level of disclosure compliance to discover if the level of compliance with IFRSs was influenced by company characteristics. Data were obtained from companies' annual reports. Table 2 summarizes the independent variables and their proxies.

Table 2. Summary of the idependent variables

Variable	Proxy	Expected sign
Company size	Total assets	+
Profitability	Return on equity (ROE) = Net profit/Total shareholders' equity	+
Leverage	Total debt to total assets ratio	+
Company age	Number of years since foundation	+
Audit firm size	Dummy variable coded 1 = a company audited by local auditor with international affiliation (Big Four), 0 = a company audited by local auditor without international affiliation (non-Big Four)	

4.4. Model development

In order to assess the effect of each corporate characteristic on the the level of Turkish companies' compliance with the mandatory IFRSs disclosure requirements, the following multiple linear regression model was fitted to the data:

$$DI = \beta 0 + \beta 1\ TA + \beta 2\ LEV + \beta 3\ ROE + \beta 4\ CA + \beta 5\ AFS + e$$
where:

      DI   = Disclosure Index;
      TA = Total Assets;
      LEV = Leverage;
      ROE = Return on Equity;
      CA = Company Age
      AFS = Audit firm size;
      e   = error term.

5. Results

5.1. Descriptive statistics

Descriptive statistics for the dependent and independent variables are reported in Table 3. The mean of the level of disclosure compliance with IFRSs of the sample companies was 79 percent with a minimum of 64 percent and a maximum of 92 percent indicating variations in the level of disclosure compliance with IFRSs in Turkey. It is lower than the level of disclosure compliance observed in Australia (0.94; Tower *et al.*, 1999), Germany (0.81; Glaum & Street, 2003), Gulf Co-Operation Member States (0.82; Al-Shammari *et al.*, 2008), Kuwait (0.82; Al-Shammari, 2011) and Bahrain (0.81; Juhmani, 2012), but higher than the level of disclosure compliance observed in Switzerland (0,74; Street & Gray, 2002), Jordan (0.63; Naser, 1998), Bangladesh (0.44; Akhtaruddin, 2005) and Saudi Arabia (0.33; Alsaeed, 2006). Table 3 also shows that the maximum level of compliance was 92 percent, indicating that no company in Turkey complied with all requirements of the IFRSs. Moreover, Table 3 reports a wide range of variation within the sample in the independent variables as indicated by the minimum and maximum values. The mean of company size was 854 TL millions with a minimum of 0,6 TL millions and a maximum of 14,800 TL millions. This size distribution was, as usual, skewed. Skewness was mitigated by utilizing the natural logarithm of size in the regression analysis, consistent with prior studies (Cooke, 1991; Wallace *et al.*, 1994).

Table 3. Descriptive statistics for the dependent and independent continuous variables

	Mean	Median	Maximum	Minimum	Std. Dev.
Dependant Variable					
Disclosure Compliance Index	0.79	0.79	0.92	0.64	0.03
Independent Variables					
Company size	8.54E+08	2.16E+08	1.48E+10	620,182	1.97E+09
Leverage	0.61	0.48	12,560	0.04	1.08
Profitability	1.73	0.08	281.85	-1.2	21.81
Company age	38.52	39	101	4	15.40

The average leverage for the sample companies was 61 percent with a minimum of 4 and a maximum of 12,560 percent. The figure of 4 percent implied that some companies had almost no debt, whereas a ratio of 12,560 percent indicated that the company had high debt. Profitability ranges from -1.2 to 281.85 with a mean of 1.73, indicating variation in profitability ratios among sample companies. The value of -1.2 implied that 1.2 times the amount of the entire equity of the company was eroded due to operations. Company age ranges from 4 to 101 with a mean of 38.52.

It is important to assess whether multicollinearity exists before estimating the model as it could cause estimation problems (Al-Shammari, 2011). Table 4 displays the correlations among the continuous independent variables. It is shown in the table that the highest correlation was between company size and audit firm size (0.402). Other variables were also correlated, but probably no correlation was sufficient to impair the regression results since the pair-wise correlation coefficients are less than 0.80 (Gujarati, 2003).

However, another method that is widely used to detect multicollinearity is the Variance Inflation Factor (VIF) (Al-Shammari, 2011). This was reported in Table 5. Since VIF did not exceed 10 for any variable in any model, it was concluded that collinearity was not a serious problem (Neter et al., 1983).

Table 4. Pearson correlation coefficients matrix for the continuous independent variables

	Company Age	Company Size	Audit firm size	Profitability	Leverage
Company Age	1.000000				
Company size	0.350097	1.000000			
	4.757066				
	0.0000				
Audit firm size	0.289589	0.402524	1.000000		
	3.850868	5.596730			
	0.0002	0.0000			
Profitability	-0.050656	0.200996	0.080814	1.000000	
	-0.645576	2.611561	1.031970		
	0.5195	0.0099	0.3036		
Leverage	-0.0083784	-0.043671	-0.051563	0.097759	1.000000
	-1.070153	-0.556373	-0.657162	1.250258	
	0.2861	0.5787	0.5120	0.2130	

5.2. Regression results

This study investigates the association between the extent of disclosure compliance with IFRSs and 5 company characteristics (companysize, leverage, profitability, company age and auditor firm size) by analyzing annual reports of sample companies listed on Istanbul Stock Exchange in 2011. Table 5 reports the regression results. The R (adj.) suggests that approximately 11 percent of the compliance level variation is explained by the independent variables. The explanatory power of this model is lower than than that of Glaum and Street, 2003 (0.29), Hodgdon *et al.*, 2009 (0.21), and Al-Shammari, 2011 (0.40). The results also show that the model was significant (F= 5.139733, p< 0.001).

Table 5. Regression results

Independent variables (expected sign)	Model Coefficients	VIF
Company size (+)	0.002310107	1.389042
Leverage (+)	-0.007234679**	1.042353
Profitability (+)	8.59E-05	1.065017
Company age (+)	-0.000117857	1.193321
Auditor (+)	0.01123463*	1.246332
Constant	0.749422944	
Adjusted R	0.110867	
F	5.139733	
Prob. (F)	< 0.001	
No. of companies	168	

significant $p < 0.10$; ***ttest (two-tailed) significant $p < 0.01$; **ttest (two tailed) significant $p < 0.05$; *ttest (two-tailed) significant $p < 0.10$.

The results provide evidence that that the extent of disclosure compliance with IFRSs is associated with company leverage and audit firm size. The remaining independent variables (profitability, company size and age) were not significant while leverage was significant but in the opposite prediction.

The results revealed that company size is not significant in explaining variation in the extent of disclosure compliance with IFRSs. Therefore, the hypothesis that there is a significant positive association between the firm size and the extent of mandatory disclosure was not supported. This finding is contradicted with that of Juhmani (2012), Akhtaruddin (2005), Hossain and Hammami (2009), Al-Shammari *et al.* (2008) and Al-Shammari (2011) which report positive association between company size and disclosure compliance with IFRSs.

Similar to Glaum and Street (2003), Al-Saeed (2006) and Juhmani (2012), we found no association between profitability and the level of compliance with IFRSs disclosure requirements. Therefore, the hypothesis that there is a significant positive association between the firm profitability and the extent of mandatory disclosure is not supported.

Since companies with higher leverage are more likely to be subject to greater shareholder demand for information it is expected that these companies comply with IFRSs. However, our findings, similar to Juhmani (2006) and Al-Shammari *et al.* (2011) reported a negative association between the leverage and the extent of disclosure compliance with IFRSs. It is opposite to the prediction. Therefore, hypothesis 2 is not supported. This finding may be explained by the fact that Turkish companies with lower levels of leverage may comply more with IFRSs in order to satisfy the needs of shareholders for information.

The results provide evidence that company age has no effect on the level of disclosure compliance with IFRSs. This result support the findings of Glaum and Street (2003), Akhtaruddin (2005), Alsaeed (2006) and Juhmani (2012) which reported no association between company age and the level of information disclosure.

Consistent with Dumontier and Raffournier (1998), Glaum and Street (2003), Hodgdon *et al.* (2009), Al-Shammari (2011) and Juhmani (2012) our results indicate a positive association between audit firm size and the level of disclosure compliance with IFRSs. This finding supports the idea that large audit firms (Big Four) which have a stronger incentive to protect their reputation and to signal to the market their higher audit quality encourage their clients to have a higher level of disclosure compliance with IFRSs.

6. Conclusions

This study examines the extent of disclosure compliance with IFRSs by 168 companies listed on the Istanbul Stock Exchange in 2011 and outlines the underlying company characteristics affecting the disclosure compliance of companies with IFRSs. The extent of disclosure compliance with IFRSs is measured using a self-disclosure compliance index. A multivariate regression analysis was employed to test the relationship between the level of disclosure compliance with IFRSs and five company characteristics.

The results showed that the level of compliance with IFRSs of Turkish companies is 0.79. It is lower than the level of disclosure compliance observed in Australia (0.94; Tower *et al.*, 1999), Germany (0.81; Glaum & Street, 2003), Gulf Co-Operation Member States (0.82; Al-Shammari *et al.*, 2008), Kuwait (0.82; Al-Shammari, 2011) and Bahrain (0.81; Juhmani, 2012). This suggests that national monitoring and enforcement mechanisms in Turkey need to be improved.

The results of multivariate analysis showed that disclosure compliance also varies by leverage and audit firm size. Other company characteristics, such as profitability, company size and age, however, are not significant in explaining the level of disclosure compliance with IFRSs. Leverage is negatively related to the level of disclosure compliance. This implies that Turkish companies which are subject to higher public equity risk due to large amount of equity financing comply more with IFRSs in order to satisfy the needs of shareholders for information. Audit firm size, as predicted, is positively associated to the level of disclosure compliance. It is infered from this result that big audit firms encourage their clients to have a higher level of disclosure compliance with IFRSs while small audit firms do not.

This study contributes to the literature by extending international accounting compliance studies in developping economies and by providing insights to compliance level of listed companies with IFRS disclosure requirements in Turkey, a code-law country with a very different cultural and institutional framework from that of common law countries. It also contributes to the literature on the relationship of company characteristics and compliance with IFRSs, by testing its application to a developing country like Turkey.

As with any research, this study has some limitations. The following limitations are the most pertinent. First, the items constituting the disclosure index do not reflect their level of importance as perceived by financial information users. Hence, the approach used in this study may not entirely capture the depth of items, thereby not measuring the disclosure properly. Second, the disclosure index includes only mandatory items. The results could have changed if voluntary items had been included. Third, the data used to test the compliance level was manually collected from the annual reports. Fourth, some firm-specific characteristics, specifically profitability and debt, were measured based on two commonly used ratios-return on equity and total debt to total assets ratios. The findings might have altered if other ratios, such as net profit to sales and total debt to equity had been applied. With these caveats in mind, much caution should be exercised when interpreting the results.

Future research could address the following suggestions:
- introduce voluntary items not addressed by the current study;
- classify mandatory disclosure into discrete groups, such as financial and non-financial information;
- incorporate other firm-specific characteristics, such as ownership concentration and international ownership;
- construct the disclosure index based on the value financial information users attach to every disclosure item.

Acknowledgement
This paper has been financially supported by Galatasaray University Research Fund.

An investigation of compliance with International Financial Reporting Standards by listed...

19

References

Akhtaruddin, M. (2005) "Corporate Mandatory Disclosure Practices in Bangladesh", *The International Journal of Accounting*, vol. 40: 399-422

Ali, M. J., Ahmed K. & Henry, D. (2004) "Disclosure Compliance with National Accounting Standards by Listed Companies in South Asia", *Accounting and Business Research*, vol. 34, no. 3: 183-199

Alsaeed, K. (2006) "The Association between Firm-specific Characteristics and Disclosure: The case of Saudi Arabia", *Managerial Accounting Journal*, vol. 21, no. 5: 476-495

Al-Shammari, B., Brown, P., & Tarca, A. (2008) "An Investigation of Compliance with International Accounting Standards by Listed Companies in the Gulf Co-Operation Council Member States", *The International Journal of Accounting*, vol. 43: 425-447

Al-Shammari, B. (2011) "Factors Influencing the Extent of Mandatory Compliance with International Financial Reporting Standards: The Case of Kuwaiti Listed Companies", *Journal of International Business and Economics*, vol. 11, no. 4: 11-31

Cooke, T. E. (1989) "Voluntary Corporate Disclosure by Swedish Companies", Journal of *International Financial Management and Accounting*, vol. 1, no. 2: 171-195

Cooke, T. E. (1991) "An assessment of voluntary disclosure in the annual reports of Japanese corporations", *International Journal of Accounting*, vol. 26, no. 3: 174-189

Demir, V., Bahadır, O., & Öncel, A.G. (2013) "What is the Best Measure of Financial Performance? Comprehensive Income versus Net Income: Evidence from Turkey", *İktisat İşletme ve Finans*, vol. 28, no. 323: 73-96.

Dumontier, P., & Raffournier, B. (1998) "Why Firms Comply Voluntarily with IAS: An Empirical Analysis with Swiss Data", *Journal of International Financial Management and Accounting*, vol. 9, no. 3: 216-245

Glaum, M., & Street, D. L. (2003) "Compliance with the Disclosure Requirements of Germany's New Market: IAS Versus US GAAP", *Journal of International Financial Management and Accounting*, vol. 14, no. 1: 64-100

Gujarati, D. N. (2003) "Basic Econometrics", 3rd ed., New York, McGraw-Hill, Inc.

Hodgdon, C., Rasoul, H. T., Adhikari, A., & Harless, D. W. (2009) "Compliance with International Financial Reporting Standards and Auditor Choice: New Evidence on the Importance of the Statutory Audit", *The International Journal of Accounting*, vol. 44: 33-55

Holthausen, R. W., & Leftwich, R. W. (1983) "The Economic Consequences of Accounting Choice", *Journal of Accounting & Economics*, vol. 5: 77-117

Hossain, M., & Hammami, H. (2009) "Voluntary Disclosure in the Annual Reports of an Emerging Country: The Case of Qatar", *Advances in Accounting, Incorporating Advances in International Accounting*, vol. 25: 255-265.

Jensen, M., & Meckling, W. (1976) "Theory of the Firm: Managerial Behavior, Agency Costs and Ownership Structure", *Journal of Financial Economics*, vol. 3, no. 3: 305-360

Juhmani, O. I. H. (2012) "Factors Influencing the Extent of Corporate Compliance with IFRSs: Evidence from Companies Listed in Bahrain Stock Exchange", *Journal of International Business and Economics*, vol. 12, no. 2: 67-79

Malone, D., Fries, C., & Jones, T. (1993) "An Empirical Investigation of the Extent of Corporate Financial Disclosure in the Oil and Gas Industry", *Journal of Accounting, Auditing & Finance*, vol. 8, no. 3: 249-273

Naser, K. (1998) "Comprehensiveness of Disclosure of non-financial Companies Listed on Amman Financial Market", *International Journal of Commerce & Management*, vol. 2, no. 8: 88-119

Neter, J, Wasserman, W., & Kunter, M. (1983) "Applied regression models", Homewood, IL: Richard D. Irwin.

Owusu-Ansah, S. (1998) "The Impact of Corporate Attributes on the Extent of Mandatory Disclosure and Reporting by Listed Companies in Zimbabwe", *The International Journal of Accounting*, vol. 33, no. 5: 605-631

Street, D. L., & Gray, S. J. (2001) "Observance of International Accounting Standards: Factors Explaining Non-compliance by Companies Referring to the Use of IAS", ACCA Research Monograph.

Street, D. L., & Bryant, S.M. (2000) "Disclosure Level and Compliance with IASs: A Comparison of Companies with and without U.S. Listings and Filings", *The International Journal of Accounting*, vol 35, no. 3: 305-329

Tower, G., Hancock, P., & Taplin, R. (1999) "A regional study of listed companies' compliance with international accounting standards", *Accounting Forum*, vol. 23, no. 3: 293-305

Wallace, R. S. O., Naser, K., & Mora, A. (1994) "The relationship between the comprehensiveness of corporate annual reports and firm characteristics in Spain", *Accounting and Business Research*, vol. 25, no. 97: 41-53

Watts, R., & Zimmerman, J. (1978) "Towards a Positive Theory of the Determination of Accounting Standards", *Accounting Review*, vol. 53, no. 1: 112-134

Appendix 1. Disclosure index

General presentation
1.   Fair presentation of financial position, financial performance and cash flows of the entity in the financial statements
2.   Financial statements that are not prepared on a going concern basis
3.   A complete set of financial statements
4.   The name of the reporting entity or other means of idendification,
5.   Whether the financial statements are of an individual entity or a group of entities
6.   Reporting date or the period covered by the set of financial statements or notes,
7.   The presentation currency and the level of rounding used in presenting amounts in the financial statements
8.   Comparative information
9.   Consistency of presentation
10. Reclassification of comparative amounts if the presentation or classification of items in the financial statements is changed
11. A brief description of the nature and principal activities of the company and its subsidiaries
12. The domicile and legal form of the entity, its country of incorporation and the adres of its registered office
13. The name of the parent and the ultimate parent of the group
14. Current vs non current distinction
15. Seperate presentation of each material class of similar items
16. For each class of share capital; the number of shares authorised, the number of shares issued and fully paid and issued but not fully paid, par value pers hare, a reconcilliation of the number of shares outstanding at the beginning and at the end of the period
17. Presentation of a statement of profit or loss and other comprehensive income either in a single statement that includes all components of profit or loss and other comprehensive income, or in the form of two seperate statements, one displaying components of profit or loss followed immediatley by another statement beginning with profit or loss and displaying componenets of other comprehensive income
18. Profit or loss for the period attributable to non-controlling interests and owners of the parent and comprehensive income for the period attributable to non-controlling interests and owners of the parent
19. Line items for amounts of other comprehensive income classified by nature
20. Reclassification adjustments relating to components of other comprehensive income
21. Circumtances that would give rise to the seperate disclosure of items of income and expense
22. An analysis of expenses recognised in profit or loss using a classification based on either the nature of expenses or their function within the entity
23. The amount of income tax relating to each component of other comprehensive income
24. The gain or loss on net monetary position of the entity (if the entity's functional currency is a currency of a hyperinflationary economy)
25. The aggregate amount of research and development expenditure recognised as an expense during the period

26. Net gains or net losses on financial assets at fair value through profit or loss, available-for-sale financial assets, held-to-maturity investments, loans and receivables and financial liabilities measured at amortised cost
27. Net gains or net losses on total interest income and interest expense
28. Net gains or net losses on fee income and expense
29. Net gains or net losses on interest income on impaired financial assets
30. Net gains or net losses on the amount of any impairment loss for each class of financial asset
31. Information that enables users of the financial statements to evaluate the financial effects of discontinued operations
32. A single amount comprising the total of the post-tax profit or loss of discontinued operations and the post-tax gain or loss recognised on the measurement to fair value less costs to sel lor on the disposal of the assets or disposal groups constituting the discontinued operation
33. An analysis of the single amount of revenue, expenses and pre-tax profit or loss of discontinued operations, the related income tax expense, the gain or loss recognised on the measurement to fair value less costs to sel lor on the disposal of the assets or disposal groups constituting the discontinued operation
34. The investor's share of the discontinued operations of an associate as part of the share of profit or loss of associates
35. Adjustments in the current period to amounts previously presented in discontinued operations that are directly related on the disposal of a discontinued operation in a prior period are classified seperately in discontinued operations
36. Gain or loss on the remeasurement of a non-current asset classified as held-for-sale that does not meet the definition of a discontinued operation
37. Total comprehensive income for the period, showing seperately the total amounts attributable to owners of the parent and non-controlling interests
38. For each component of equity, the effects of retrospective application or retrospective restatement
39. For each component of equity, a reconciliation between the carrying amount at the beginning and the end of the period, seperately disclosing changes resulting from profit or loss, other comprehensive income and transactions with owners in their capacity as owners
40. The amount of dividends recognised as distributions to owners during the period and the related amount of dividends per share
41. The amount of transaction costs accounted for as a deduction from equity
42. The increase or decrease in the carrying amount of non-cash distributed to owners recognised in the period as a result of the change in the fair value of the assets to be distributed
43. Cash flows during the period classified as operating, investing and financing activities
44. Cash flows arising cash receipts and payments on behalf of customers when the cash activities of the customer rather than those of the entity
45. Cash flows arising from cash receipts and payments for items in which the turnover is quick, the amounts are large and the maturities are short
46. Cash flows arising from cash receipts and payments for the acceptance and repayment of deposits with a fixed maturity date
47. Cash flows arising from the placement of deposits with and withdrawal of deposits from other financial institutions

48. Cash flows arising from cash advances and loans made to customers and the repayment of those advances and loans
49. Cash flows from operating, investing and financing activities
50. Cash flows from interest and dividends received and paid
51. Cash flows from taxes on income in operating activities
52. Investing and financing transactions that are excluded from the statement of cash flows because they do not require the use of cash or cash equivalents
53. Cash flows from obtaining or losing control of subsidiaries or other businesses
54. Information about the basis of preparation of the financial statements and the specific accounting policies used
55. An explicit and unreserved statement of compliance with IFRS
56. Material uncertainties related to events or conditions that may cast significant doubt upon the entity's ability to continue as a going concern
57. The measurement basis used in preparing the financial statements
58. The accounting policies used
59. The judgements made by management in the process of applying the accounting policies that have most significant effect on the amounts recognised in the financial statements
60. Information about assumptions made about the future, and other major sources of estimation uncertainty at the reporting date
61. Information that enables users of the consolidated financial statements to understand the composition of the group and the interest that non-controlling interests have in the group's activities and cash flows, and to evaluate the nature and extent of significant restrictions on the ability to Access or use assets, and setle liabilities of the group
62. The functional currency and the reason for using different presentation currency
63. The nature and amount of a change in accounting estimate
64. The nature of the prior period error
65. The date that financial statements were authorised for issue and who gave that authorisation

Statement of financial position
66. For each class of property, plant and equipment; the gross carrying amount and the accumulated depreciation at the beginning and end of the period
67. For each class of property, plant and equipment; a reconcilliation of the carrying amount at the beginning and end of the period showing additions, assets classified as held-for-sale, acquisitions through business combinations, increases or decreases resulting from revaluations, decreases resulting from impairment losses recignised, increases resulting from impairment losses reversed, depreciation, the net exchange differences arising on the translation of the financial statements from the functional currency into a different presentation currency
68. Restrictions on title and property, plant and equipment pledged as security for liabilities
69. The amount of expenditures recognised in the carrying amount of an item of property, plant and equipment in the course of construction
70. For revalued property, plant and equipment; the effective date of the revaluation
71. For revalued property, plant and equipment whether an independent valuer was involved
72. For revalued property, plant and equipment; the carrying amount that would have been recognised had the assets been carried under the cost model, the revaluaion surplus

73. For each class of intangible assets; the gross carrying amount and any accumulated amortisation at the beginning and end of the period,

74. For each class of intangible asstes, the line items of the statement of profit or loss and other comprehensive income in which any amortisation of intangible assets is included

75. For erach class of intangible assets, a reconciliation of the carrying amount at the beginning and end of the period

76. For an intangible asset assesed as having an indefinite useful life, the carrying amount of that asset and the reasons supporting the assessment of an indefinite life

77. For revalued intangible assets; the effective date of the revaluation

78. For revalued intangible assets; whether an independent valuer was involved

79. For revalued intangible assets; the carrying amount that would have been recognised had the assets been carried under the cost model, the revaluaion surplus

80. A reconciliation of the carrying amount of goodwill at the beginning and en of the reporting period showing seperately the gross amount and accumulated impairment losses at the beginning period, additional goodwill recognised during the period, adjustments resulting from the subsequent recognition of deferred tax assets during the period, goodwill included in a disposal group, goodwill derecognised during the reporting period, impairment losses recognised during the reporting period, net exchange differences arising during the reporting period, the gross amount and accumulated impairment losses at the reporting period

81. Cash-generating unit (group of units) for which the carrying amount of goodwill or intangible assets with indefinite useful lives allocated

82. The amounts recognised in profit or loss for rental income from investment property, direct operating expenses arising from investment property that generated rental income during the period,

83. The existence and amounts of restrictions on the realisability of investment property or the remittance of income and proceeds of disposal

84. A reconciliation of the carrying amount of investment property at the beginning and end of the period

85. The depreciation methods used, the useful lives, the gross carrying amount and the accumulated depreciation of investment property (when the cost model is applied)

86. Information that enables users of the financial statements to evaluate the nature of, and risks associated with the interests in other entities

87. Information about significant judgements and assumptions made in determining that the entity has significant influence over another entity

88. Information that enables users of the financial statements to evaluate the nature, extent and financial effects of the interests in associates

89. For each associate that is material to the reporting entity; the name of the associate, the nature of the entity's relationship with the associate, the principal place of business of the associate, the proportion of ownership interest or participating share held by the entity, whether the investment in the associate is measured under the equity method or at fair value, dividends received from the associate, summarised financial information for the associate

90. Information that enables users of the financial statements to evaluate the nature, extent and financial effects of the interests in joint arrengements

91. For each joint arrangement that is material to the reporting entity; the name of the joint arrengement, the nature of the entity's relationship with the joint arrangement, the principal place of business of the joint arrangement, the proportion of ownership

interest or participating share held by the entity, whether the investment in the joint arrangement is measured under the equity method or at fair value, summarised financial information for the joint arragement

92. The amount reclassified into and out of each category and the reason fort hat reclassification when the entity has reclassified a financial asset

93. The carrying amount of financial assets that the entity has pledged as collateral for liabilities or contingent liabilities

94. The fair value of the collateral held

95. For designated fair value hedges, a description of the hedges, a description of the financial instruments designated as hedging instruments and their fair values at the reporting date and the nature of the risks being hedged

96. Gains or losses on the hedging instrument and on the hedged item attributable to the hedged risk

97. For designated cash flow hedges, a description of the hedges, a description of the financial instruments designated as hedging instruments and their fair values at the reporting date, the nature of the risks being hedged, the periods when the cash flows are expected to ocur and when they are expected to affect profit or loss, a description of any forecast transaction for which hedge accounting had previously been used, the amount that was recognised in other comprehensive income during the period, the amount that was reclassified from equity to profit or loss for the period

98. For hedges of net investments in foreign operations, a description of the hedges, a description of the financial instruments designated as hedging instruments and their fair values at the reporting date, the nature of the risks being hedged and the ineffectiveness recignised in profit or loss

99. For each class of financial assets and financial liabilities, the fair value of that class of assets and liabilities in a way that permits it to be compared with its carrying amount

100. For financial instruments whose fair value could not previously be neasured reliably are derocognised, their carrying amount at the time of derecognition and the amount of gain or loss recognised

101. Information to help users of the financial statements make their own judgements about the extent of possible differences between the carrying amount of those financial assets and their fair value

102. Information that enables users of the entity's financial statements to evaluate the nature and extent of risks arising from financial instruments to which the entity is exposed at the reporting date.

103. The exposures to the market risk and how they arise

104. The exposures to the liquidity risk and how they arise

105. The exposures to the credit risk and how they arise

106. For financial assets at fair value through profit or loss; the maximum exposure to credit risk of the loan or receivable, the amount by which any related credit derivatives or similar instruments mitigate that maximum exposure to credit risk, the amount of change in the fair value of the loan or receivable

107. For financial liabilities at fair value through profit or loss; the amount of change in the fair value of liability

108. The total carrying amount of inventories and the carrying amount in classifications appropriate to the entity, the carrying amount of inventories carried at fair value les costs to sell, the amount of inventories recognised as an expense during the period, the amount of any write-down of inventories recognised as an expense in the period, the

amount of any reversal of any write-down that is recognised as a deduction in the amount of inventories recognised as expense, the carrying amount of inventories pledged as security for liabilities

109. The amount of dividends proposed or declared before the financial statements were authorised for issue but not recognised as a distribution to owners during the period, the amount of any cumulative preference dividends not recognised

110. For each class of provision; the carrying amount at the beginning and en of the period, additional provisions made in the period, amounts used during the period, unused amounts reversed during the period

111. For each class of provision; a brief description of the nature of the obligation and the expected timing of any resulting outflows of economic benefits, an indication of the uncertainties about the amount and timing of those outflows

112. Major components of tax expense (including curent tax expense, any adjustments recognised in the period for current tax of prior periods, the amount of deferred tax expense or income relating to the origination and reversal of temporary differences, the amount of deferred tax expense or income relating to changes in tax rates)

113. The aggregate current and deferred tax relating to items that are charged or credited to equity, the amount of income tax relating to each component of other comprehensive income

114. For each class of contingent liability, a brief description of the nature of the contingent liability and an estimate of its financial effect

115. For each class of contingent asset, a brief description of the nature of the contingent asset and an estimate of its financial effect

116. For contingent consideration assets acquired and contingent consideration liabilities assumed in a business combination; any changes in the recognised amounts, any changes in the range of outcomes and the valuation techniques and key model inputs used to measure contingent consideration

Statement of profit or loss and other comprehensive income
117. The amount of each significant category of revenue recognised during the period including revenue arising from the sale of goods, the rendering of services, interest, royalties and dividends

118. The amount of contract revenue recognised as revenue in the period

119. For contracts in progress at the reporting date; the aggregate amount of costs incurred and recognised profits, the amount of advances received and the amount of retentions

120. Information about how the entity determines which agreements meet al the criteria as construction progresses, the amount of revenue arising from such agreements in progress, the methods used to determine the stage of completion of agreements in progress

121. The effect of the grants on any item of income or expense

122. The nature and extent of government grants recognised in the financial statements and an indication of other forms of government assistance from which the entity has benefited directly and unfulfilled conditions and other contingencies attaching to government assistance that has been recognised

123. The amount recognised as an expense for defined contribution plans

124. Information abput contributions to defined contribution plans for key management personel

125. Information that explains the characteristics of the defined benefit plans and risks associated eith them, identifies and explains the amounts in the financial statements arising from the defined benefit plans and describes how the defined benefit plans may affect the amount, timing and uncertainty of the entity's future cash flows

126. A reconciliation from the opening balance to the closing balance for the net defined benefit liability (assets) showing seperate reconciliations for plan assets, the present value of the defined benefit obligation and the effect of the asset ceiling and any reimbursement rights

127. In each reconciliation relating to the net defined benefit liability (asset); curent service cost, interest income or expense, past service cost and gains and losses arising from settlements, remeasurements of the net defined benefit liability (asset) showing seperately the return on plan assets, acturial gains and losses arisinf from changes in demographic assumptions and acturial gains or losses arising from changes in financial assumptions

128. The entity's own transferable financial instruments held as plan assets and the fair value of plan assets that are property occupied by, or other assets used by, the entity

129. The significant acturial assumptions used to determine the present value of the defined benefit obligation

130. A sensitive analysis for each significant acturial assumption as of the reporting date, showing how the defined benefit obligation would have been affected by changes in the relevant acturial assumption that were reasonably possible at that date

131. If the antity participates in a multi-employer defined benefit plan; a description of the funding arrangements

132. If the entity participates in a defined benefit plan that shares risks between entities under common control; the contractual agreeement or stated policy for charging the net defined benefit cost or the fact that there is no such policy

133. Related party transactions with posy-employment benefit plans and post-employment benefits for key management personnel.

134. Information about contingent liabilities arising from post-employment benefit obligations

135. Information that enables users of the financial statements to understand the nature and extent of share-based payment arrangements that existed during the period

136. A description of each type of share-based payment arrangement that existed at any time during the period, the number abd weighted-average exercise prices od share options for each group of options

137. Information that enables users of the financial statements to understand how the fair value of the goods or services received, or the fair value of the equity instruments granted

138. Information that enables users of the financial statements to understand the effect of share-based payment transactions on the entity's profit or loss for the period and on its financial position

139. The total expense recognised fort he period arising from share-based payment transactions in which the goods or services received did not qualify for recognition as assets and hence were recognised immediately as an expense

140. For liabilities arising from share-based payment transactions; the total carrying amount at the end of the period and the total intrinsic value at the end of the period of liabilities for which the counterparty's right to cash or other assets had vested by the end of the period

141. The amount of borrowing costs capitalised during the period
142. The capitalisation rate used to determine the amount of borrowing costs eligible for capitalisation

Special topics
143. For each class of financial lease asset; the net carrying amount at the reporting date and a reconciliation between the total future minimum lease payments at the reporting date and their present value
144. The total minimum finance lease payments at the reporting date and their present value for each of the following periods: no later than one year, later than one year and not later than five year and later than five years
145. Contingent rents recognised as expense in the period
146. The total future minimum sub-lease payments expected to be received under non-cancellable sub-leases at the reporting date (for finance leases)
147. A general description of the lessee's material leasing arrangements including the basis on which contingent rent payable is determined, the existence and terms of renewal or purchase options and escalation clauses and restrictions imposed by lease arrangements (for finance leases)
148. The total minimum operating lease payments at the reporting date and their present value for each of the following periods: no later than one year, later than one year and not later than five year and later than five years
149. The total future minimum sub-lease payments expected to be received under non-cancellable sub-leases at the reporting date (for operating leases)
150. Lease and sub-lease payments recognised as an expense in the period, with seperate amounts for minimum lease payments, contingent rents and sub-lease payments (for operating leases)
151. A general description of the lessee's significant leasing arrangements including the basis on which contingent rent payments are determined, the existence and terms of renewal or purchase options and escalation clauses and restrictions imposed by lease arragements (for operating leases)
152. A reconciliation between the total gross investment in the lease at the reporting date and the present value of minimum lease payments receivable at the reporting date (lessor-financie leases)
153. The total gross investment in the lease and the present value od minimum lease payments receivable at the reporting date for each of the following periods: not later than one year, later than one year and not later than five years and later than five years (lessor-finance leases)
154. Unearned finance income (lessor-finance leases)
155. The un-guaranteed residual values accruing to the benefit of the lessor (lessor-finance leases)
156. The accumulated allowance for uncollecteable minimum lease payments receivable (lessor-finance leases)
157. Contingent rents recognised as income in the period (lessor-finance leases)
158. A general description of the lessor's material leasing arrangements (lessor-finance leases)
159. The future minimum lease payments under non-concellable operating leases in the aggregate and for each of the following periods: not later than one year, later than one year and not later than five years and later than five years (lessor-operating leases)

160. Total contingent rents recognised as income in the period (lessor-operating leases)
161. A general description of the lessor's leasing arrangements (lessor-operating leases)
162. A description of the arrangement (service concession arrangements)
163. Significant terms of the arragement that may affect the amount, timing and certainty of future cash flows (service concession arrangements)
164. The nature and extent of rights to use specified assets, obligations to provide or rights to expect provision of services, obligations to acquire or build items of property, plant and equipment, obligations to deliver or rights to receive specified assets at the end of the concession period, renewal and termination options and other rights and obligations (service concession arrangements)
165. Changes in the arrangement during the period (service concession arrangements)
166. How the service arrangement has been classified (service concession arrangements)
167. Revenue and profits or losses recognised on exchanging construction services or a financial asset or an intangible asset
168. Information to enable users of financial statements to evaluate the nature and financial effects of the business activities in which the entity engages and the economic environments in which it operates
169. Factors used to idebtify the entity's reportable segments
170. Types of products and services from which each reportable segment derives its revenues
171. The measure of profit or loss for each reportable segment
172. The measure of total assets and liabilities for each reportable segment if such amounts are regularly provided to the chief operating decision maker
173. Revenues from external customers (for each reportable segment)
174. Revenues from transactions with other operating segments of the same entity (for each reportable segment)
175. Interest revenue (for each reportable segment)
176. Interest expense (for each reportable segment)
177. Depreciation and amortisation (for each reportable segment)
178. Material items of income and expense (for each reportable segment)
179. The entity's interest in the profit or loss of associates and joint ventures accounted for by the equity method (for each reportable segment)
180. Income tax expense or income and material non-cash items other than depreciation (for each reportable segment)
181. An explanation of the measurements of segment profit or loss, segment assets and segment liabilities for each reportable segment
182. The basis of accounting for any transactions between reportable segments
183. The nature of any differences between the measurements of the reportable segments' profits or losses and the entity's profit or loss before income tax expense or income and discontinued operations
184. The nature of any differences between the measurements of the reportable segments' assets and the entity's assets
185. The nature of any differences between the measurements of the reportable segments' liabilities and the entity's liabilities
186. The nature of any changes from prior periods in the measurement methods used to determine reported segment profit or loss and the effect of those changes on the measure of segment profit or loss
187. The nature and effect of any asymmetrical allocations to reportable segments

188. Reconciliations of the following: the total of the reportable segments' revenues to the entity's revenue, the total of the reportable segments' measures of profit or loss to the entity's profit or loss before tax expense and discontinued operations, the total of the reportable segments' assets to the entity's assets, the total of the reportable segments' liabilities to the entity's liabilities, the total of the reportable segments' amounts for every other material item of information disclosed to the corresponding amount for the entity

189. Basic and diluted earnings pers hare

190. The amounts used as the numerators in calculating basic and diluted earnings pers hare and a reconciliation of those amounts to the profit or loss attributable to the parent entity fort he period

191. The weighted-average number of ordinary shares used as the denominator in calculatinf basic and diluted earnings per share, and a reconciliation of these denominators to each other

192. Instruments that could potentially dilute basic earnings pers hare in the future

193. A description of ordinary share transactions or potential ordinary share transactions

194. The classification, presentation and measurement requirements to a non-current asset (or disposal group) that is classified as held-for-sale

195. Information that enables users of the financial statements to evaluate the financial effects of non-current assets (or disposal groups)

196. For a non-current asset or disposal group classified as held-for-sale; the major classes of assets and liabilities classified as hel-for-sale seperately from other assets

197. Related party relationships between parent and subsidiaries irrespective of whether transactions have taken place between those related parties

198. The fact that the related party transactions were made on terms equivalent to those that prevail in arm's length transactions

199. Information about the transactions and outstanding balances between related parties

200. The amount of the transactions, the amount of outstanding balances, provisions for doubtful debts related to the amount of outstanding balances and the expense recognised during the period in respect of bad or doubtful debts due from related party transactions

201. Key management compensation of the entity in total for each of the following categories: short-term employee benefits, post-employment benefits, other long-term benefits, termination benefits and share-based payments

202. Information that identifies and explains the amounts in the financial statements arising from insurance contracts

203. The accounting policies adopted for insurance contracts and related assets, liabilities, income and expenses

204. The recognised assets, liabilities, income and expense arising from insurance contracts

205. The process used to determine the assumptions that have the greatest effect on the measurement of the recognised amounts relating to insurance contracts

206. The effect of changes in assumptions used to measure insurance assets and insurance liabilities

207. Reconciliations of changes in insurance liabilities, reinsurance assets and related deferred acquisition costs

208. Information that enables users of the financial statements to evaluate the nature and extent of risks arising from insurance contracts

209. Information about exposures to interest rate risk or market risk under embedded derivatives conrtained in a host insurance contract
210. Information about market risk arising from insurance contracts
211. Information about liquidity risk arising from insurance contracts
212. Information about credit risk arising from insurance contracts
213. Information that identifies and explains the amounts recognised in the financial statements arising from the exploration for and evaluation of mineral resources
214. The amounts of assets, liabilities, income and expense and operating and investing cash flows arising from the exploration for and evaluation of mineral resources
215. Amount of any impairment loss arising from the impairment test of exploration and evaluation assets

---

[1] In 2012 Turkish Accounting Standards Board was remplaced by Public Oversight Accounting and Auditing Standards Authority. From beginning with 2012, Public Oversight Accounting and Auditing Standards Authority is charged with the issuance of Turkish Financial Reporting Standards which are compatible with International Financial Reporting Standards.

2

The reputation driven interplay of relationships between clients and auditors in an auditor selection process: A multilevel network approach

Slobodan Kacanski[1]

Roskilde University, Denmark

Abstract: This study investigates the reputation-based interplay between auditor selection and interlocking directorships from a multilevel network perspective. The aim of this article is to explore how and under what conditions reputation influences patterns of social selection processes in an assurance service context. To empirically determine the impact of reputation on establishing relational ties, this study applies exponential random graph models (ERGMs) for multilevel networks. The case study was carried out in the Danish field of mandatory audits, and findings here make a valuable contribution to the literature on auditor selection. A total of 774 annual reports were collected from 145 - 165 Danish public listed companies, and the relational data of companies was assembled, as comprised of the members of supervisory boards and partners who signed audit reports during the five-year period from 2010 to 2014. In this study, mechanisms for auditor selection were controlled by mechanisms for interlocking directorships in order to obtain a broader picture of the conditions under which board members have tendencies to select reputable auditors. The findings suggest that reputation has a significant impact on both observed processes, however, results reveal that reputation has a compensatory nature, as it drives both mechanisms of social selection but never simultaneously.

Keywords: reputation, board of directors, interlock directorship, network, ERGMs

---

[1] *Corresponding author*: Department for Social Sciences and Business, Roskilde University; Universitetsvej 1, 4000 Roskilde; email address: kacanski@ruc.dk

1. Introduction

There are two mechanisms that drive customer demands: (1) experience (Granovetter, 1973; Davis & Robins, 2004; Powell, 1990; Podolny, 2001), and (2) reputation. In today's auditing, it is argued that reputation plays a role in setting up market structure (OECD, 2009).

Brazel and Bradford (2011) argued that before the Sarbanes-Oxley (SOX) era, external auditors were entitled to select and dismiss their clients. However, after the announcement of the SOX, when clients became able to select which auditor to use, many questions were raised in relation to the factors and reasons that clients consider when selecting or changing their auditors (Beattie & Fearnley, 1998; Magri & Baldacchino, 2004; Woo & Koh, 2001). Although, the literature in this academic field at first claimed that audit fees were the main driver influencing the selection of auditors, Beattie and Fearnley (1998) argued that fees are only the most frequently cited reason. In fact, clients who change auditors are less likely to consider economical factors (Beattie & Fearnley, 1998), but Magri and Baldacchino (2004) found that the availability of auditors and a client's perception of their behavioral characteristics were the most important factors in the selection of an auditor. The selection and change of an auditor might have negative consequences for companies, such as to their public image (Neveling, 2006) or stock price (Asthana et al., 2010). The literature has reported that client might expect to gain better reputation if they select reputable auditor (Magri & Baldacchino, 2004). The literature has only initiated the question of reputation and the role it might have on auditor selection, however, and no study yet examined the significance of reputation on a client's choice.

The literature on the structure of supervisory boards (Palmer et al., 1986) and strategies for interlocking directorships has emphasized that boards are responsible for auditor selection (PwC, 2012). Board structures and interlocking directorships (Mizruchi, 1996) have been of a special interest to researchers ever since the concepts were first seen in the US economy. By definition, "interlocking" involves the participation of a single director in a supervisory board of at least two companies at the time (Mizruchi, 1996). Studies have showed that the existence of interlocks is an integral part of company strategies and goals, such as: capital allocation (Mizruchi & Stearns, 1988; Pfeffer, 1972), business control (Allen, 1978, 1974; Stokman et al., 1985; Zeitlin, 1974), the formation of interdependencies between companies (Pfeffer & Salanc, 1978) and upper class cohesion (Palmer, 1983; Useem, 1982; Zeitlin, 1974), however, Galaskiewicz et al. (1985) hypothesized that increasing prestige might be an alternative strategy to interlocking, arguing that companies select other companies that are better perceived.

Both streams of the literature have suggested that reputation might impact both selection mechanisms. Thus, regarding the assumptions that (1) reputation, as a social perception, might both be positive and negative (Brewer *et al.*, 2002), and (2) companies that share a board member are likely to select the same audit firm (Davison *et al.*, 1984), this paper argues that reputation has a significant impact on both selection processes (auditor and company with which to interlock), and that those processes are mutually interdependent. By adopting a network methodology, this paper aims to provide an examination of how reputations are distributed across the network of inter-company and auditor-client relational ties. The network approach used here offers a unique opportunity to challenge the previous two literature streams, and therefore, the analysis is centered on the following research question: *How does reputation affect the social selection process in the auditing context?*

The paper is structured as follows. First, I present the research area, motivations behind the investigation and the research question in the introduction of the paper. Second, the background outlines relevant literature on the topic, including the theoretical background of the study. The methodology, data collection and method are then described. I present the findings of the analysis, followed by a discussion involving the theoretical background of the study. Finally, the conclusions explicitly answer the research question and delineate the limitations of the study, and an agenda is offered for future research.

2. Literature review, hypotheses development and theoretical background

2.1. Reputation in the contexts of auditing and interlocking directorships

Recent research has emphasized the importance of reputation through the role it has in determining social relations across different social contexts. Various studies have deployed their own definitions of the concept, but for this study I readapt the definition developed by Fombrun (1996:72) who defined reputation as *'a perceptual representation of a social actor's past action and future prospects that describes its overall appeal'*. Reputation is recognized as an intangible asset (Goldberg *et al.*, 2003) which is a reflection of a person's or social group's perception.

Researchers studying corporative contexts were interested in various aspects of reputation (Barnett *et al.*, 2006). In the business world, reputation is predetermined as a fundamental resource for achieving competitive advantages, which ensure the sustainability of the business entity (Barney, 1991; Deephouse, 2000; Martínez & Olmedo, 2010). Several studies have showed that self-perception might provide insights into someone's own reputation, but the concept recognizes that reputation emerges in the eyes of others (Stuart et al., 1999; Turban & Cable, 2003). Miles and Covin (2002) stated that reputation is fragile commodity as a result of perception, and is difficult to achieve but easily lost.

Unlike prestige which is subjective and can be only a positive value (Maner & Case, 2016; Henrich & Gil-White, 2001; Norredam & Album, 2007), reputation is an objective social concept that can be both positive and negative (Brewer et al., 2002: 27-8; Henrich & Gil-White, 2001; Highhouse et al., 2009: 1482), and the value of it emerges from the summative perception of an entire community et al. 2010). This study will thus focus on reputation due to its objective nature, and since the collected data and the scale of the observed network did not enable subjective perceptions to be either observed or analyzed.

Various studies in auditing have discussed the implications of reputation for auditing firms and auditors. Linthicum et al. (2010) argued that auditor reputation is important for clients, and asserted that clients tend to compensate for the diminished reputation level of auditors by investing in corporate social responsibility in order to stabilize or enhance their own social position. Magri and Baldacchino (2004) assumed that clients tend to overpay in order to have their annual reports audited by reputable auditors, which implies that, in both cases clients are likely to pay more, but might select either reputable or disreputable auditors according to the incentives. Magri and Baldacchino (2004) assumed that a client's selection of a reputable auditor might also enhance their reputation, and compensate for the negative consequences of the change. Kanagaretnam et al. (2010) reported that an auditor's reputation and their earnings management are negatively correlated. This is because reputable auditors tend not to risk their own reputation, and they refuse bribes offered by clients to report favorable opinions. Sucher et al. (1999) argued that audit firm reputation is primarily based on technical and functional properties, where the size of the firm is what indicates the quality of service (DeAngelo, 1981; Salehi & Kangarlouei, 2010). Aronmwan et al. (2013) reported that the reputation of an audit firm might affect the corporate image of a client, which implies that the selection of a Big 4 firm might enhance the credibility of a client's financial statements, compared to that of a non-Big 4 firm (Simunic & Stein, 1987; Francis & Wilson, 1988). The first stream of literature therefore shows that audit firm reputation might be of importance to clients, since clients might perceive selecting reputable auditors as increasing their own social standing.

On the other hand, the literature on reputation-driven interlocks has argued that increased reputation is a sign of improved legitimacy and trustworthiness (Parkhe, 1993). Board members perceive that the formation of an interlock with reputable companies might have a positive impact on their own reputation as well. Boards might therefore employ a cooptation strategy for business alliance formation in order to gain legitimacy (Gu & Lu, 2014), which might further be manifested in tendencies to increase proximity to those that are generally perceived as reputable (Gu & Lu, 2014). Podolny (2001) suggested that status is relationally reflexive and an awareness of its sensitivity urges actors to carefully select the other social actors, because low-status holders might lower the status of those holding a better position. This corresponds to the mechanism of opportunities and needs, and suggests that cooptation is less likely to occur if differences in perceived levels of reputation or other attributes are apparent between focal actors (Galaskiewicz et al., 1985; Gu & Lu, 2014). Overall, studies have revealed that, in the context of corporate governance, interlocks are likely to emerge between companies that hold similar socially perceived reputations.

To the author's knowledge, there were only two studies that have examined the contexts of auditor selection and interlocking directorships. In an Australian context, Davison et al. (1984) found that links between companies audited by the same audit firm can, to a considerable extent, be explained by links between those same companies when they have a director in common. On the other hand, by focusing on an experience-based demand mechanism, Johansen and Pettersson (2013) found that interlocks in Denmark have a strong impact on the selection of auditors and audit fees. The gap found in previously proposed framework urges bridging the seemingly disparate bodies of theory by discussing the question of how two reputation-driven demands are mutually negotiated through mechanisms of interlocking directorships and auditor selection.

To tackle some of the limitations of the previous literature, and theorize about the mechanism of auditor selection through mechanisms of interlocking directorships, I define two hypotheses that will be tested by conducting network studies.

> *H1: Reputation plays an important role in driving the demand mechanisms of auditor selection and interlocking directorships.*
> *H2: Clients tend to select reputable auditors when they want to compensate for a lack of homophily at the level of interlocks.*

2.2. Theoretical perspectives

This subsection presents the main theoretical background where the aim is to frame the space and conditions within which results of the study are discussed. Use of social network analysis, as a research method, is theoretically insufficient and the engagement of the respective theory that will provide generalizations of findings is crucial (Robins, 2015: 216). I outline the theory which, I believe, will provide a meaningful framework for the discussion of empirical results.

I justify the selection of a theoretical background on the following assumption. Market demands that evolve under the condition of egocentric uncertainties, when social actors tend to select other actors who hold higher social status, occurs only when selectors are unaware of the quality that selected actor provides (Podolny, 2001). DeAngelo (1981) argued that the audit market is just like that, because clients are unable to gather insight into the quality of the audit service. In general, social actors might enhance their legitimacy in the eyes of the others by forming relationships with those that are reputable (Baum & Oliver, 1992), selecting those of higher rather than lower status (Podolny, 1993). In such a way, they are being influenced by previous quality uncertainties to enter the zone of "conspicuous consumption" (Podolny, 2001), which they use to demonstrate their belonging to the group of those that are reputable. Consequently, it appears that social actors tend to connect and identify themselves with others as they use the status of others to increase recognition within their own environment. According to Zuckerman (1999), patterns of relationships formed by firms are not only relevant for the exchange of, for example, information or services, but for those patterns might have an impact on the perception that third parties have of social actors and their engagement in relationships with others. Taking that into account, in addition to auditor selection companies establishing interlocks, it is questionable how patterns of relational ties emerge at the network level.

Correspondingly, the theoretical framework of this study is given by a combination of elements that have been outlined by reputation and identity theory. Despite notable similarities in conceptualizations of reputation across various theoretical standpoints, theorists have occupied different perspectives and grounded their theories on different assumptions, allowing researchers to select the most appropriate one (Musum & Tovey, 2011; Burke et al., 2011; Craik, 2009). Central to this study is the viewpoint of Craik (2009) who argued that the concept of reputation always operates within networks of social relations. His assertion was that reputation is not located on or in a person, but it is a dispersed phenomenon found in the beliefs and assertions of groups. It is therefore a part of the social environment that is uniquely referenced to a specific social actor. In general, any discussions related to reputation are often vague in terms of who it is that holds beliefs and assertions, but the subjects of the reputation are clearly specifiable, finite in number, and unique to each social actor. More specifically, Craik (2009) developed a network-based model of reputation, and asserted that it has systematic implications for the diversity of disciplines, including the social network analysis. In this theory, he suggested that a change in reputation network might emerge as an initiative that is triggered by social actors. Such a premise implies that reputation might recreate structures of social relationships, where a particular actor's incentives determine the distribution of network dynamics. Craik's (2009) theory conceptualizes reputation network as a structure of relational ties where social incentives, which might be different in nature and contextually independent, determine and restructure the network configuration. In this study, reputation is understood as a variable that is independent from network ties as it gives an opportunity to observe the change of the network structure over time, which is the main unit of the analysis, and context specific.

To reflect the incentives of social actors, reputation theory requires the support of an additional theory that will enable the proper discussion of findings. According to Fombrun (1996) five factors are critical for establishing reputation at the corporate level, and one of these is *identity*, which Fombrun interprets as seeing an organization as genuine. To integrate the notion of identity into the network study of reputation in terms of the dynamic nature of relationships between social actors, I assume that it is legitimate to inspect how social actor incentives could be linked to particular social identity scenarios, and which scenarios could be particularly ascribed to incentives for social identification by observing the characteristics of network configurations. Bringing this closer, the use of this theory will enable a determination of whether reputation might be asserted to serve as a mechanism or a tool for boosting social identification.

I use theory developed by Tajfel and Turner (1979) who grounded their main propositions on theories of intergroup behavior and intra-group morale, cohesiveness and cooptation. Three principles are fundamental for actor entities seeking social identity: (1) individuals always strive for positive social identity; (2) which is, to a large extent, based on favorable comparison; (3) but in the event it becomes perceived as unsatisfactory, social actors might switch to others that are perceived as more positively distinct. Tajfel and Turner (1979) define three strategies for enhancing identity: (1) individual mobility - as a strategy for dissociating from the erstwhile group and joining the other, (2) social creativity - to seek alternative criteria for comparison when no change occurs, and (3) social competition - as an aggressive scenario of seeking positive distinctiveness through direct competition of the out-group.

To conclude, if it is accepted that reputation has a given value that drives network structure, and that incentives for acquiring reputation are changeable and conditioned on relationships, and that establishing relationships with reputable actors might be used as a tool for boosting social position by identifying through that relationship, it could be argued that the network theory of reputation and identity theory might give a solid basis for the interpretation of findings.

3. Methodology

3.1. The Danish regulation and corporate context related to auditor selection

The Danish corporate governance system of publicly listed companies involves two tiers, and comprises a supervisory board, which appoints an executive board.

Depending on which type of top tier is employed, the Danish corporate governance system might be categorized as either a 'classical' or 'modified' two-tier system, and accordingly, representatives sitting on those boards have different responsibilities. In Denmark, public listed companies follow a classic two-tier structure, and the modified system is also applied to some extent. Disregarding the previous categorization, representatives of the top tier boards have different responsibilities, such as determining business principles and strategies, ensuring proper organization, deciding on risk policies and supervising the performance of the executive management.

In addition to responsibilities, Article 41 from the 2006 amendment of the European Directive on statutory audit prescribes an obligation for the board to make a decision of appointment of the auditor, which, once made, should be announced at the annual general meeting (AGM). In practice, supervisory board members make the final decision on auditor appointment, but their decision might to some extent be moderated by the recommendation of an audit committee, if present.

Only a small sample of companies has separately appointed audit committees, however, which, if present, usually consist of members of the supervisory boards. If an audit committee is not appointed, the board of directors must be explicit in announcing that they take the overall responsibilities that are in jurisdiction of the audit committee.

For the purpose of this study I take into consideration only representatives of supervisory boards, since they are fully liable for appointing an external auditor. I do not distinguish the formal positions of members on boards, and assume that each member might equally effect a decision about the appointment of the auditor. The top tier in the corporate governance structure was selected for this study, as their representatives might simultaneously occupy multiple positions on the boards of different companies, and by chairing at multiple tables might equally impact multiple auditor selection processes, by choosing the same auditor.

Some features of regulation have affected the research design. From 1930 all listed companies in Denmark were obligated to appoint two audit firms, but joint audits were abandoned in 2005. In Denmark, information on the audit partners that signed the audit report is transparent, and it is not uncommon that two partners sign off on the same audit report. This has enabled me to identify the audit partners that were responsible for the audits and relate that information to a particular company, instead of the information of the auditing firm. Usually, up to two partners put their signatures on the report, but there are some examples where two audit firms collaborated on a single engagement, which resulted in four partner signatures on a single audit report.

3.2. Data collection

The data here covers the five year period from 2010 to 2014. I selected that period because there were no changes in regulations for mandatory audits in Denmark, and the period was uninterrupted by mergers, which were, by all means, very specific to the Danish audit context, since two huge mergers took place in 2008 (PwC) and in 2014 (KPMG), in Denmark.

In order to investigate interdependencies among the relationships between two types of social relations, companies sharing board members and their relationships with auditors in the context of auditor selection, I collected and extracted relational data from publically available annual reports for the purpose of this study. Relationships were extracted from the reports that were taken from the sample of Danish companies listed at Nasdaq OMX Copenhagen in each year of the observed period. A complete list of companies representing the sample was taken from a monthly report on equity trading from the 31st of December in each of the five consecutive years. All relevant annual reports were either collected from the official websites of companies, or via the online registry of Danish business entities, *Virk.dk*, which contains information and documents, such as annual reports, for all business entities in Denmark. Investor relationships departments delivered missing data via e-mail.

For this study 774 annual reports were collected in total, respectively 165, 162, 153, 149 and 145 for each year of observation from 2010 to 2014. As the number of collected annual reports corresponded to the size of the sample of business entities included in observations, a condition of completeness for network studies was fulfilled. The sample includes both financial and non-financial organizations, and a total of 191 unique business entities were included in the study. The structure of business entities slightly varied over the period, however, since some companies were listed and delisted during the time, which suggests that the inventory was not entirely stable. In total, information about 1761 board members was extracted and the data included 297 audit partners who signed off on the reports of 191 company, which were affiliated to, in total, 17 audit firms.

Reputation data was collected from two separate sources. At first, information related to company reputation scores was extracted from the annual RepTrak® reports issued by the Danish branch of the Reputation Institute in each respective year. The institute provides quantitative measures of company reputation scores that are appraised based on the following seven categories: product/service, innovation, workplace, governance, citizenship, leadership and performance. The quantification of each of these categories was used as an independent measure whose sum gives the final score reported in percent, and refers to both private and public companies. For the purpose of this study, only reputation scores related to relevant companies were extracted, but since the observed sample did not match the list of companies being appraised by RI, the entities omitted were assumed to be disreputable. This further supported the assumption that prestige, which is a highly subjective perception, could not be used in this study. On the other hand, in relation to the reputation of audit firms and auditors, I followed the arguments of Kanagaretnam *et al.* (2010) and McLennan and Park (2016), who primarily used a two-type classification of audit firms as a reputation proxy, Big 4 and non-Big 4 (Fuerman & Kraten, 2008; Aronmwan *et al.*, 2013). This classification implied that the first group was reputable, and the latter were disreputable audit firms. Following that classification, and since this study deals with individual auditors rather than audit firms, I used auditor affiliations to proxy their individual reputation scores.

To put the data in a form appropriate for statistical modeling, raw relational data was first extracted to a unique spreadsheet from which relevant information was selected and converted to a .csv format readable by Visone, which is a network visualization tool. In addition to visualizations it also provides an opportunity to export relational data from a visual form to an adjacency matrix in .txt format that is further readable by MPNet (Wang *et al.*, 2013), which is the software used here for statistical modeling. The extracted data finally produced estimations for five statistical models that will be discussed below, from which theoretical inferences were drawn.

3.3. Method

To extract findings from this case study it was crucial to select the appropriate method for the analysis. The aim of this study was to identify patterns of network configurations assembled from relationships between companies sharing directors and auditors with regard to reputation-based auditor selection. This case was selected to enable a better understanding of whether and how immaterial commodities govern social selection processes. With that focus, this study finds that social network analysis (SNA) is the most appropriate method for conducting an examination of the collected data, as it enables the identification of the structure and evolution of network patterns assembled around mutually interdependent social relationships.

According to Wassermann and Faust (1994: 11) social network analysis is a quantitative-based method, which emerged as a combination of empirical, theoretical and mathematical aspects of social relations, when different disciplines struggled to make sense of their relational data. There are different techniques in the research methodology of social network analysis, but technique selection is primarily driven by the nature of the observed network (one-mode, multiple, bipartite, multilevel, etc.) and boundaries predetermined by the researcher (Robins, 2015). So far, SNA has been widely used as a research method in fields such as sociology, psychology, business, organization, politics, etc. An advantage of this method is that it provides estimations on network statistics with regard to observed network patterns (configurations) and attributes, and the statistical results it produces represent estimations of how particular network configurations or observed attributes play a role in structuring the entire network. A particular advantage of this method is that it enables simultaneous estimation to be conducted over a range of selected network parameters, through which it is possible to identify interdependencies between individual observations. Importantly, the method does not conflict with the classical statistical methods, but rather adds to previous statistical approaches.

This study aims to simultaneously observe social processes existing between relationships among homogeneous (company to company) and heterogeneous (company to auditor) social actors. This network is thus most appropriately categorized as multilevel, since two types of relationships were observed between two types of actors. Although the network is configured as multilevel, relationships between homogeneous social actors have not been observed at both levels, so auditor-to-auditor relationships were excluded as no reputation effect was expected at the bottom level of the network.

Figure 1: Board interlocks and auditors - simplified visualization of the observed network

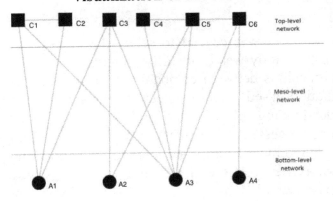

Note: In Figure 1 squares represent companies (C) and circles represent auditors (A) together with their respective IDs. The figure here is a simplification of the multilevel network analyzed in this paper. This study considers only top (company-to-company / interlock) and meso-level (company-to-auditor / mandatory audit) networks. Ties at both network levels are non-directional.

This study used recently developed exponential random graph models (ERGMs) for multilevel networks (Wang et al., 2013), which is a cutting-edge statistical model to produce the network statistics. The model will project the structure of network ties by using information on relationships between observed actors, supporting them with theoretically selected attributes to serve as predictors of ties. ERGM works as a pattern-recognition device, which was originally developed for examination of one-mode networks by Frank and Strauss (1986) and Wasserman and Pattison (1996). ERGMs are concerned with explaining the patterns of ties in a social network (Lusher et al., 2013), and assume that stochastic processes generate relational ties between them, which fits the theoretical conceptualization of reputation. ERGMs assume that ties in networks emerge through two distinctive processes: (1) network self-organization - presence or absence of other ties, and (2) social selection - due to the attributes of social actor. This study focuses on the latter, and specifically on the association of exogenous attributes and propensity of tie formation (Lusher *et al.*, 2013). One major example of such a process is the 'homophily' effect where ties tend to emerge between actors holding the same attribute (McPherson *et al.*, 2001). ERGMs hold the premise that the overall network structure is comprised of small mechanisms that lead to tie formation processes. This study considers network statistics in order to capture those network patterns whose emergence is not likely to occur at random. The network parameters observed in this study fully correspond to theoretically conditioned relational mechanisms. Finally, I estimate network statistics by integrating both top and meso-level parameters into the single model, and develop network estimations for each observed year. These estimations will enable an understanding of the drivers of local structural patterns, while their occurrence is conditioned on the likelihood of observing the overall network (Robins *et al.*, 2007).

4. Analysis of results

4.1. Sample description

Table 1 provides a summary of the descriptive statistics for the observed network models, and Table 3 reports the model estimations for network structural parameters and selected social actor attributes. It captures the most important properties of the two-mode interlock and auditor selection multilevel network for each of five observed years in order to identify the essence that is crucial for understanding the models. All networks are structurally different in regard to the number of companies (145 - 165), total numbers of board members (898 - 970) and auditors (161 - 189). Nevertheless, the presented ratios differ across observed network structures.

The densities of each network and in each year are below 1% (0.73% - 0.86%), which signifies low-density networks. That might be a consequence of regulation which determines the number mandatory engagements per year and number of partners per engagement, which could be assembled between auditors and companies. Across the observed years the average number of supervisory board members was below 7 ($m = 6.54 - 6.86$ / $SD = 2.52 - 2.73$), which in comparison with the size of supervisory boards in other countries, such as the US, may be considered relatively small. The average number of interlocks per board ranges from 1.11 - 1.16 ($SD = 0.42 - 0.44$), which implies the stability of an interlock network across the time, and rarely more than one director that interlocks at one board of directors. Finally, on average 1.82 - 1.91 ($SD = 0.38$ - 0.54) audit partners were engaged per client per year, while each auditor had 1.63 - 1,75 ($SD = 1.08$ - 1.17) audit engagements per year.

Table 1. Sample description

	2010	2011	2012	2013	2014
Number of companies (clients)	165	162	153	149	145
Number of board members (Individuals / with overlaps)	970 (1086)	963 (1074)	922 (1026)	898 (1000)	899 (994)
Number of audit firms	13	12	10	10	10
Number of auditors (Individuals / with overlaps)	189 (315)	189 (310)	167 (290)	161 (282)	163 (265)
Ratio auditors to audit firms	14.54 (24.23)	15.75 (25.83)	16.7 (29)	16.1 (28.2)	16.3 (26.5)
Average number of members per board of directors (supervisory board)	m=6.54 SD=2.62	m=6.63 SD=2.52	m=6.71 SD=2.61	m=6.71 SD=2.73	m=6.86 SD=2.61
Average number of interlocks per board of directors (supervisory board)	m=1.12 SD=0.42	m=1.16 SD=0.43	m=1.11 SD=0.44	m=1.11 SD=0.44	m=1.11 SD=0.43
Average number of audit partners per company (client)	m=1.91 SD=0.54	m=1.91 SD=0.46	m=1.89 SD=0.42	m=1.89 SD=0.48	m=1.82 SD=0.38
Average number of audit engagements per auditor	m=1.67 SD=1.13	m=1.64 SD=1.17	m=1.73 SD=1.23	m=1.75 SD=1.08	m=1.63 SD=1.17
Total density of two-mode multilevel interaction network	0.73%	0.73%	0.84%	0.86%	0.82%

Note: m - mean; *SD* - standard deviation.

4.2. Model estimations

Table 3 provides estimations of the five respective models for each observed year, which are organized into three horizontal sections. The first and second sections represent statistics related to network structural effects. Specifically, they give estimations of parameters related to ties between companies sharing directors (one-mode) and companies selecting auditors (two-mode). The third section outlines estimations related to variables (reputation, net income and company size), which are integrated into the model together with network structural parameters that are theoretically determined. Attributes are further distinguished in two subsections in order to enable the transparency of both one-mode and two-mode network attribute effects. All models are discussed to provide an understanding of the interdependence between network structures and observed attributes.

Overall, model estimations reveal that observed network is characterized by the presence or the absence of a certain number of patterns. Significant patterns are those that are likely to occur more or less often than could be expected by chance. The presence and significance of attribute effects indicates the extent to which a particular attribute contributes to the network formation process. Despite the fact that findings are partially inconsistent across observations, a trend in regard to how the social selection process unfolds is identifiable across the network statistics. Table 2 presents the network patterns that were included in model estimations, which are derived based on previously delineated theoretical assumptions.

Table 2. Network patterns included in the models

Visualization	Parameter (MPNet)	Interpretation
	Edge - 1-mode network edge	Tie between two companies sharing a board member (Control effect)
	ATA - 1-mode network closure effect	Companies forming closure effect through ties of interlocks
	XEdge - 2-mode network edge	Tie between company and auditor (Control effect)
	XACB - 2-mode network clustering effect	Interlock has no impact on selection of the same auditor
	ATXAX - 2-mode network closure effect	Interlock has an impact on selection of the same auditor
Control effects		
	Star2A - 1-mode network	Companies tend to share a board member between two companies (Markov model effect)
	A2PA - 1-mode network	Companies forming clustering effect through ties of interlocks
	XStar3B - 2-mode network	Auditor tends to audit three clients (Markov model effect)
	XASB - 2-mode network	Auditor popularity effect

Visualization	Parameter (MPNet)	Interpretation
	XASA - 2-mode network	Company selecting more auditors

In the following, I provide with an overview of the results for each separate network, together with an overview of the entire period of observation to enable a dynamic approach.

4.3. Structuring principles of shared directorship network

The results of network parameter estimations related to the top-level network indicate that companies are likely to have a shared board member(s) in the structure of the supervisory boards (board of directors). In network terms, this implies that relational ties are likely to become established between companies through interlocking directorships. More specifically, the positive and significant statistics of the observed network parameter shows that the interlocking directorship network is rather structured according to a more complex rule than a single tie observation might reveal.

The focal network structuring parameter shows that relational ties between companies tend to create a strong closure effect, which is both positive and significant in all five models across the entire period. The significant parameter value indicates that an interlock network is characterized by the presence of small regions where two companies that share at last one board member are likely to share their board members with the same other companies, if more than one other interlock is established with more than one additional company. This implies that the emergence of interlocks with the same companies might be directly ascribed to an already existing interlock between two focal companies, where the interlock also affects the emergence of other interlocks.

The closure effect is an alternating triangle-like form network configuration where the number of triangles, interlocks with the same other companies, is rather flexible, and does not specify the direction, origin, which particular individual board member represents the interlock, or whether the common actor mediates multiple interlocks. It also reveals the path that board members tend to take when they structure a network of interlocks. The results here show that a closure effect is the main structuring principle, which might create a condition for the direct information flow between boards comprising the network. It is also possible to assume that, due to the information flow, companies that are structuring the closure might be engaged with similar decisions related to other possible relationships, such as auditor selection.

In three out of five observations, models were controlled by the *Markov* two-star effect in order to achieve model convergence, which represents the approach to network statistics at the common point. Good convergence is indicated by the t-ratios being close to zero. In all three cases negative and significant statistics were produced, and those results showed that companies, in general, are not likely to have exactly two interlock ties with other companies, which corresponds to the information on the average number of interlocks per board of directors (supervisory board) presented in Table 1. Those results correspond with the social circuit network parameter (closure), where the significance of a complex network structure requires more than two interlock ties to emerge from a single entity in order to form a particular configuration.

The second part of the analysis is driven by the assumption that social selection processes within social networks are conditioned by similarities in attributes that actors in the network hold. In this step I inspect the extent to which different attributes drive the homophily effect in relation to interlock emergence, taking into account a condition of attribute interdependence. For this purpose I integrated company size, total earnings (net income) and reputation scores for each company as main variables. The attributes of company size and net income are categorized as continuous, while reputation is predetermined as a binary variable. The aim of these attributes is to examine how the strength of similarities in particular characteristics determines the emergence of relational ties. The incorporation of all three attributes to network structural parameters allowed an examination of whether, and if so which, previously selected attributes surpass the others in terms of significance, and therefore might be described as the model's most influential attribute regarding tie emergence.

The results in all five estimations showed that similarity in company size and financial results have no significant effect on predetermining the interlock emergence when reputation is integrated in the model as a separate variable. The results indicate that interlocks tend not to emerge between companies that are similar in number of employees, which were used here as a proxy for company size, nor at the level of the bottom line result. Although the observed models demonstrated mainly positive network statistics, all previous attributes were insignificant, and thus the size and income-based homophily effects on interlock emergence tend to occur at random.

Table 3. Results of the exponential random graph models for selected years

Network level	Parameter	2010 Estimate (S.E.)	2011 Estimate (S.E.)	2012 Estimate (S.E.)	2013 Estimate (S.E.)	2014 Estimate (S.E.)
Client-level: shared directorship networks (Control)	Tie between two companies sharing board member (Edge)	-5.5063* (0.219)	-5.7073* (0.203)	-3.4894* (0.35)	-5.477* (0.203)	-5.7107* (0.174)
	Companies forming closure effect through ties of interlocks (ATA)	1.6745* (0.106)	1.8902* (0.123)	0.2446* (0.119)	2.0358* (0.127)	1.7440* (0.109)
	Companies forming clustering effect through ties of interlocks (A2PA)	-0.0378 (0.028)	-	-	-	-0,0497 (0,031)
	Companies tend to share board member with two companies (Markov model effect) (Star2A)	-	-0.0549* (0.025)	-0.1117* (0.045)	-0.0945* (0.036)	-
Auditor-client interaction network: (Control)	Tie between company and auditor (XEdge)	-3.8575* (0.376)	-7.2185* (1.24)	-4.3094* (0.37)	-7.1716 (3.859)	-6.4880* (1.010)
	Interlock has no impact on selection of the same auditor (XACB)	-0.4172* (0.19)	-0.2074 (0.226)	0.1453 (0.081)	0.6582* (0.252)	-0.2334* (0.089) (λ = 6)
Meso-level network	Interlock has an impact on selection of the same auditor (ATXAX)	0.0086 (0.023)	1.1727* (0.221)	-0.4127 (0.605)	0.7037 (0.444)	1.2593* (0.342)
	Auditor popularity effect (XASB)	-	2.0162* (0.909)	-	-	-
	Companies selecting more auditors (XASA)	-	-	-	-	-7,5249* (0,843)
	Auditor tends to audit three clients (XStar3B)	-0.0461 (0.056)	-	-	-0.1103 (0.083)	-
Attributes at the shared directorship network	Reputation-based interlock effect	1.0594* (0.279)	1.0055* (0.277)	-0.2661 (0.978)	0.3443 (0.944)	0.1135 (1.088)
	Company size-based interlock effect	0.1189 (0.121)	0.0733 (0.102)	0.244 (0.172)	-0.0397 (0.042)	0.1454 (0.106)
	Financial result-based interlock effect	-0.0146 (0.063)	0.0321 (0.041)	-0.0247 (0.075)	0.064 (0.043)	0.0271 (0.051)
Attributes at meso-level network	Reputation-based selection of auditors	-0.5137* (0.221)	1.1265 (1.024)	0.4613 (0.348)	2.2883 (3.877)	0.449* (0.202)

Goodness of fit All t-statistics for each parameter at all selected years were below the threshold value of 0.1 and such indicates a good model fit (Robins *et al.*, 2009; Wang *et al.*, 2013).

Notes: All reported coefficients are unstandardized. Z score was used only to convert client size and net-income values into a narrower span relative to their original values. Statistically significant effects were captured at or beyond 0.05 level. The value of λ = 2 has been used here as an initial value as it been proven to be reasonable for many ERGMs estimations, however higher values, as indicated (λ = 6), contribute convergence in the case of highly skewed degree distributions (Koskinen & Daraganova, 2013; Robins *et al.*, 2007). Omitted parameters at both network levels were excluded either because the model convergence could be reached without them or could not be, if otherwise.

4.4. The impact of company attributes on one-mode network social selection process

Model estimations, on the other hand, show that reputation scores might affect interlock emergence. Based on the estimations, in the first two models (2010 and 2011) the reputation-based homophily effect is both positive and significant, and reputation effect was either positive or negative, but insignificant in the following three models. Comparing those results to the network structuring parameters it could be inferred that a strong positive closure effect is present between reputable companies in years when reputation effect was significant, but as the closure effect is durable over time because decisions for establishing alliances are strategic, the diminished significance of reputation statistics might not be a sign of the reduced importance of reputation effect on alliance emergence, but rather a sign of diminished levels of reputation scores between companies making closures, which further disturbs the effect of reputation-based homophily. Potentially reduced reputation scores between members of highly closured network areas might suggest the irrelevance of reputation for interlock emergence. However, this might require additional inspection of whether and how, on the other levels of the network, reputation effect might potentially be compromised or regained.

4.5. Structuring principles of auditor selection network

Continuing with presentation of estimated models, in one part of the observation it was estimated whether the selection of auditor can be determined by the presence of interlocks, and in particular, the selection of the same auditor. The effect of an interlock on auditor selection was examined by testing the two opposite network structuring principles, through which it was possible to identify the prevalent significance. In particular, whether the presence of an interlock has an impact on auditor selection or not. These two effects differ in regard to the presence or absence of a tie between companies (clients) in relation to the same auditor selection. The results of simultaneous inspection of the top-level and meso-level network showed that across the entire observed period, apart from 2012, interlocks had a positive and significant effect on selection of the same auditor. Although the 2012 model produced insignificant statistics, the positive parameter value shows that the tendency is present, but the insignificant statistics might be a result of changes in the structure of companies being listed at particular time. Overall, the results here imply that interlocks have a positive and significant impact on auditor selection, and this might be a result of previously discussed closure effect which implies that the transmission of information between boards of directors is established through interlocks.

Additional network structuring principles were included within several models to enable network convergence. They included auditor popularity effect, auditor tendencies to select three clients (which is a *Markov* 3-star effect) and company tendencies to select more auditors. Each of these network parameters was insignificant except the last, which was significant and negative, which was expected since regulatory requirements prevent companies from selecting an arbitrary number of auditors.

4.6. The impact of auditor reputation on client choice

Finally, to encompass the entire model estimations and reflect on the previously defined hypotheses, I report the following findings related to reputation in earlier discussions about findings of the observed models. The findings here prompt inconsistent but rather interesting reflections on whether and how reputation plays a role in social selection processes.

Network statistics show that the impact of an auditor's reputation on client selection varies across models over the observed period. The first of five models shows negative and significant statistics for the reputation-driven selection of auditors, implying that the companies were less likely to select auditors with positive reputation scores, or who are considered reputable. In the following three models, the reputation statistics started gathering positive values, but were still insignificant, however, in the very last model the effect of reputation on auditor selection became positive and significant. Regardless of the fact that the model statistics gave cross-sectional estimations of network observations, it is clearly seen that there are tendencies for clients in this case to be prone to altering incentives for selecting reputable auditors.

Overall, the effect of the changed and increased significance of auditor reputation scores on the client selection process could be directly related to the emergence of a reputation-based interlock. Considering two reputation based social selection processes, homophily for interlock emergence and the selection of an auditor, it is possible to identify an interplay in which a single attribute type is produced between two network levels, and finally to identify cross-level reflections on relational tie emergence. In models where the reputation-based interlock effect was positive and significant, the effect of reputation-based selection of the auditor was negative and significant or either insignificant. This could be interpreted as meaning that companies might not be interested in selecting reputable auditors when they have established ties with reputable companies through interlocks, or in other words, when interlock cluster representatives hold similar reputation levels. The finding here supports the assumption that in the latter models, when the reputation effect between companies became insignificant, reputation-based effect on the selection of auditor was the opposite, positive and significant. It might seem that the ease of auditor reselection and a change towards those that are reputable might be used as the tool to compensate for the lack of reputation effect at the company level network, because interlock alliance formation is relatively more durable and hard to disrupt.

It is possible to confirm that reputation, in general, has an important and significant role in social selection processes within actors of the same, and between actors of different, types. More specifically, auditor reputation plays an important role in the selection process of clients, but only when diminished reputation scores disturb the reputation effect at the interlock level. Acknowledging this, it could be argued that both hypotheses, *H1* and *H2*, have been proved.

4.7. Goodness of fit analyses

As recommended by Robins *et al.* (2009) and Wang *et al.* (2013), each model presented has been tested for goodness of fit. *T*-values have been estimated for all available network configurations, and estimates for observed network parameters were below 0.1, and below 2 in absolute values for all the other network configurations, suggesting reliable results (Appendix 1).

5. Discussion

In agreement with two streams of literature that an immaterial commodity such as reputation might have a significant effect on social selection processes in the contexts of interlocking directorships (Galaskiewicz *et al.*, 1985) and auditor selection (Magri & Baldacchino, 2004), the study here examined whether and how reputation mutually negotiates between the two contexts. Although the literature only hypothesized an impact of reputation on social tie emergence, a separate examination of those two contexts would result in limited understanding of the reputation effect in an audit context. Arguing that reputation might negotiate between two social selection processes, reputation-driven tension prompted an investigation of how such interdependence drives the interplay of social selection processes. To jointly examine the effect of reputation on relation emergence, I utilized exponential random graph models (Wang *et al.*, 2013) to quantify the interdependence and identify the mutual impact of two separate, but arguably contingent, reputation-driven tendencies. This was done through an examination of relational ties and the network configurations that they have formed across five separate models that were captured across the observed period.

The results of the analysis suggest that reputation has a significant effect on the emergence of both interlocks and auditor selection, but the emergence of relationships is causal and reputation effect is compensatory.

Initially, this study confirmed that interlocks impact auditor selection (Davison *et al.*, 1984; Johansen & Pettersson, 2013), but also that Danish interlocks have a strong tendency to form complex, closure-like network configurations, which might enable information flow and managing decisions across the alliances. In respect to other studies on strategies for establishing interlocking directorships (Mizruchi & Stearns, 1988; Stokman *et al.*, 1985; Pfeffer & Salanc, 1978; Useem, 1982) and reasons for auditor selection and change (Beattie & Fearnley, 1995; Magri & Baldacchino, 2004; Woo & Koh, 2001), the findings showed that, in both contexts, relationships tend to either exist between those that are reputable, or to emerge towards those that are reputable. The social selection process is characteristic of network studies, as ties between homogeneous actors exist and emerge through the homophily effect, and the results here demonstrate that no material elements drove the effect of emergence, while the reputation, as an immaterial element, did. Not all models showed that reputation had a significant effect on interlock emergence, however, the results here challenged the argument of Gu and Lu (2014) who claimed that in a lack of homophily it is hard to establish proximity with the others social actors. Their argument is questionable due to the durability of interlock ties, which implies that the actors involved in social networks might experience changes in attributes over time. In this regard, the diminished significance of reputation, which is a result of changed reputation scores between companies forming closures, does not result in redistribution of ties representing interlocking directorships towards those that were re-evaluated as reputable, but rather keeps them stable despite the unequal distribution of reputation scores.

The duration of interlock alliances and investigation of homophily effects to determine the relevance of reputation by inspecting only the network of interlocks, would bring concern about whether reputation has durability in terms of significance, or is rather random since it depends on current evaluation scores. An inspection of how a level of auditor reputation becomes relevant to companies when closure effects do not sustain homophily effect between those that assemble closure becomes a crucial part of the investigation. Results revealed the existence of an alternative mechanism that companies undergo in order to compensate for an imbalance at the homogeneous actor level of the network. This mechanism of compensation brought complexity to strategies for establishing ties, in this case, with auditors. This indicated that a deficit of reputation-based homophily drives changes of relationships between companies and auditors, particularly those that are also carriers of the focal attribute, but at the other network level. Divergences in durations of interlock-based alliances and client engagement with auditors enables companies to use auditor reputation as a temporary mechanism to compensate for the current lack of reputation-based homophily. This study further extends the argument of Gu and Lu (2014) and Galaskiewicz *et al.* (1985), as it touches upon how companies deal with the issue of unequal distribution of reputation in order to protect their social position from being perceived as either disreputable, or being connected with those that are disreputable.

This study also gives an indication that social actors might find that their relationships with other social actors may contribute to the social perception of themselves, as they tend to navigate through relationships in order to eliminate the negative effects that more durable relationships (interlocks) might bring. This offers a rationale for discussing the results of reputation networks from the perspective of identity theory, as social environments are comprised of stratified social groups, and social actors might use such mechanisms to signify their identification through others, which might enhance their social standing. Reflecting on identity theory, it is notable that board members, in fact, use reputation as a strategy for identification, since they tend to establish relationships with those that are reputable if they are perceived as reputable, as well. Put differently, companies establish relationships with heterogeneous social actors to compensate for an imbalance in reputation between the homogeneous group, which they use as a tool for re-identification.

Giving empirical context to the theoretical categorization of social processes in alignment with identity theory, the case here reveals that two strategies are characteristic of this context. In fact, two processes resemble the strategies of social creativity and individual mobility (Tajfel & Turner, 1979) as they give complementary perspectives on scenarios that social actors tend to pursue at the multilevel network level. The strategy of social creativity enables network participants to seek positive distinctiveness through an alternation of criteria for comparison, while the mobility strategy enables them to make movements towards higher-status groups. More specifically, companies, while still holding interlocks, tend to seek an alternative source of comparison in order to enhance their own social standing. This means that the social creativity strategy enables companies (clients) to locate the source of reputation to alternative groups of social actors, because the ability to manipulate relational ties enables them to react promptly to reputation imbalance by switching to reputable auditors. This means that, at the level of homogeneous networks, companies use social creativity strategy to distinguish themselves from the group, and there is no change in interlock structure, however, at the heterogeneous level, companies tend to switch to reputable auditors by using this as a mechanism to improve previous standing in the group to which they belong.

6. Conclusion

The paper here addressed the research question: *How does reputation impact the social selection process in an auditing context?* The objective of this study was to consider two assumptions on reputation in the context of the interlock-based selection of auditors, to investigate whether and under what conditions reputation creates interplay between two social selection processes. The investigation was conducted by application of exponential random graph models, and the findings of the study have extended what we know from the literature about the impact of interlocking directorships on auditor selection.

The results of the study outline that, within the interlocking directorship network, companies tend to form closure-like strategic network configurations between reputable companies. More importantly, when the level of reputation becomes unequal among the members assembling closures, companies tend to use the opportunity to establish relationships with reputable auditors, which previously had not been considered. The study revealed that actual relationships and the reputation of those with whom companies form relationships, play significant roles in how social actors imagine themselves to be perceived by others. In other words, the reputation-based social selection model produces dynamics in the structure of the multilevel network ties between homogeneous and heterogeneous social actors. It is thus possible to conclude that companies tend to use auditor reputation as a tool to compensate for a lack of balance at the level of reputation, experienced through those with who they interlock, and enhance their perception in the eyes of others.

By pointing out how reputation reveals the interplay of relationships between interlocks and auditors, this study contributes to the existing literature on auditor selection and change. In fact, it responds to the call for research into the demand mechanism of auditor selection based on reputation (Johansen & Pettersson, 2013), and therefore adopts a relational perspective to estimating network statistics by involving two types of social actors that are interrelated by two types of relational ties, which were used here as the unit of the analysis. In this regard, this study investigated the interdependencies between several observed multilevel network configurations over five consecutive years within an auditing context, where individual mobility and social creativity together characterized patterns of the evolution of the reputation network. Finally, this study used identity theory to discuss the results, which led to a discussion of how we might understand the observed network patterns, and simultaneously how these two theoretical perspectives could be used to discuss the results of multilevel networks structures.

Nevertheless, this study is not free of limitations. On the one hand, even though the sample comprised the entire population of companies listed on the Nasdaq OMX, subsidiary Copenhagen, at the particular time of each consecutive year observed, the results are only country specific and a wider geographical extent of the analysis would be welcome. On the other hand, this study provided insights into network patterns and network tendencies over time, and it would be worth investigating the perceptions of board members, both those that interlock and those that do not, and auditors from both Big/non-Big 4 companies, and intersect their arguments against the previous results. Finally, this study was limited to the extent that reputation regain was not observed, but which could be overcome through the integration of a larger number of models.

References

Allen, M. P. (1974) "The structure of interorganizational elite cooptation: Interlocking corporate directorates", *American Sociological Review*, vol. *39*(3): 393-406

Allen, M. P. (1978) "Economic interest groups and the corporate elite structure", *Social Science Quarterly*, vol. *58*(4): 597-615

Aronmwan, J. E., Oghenekome, T. A., & Chijioke, O. M. (2013) "Audit Firm Reputation and Audit Quality", *European Journal of Business and Management*, vol. 5(7): 66–75

Asthana, S. C., Balsam, S., & Krishnan, J. (2010) "Corporate Governance, Audit Firm Reputation, Auditor Switches, and Client Stock Price Reactions: The Andersen Experience", *International Journal of Auditing*, vol. 14(3): 274-293

Autore, D. M., Billingsley, R. S., & Schneller, M. I. (2009) "Information uncertainty and auditor reputation", *Journal of Banking and Finance*, vol. 33(2): 183-192

Barnett, M. L., Jermier, J. M., & Lafferty, B. A. (2006) "Corporate reputation: The definitional landscape", *Corporate Reputation Review*, vol. 9(1): 26-38

Baum, J. & Oliver, C. (1992) "Institutional embeddedness and the dynamics of organizational populations", *American Sociological Review*, vol. 57(4): 540-559

Beattie, V. & Fearnley, S. (1995) "The importance of audit firm characteristics and the drivers of auditor change in UK listed companies", *Accounting and Business Research*, vol. 25(100): 227-239

Beattie, V. & Fearnley, S. (1998) "Audit market competition: Auditor changes and the impact of tendering", *The British Accounting Review*, vol. 30(3): 261-289

Brewer, D. J., Gates, S. M., & Goldman, C. A. (2002) "In Pursuit of Prestige: Strategy and Competition in US Higher Education", Unpublished manuscript

Brazel, J. F., & Bradford, M. (2011) "Shedding New Light on Auditor Switching", *Strategic Finance*, vol. 92(7): 49-53

Burke, R., Martin, G., & Cooper, C. (2011) *Corporate Reputation: Managing Opportunities and Threats*, Gower Publishing Limited

Craik, K. (2009) *Reputation: A Network Interpretation*, Oxford University Press

Davison, A. G., Stening, B. W., & Wai, W. T. (1984) "Auditor concentration and the impact of interlocking directorates", *Journal of Accounting Research*, vol. 22(1): 313-317

Davis, G. F. & Robbins, G. (2004) "Nothing but net? Networks and status in corporate governance", In K. K. Cetina &A. Preda (Eds.) *The sociology of financial markets*, Oxford University Press, pp. 290-311

DeAngelo, L. E. (1981) "Auditor size and audit quality", *Journal of Accounting and Economics*, vol. 3(3): 183-199

Francis, J. R., & Wilson, E. R. (1988) "Auditor changes: A joint test of theory relating to agency costs and auditor differentiation", *Accounting Review*, 63(4): 663-680

Frank, O., & Strauss, D. (1986) "Markov graphs", *Journal of the American Statistical Association*, vol. 81(395): 832-842

Frendy, & Hu, D. (2014) "Japanese stock market reaction to announcements of news affecting auditors' reputation: The case of the Olympus fraud", *Journal of Contemporary Accounting and Economics*, vol. 10(3): 206-224

Fombrin, C. (1996) *Reputation: Realizing value from the corporate image*, Harward Business School Press

Galaskiewicz, J., Wasserman, S., Rauschenback, B., Bielefeld, W., & Mullaney, P. (1985) "The affect of corporate power, social status, and market position on corporate interlocks in a regional network", *Social Forces*, vol. 64(2): 403-431

Goldberg, A. I., Cohen, G., & Fiegenbaum, A. (2003) "Reputation building: Small business strategies for successful venture development", *Journal of Small Business Management*, vol. 41(2): 168-186

Granovetter, M. (1985) "Economic action and social structure: The problem of embeddedness", *American Journal of Sociology*, vol. 91: 481-510

Gu, Q., & Lu, X. (2014) "Unraveling the mechanisms of reputation and alliance formation: a study of venture capital syndication in China", *Academy of Management Journal*, vol. 35(2): 739-750

Henrich, J., & Gil-White, F. J. (2001) "The evolution of prestige: Freely conferred deference as a mechanism for enhancing the benefits of cultural transmission", *Evolution and Human Behavior*, vol. 22(3): 165-196

Highhouse, S., Brooks, M. E., & Gregarus, G. (2009) "An organizational impression management perspective on the formation of corporate reputations", *Journal of Management*, vol. 35(6): 1481-1493

Johansen, T. R., & Pettersson, K. (2013) "The impact of board interlocks on auditor choice and audit fees", *Corporate Governance (Oxford)*, vol. *21*(3): 287-310

Kanagaretnam, K., Lim, C. Y., & Lobo, G. J. (2010) "Auditor reputation and earnings management: International evidence from the banking industry", *Journal of Banking and Finance*, vol. *34*(10): 2318-2327

Linthicum, C., Reitenga, A. L., & Sanchez, J. M. (2010) "Social responsibility and corporate reputation: The case of the Arthur Andersen Enron audit failure", *Journal of Accounting and Public Policy*, vol. *29*(2): 160-176

Lopez, J., Roman, R., Agudo, I., & Fernandez-Gago, C. (2010) "Trust management systems for wireless sensor networks: Best practices", *Computer Communications*, vol. *33*(9): 1086-1093

Lusher, D., Koskinen, J., Robins, G. (2013) *Exponential Random Graph Models - Theory, Methods, and Application*, Cambridge University Press

Magri, J., & Baldacchino, P. J. (2004) "Factors contributing to auditor-change decisions in Malta", *Managerial Auditing Journal*, vol. *19*(7): 956-968

Maner, J. K., & Case, C. R. (2016) "Dominance and prestige: Dual strategies for navigating social hierarchies", *Advances in experimental social psychology*, (1st ed.). Elsevier

Martínez, I., & Olmedo, I. (2010) "Revisión teórica de la reputación en el entorno empresarial", *Cuadernos de Economía Y Dirección de La Empresa*, vol. *13*(44): 59-77

Masum, H., Tovey, M. (2011) *The Reputation Society, How Online Opinions are Reshaping the Offline World*, The MIT Press

McLennan, A., & Park, I.-U. (2016) "The market for liars: Reputation and auditor honesty", *International Journal of Economic Theory*, vol. *12*(1): 49-66

McPherson, M., Smith-Lovin, L., & Cook, J. M. (2001) "Birds of a feather: Homophily in social networks", *Annual Review of Sociology*, vol. *27*(2001): 415-444

Miles, M. P., & Covin, J. G. (2002) "Exploring the practice of corporate venturing: some common forms and their organizational implications", *Entrepreneurship Theory and Practice*, vol. 26: 21-41

Mizruchi, M. S. (1996) "What do interlocks do? An analysis, critique, and assessment of research on interlocking directorates", *Annual Review of Sociology*, vol. *22*(1): 271-298

Mizruchi, M. S., & Stearns, L. B. (1988) "A longitudinal study of the formation of interlocking directorates", *Administrative Science Quarterly*, vol. 33(2): 194-210

Neveling, N. (2006) "Changing auditors: Switch hitch", *Accountancy Age*, Retrieved on 18.03.2016 from http://www.accountancyage.com/aa/feature/1779588/changing-auditors-switch-hitch

Norredam, M., & Album, D. (2007) "Prestige and its significance for medical specialties and diseases", *Scandinavian Journal of Public Health*, vol. *35*(6): 655-661

OECD (2009) *Competition and regulation in auditing and related professions*, Available at www.oecd.com/competition, retrieved on 19.02.2016

Palmer, D. (1983) "Broken ties: Interlocking directorates and intercorporate coordination", *Administrative Science Quarterly*, vol. *28*(1); 40–55

Palmer, D., Friedland, R., & Singh, J. V. (1986) "The ties that bind: Organizational and class bases of stability in a corporate interlock network", *American Sociological Review*, vol. *51*(6): 781

Parkhe, A. (1993) "Strategic alliance structuring: A game theoretic and transaction cost examination of interfirm cooperation", *Academy of Management Journal*, vol. 36(4): 794-829

Pfeffer, J. (1972) "Size and composition of corporate boards of directors: The Organization and its Environment", *Administrative Science Quarterly*, vol. *17*(2): 218-228

Pfeffer, J., & Salanc, G. R. (1978) *The external control of organizations*, Book Stratford Press.

Podolny, J. M. (2001) "Networks as the pipes and prisms of the market", *The American Journal of Sociology*, vol. *107*(1): 33-60

Powell, W.W. (1990) "Neither Market nor Hierarchy: Network Forms of Organization", *Research in Organizational Behavior*, vol. 12: 295-336

PwC (2012) "How audit committee members add value", *Audit Committee Guide*, pp. 1-154

Robins, G., Pattison, P., Kalish, Y., & Lusher, D. (2007) "An introduction to exponential random graph (p*) models for social networks", *Social Networks*, vol. *29*(2): 173-191

Robins, G. (2015) *Doing Social Network Research: Network-based Research Design for Social Scientists*, Sage Publication Inc.

Salehi, M., & Kangarlouei, S. J. (2010) "An investigation of the effect of audit quality on accrual reliability of listed companies on the Tehran Stock Exchange", *Review of International Comparative Management*, vol. *11*(5): 940-960

Simunic, D. A., Stein, M. (1987) *Product of Differentiation in Auditing: a Study of Auditor Choice in the Market for Unseasoned New Issues*, Canadian certified general accountant's research foundation

Stokman, F. N., Ziegler, R., & Scott, J. (1985) *Networks of corporate power: A comparative analysis of ten countries*, Polity Press

Stuart, T., Hoang, H., & Hybels, R. (1999) "Interorganizational endorsements and the performance of entrepreneurial ventures", *Administrative Science Quarterly*, vol. *44*(2): 315-349

Sucher, P., Moizer, P., & Zarova, M. (1999) "The images of the Big Six audit firms in the Czech Republic", *European Accounting Review*, vol. *8*(3): 499-521

Tajfel, H., & Turner, J. (1979) "An Integrative Theory of Intergroup Conflict", *The Social Psychology of Intergroup Conflict*, CA: Brooks, Monterey, pp. 7-24

Turban, D. B., & Cable, D. M. (2003) "Firm reputation and applicant pool characteristics", *Journal of Organizational Behavior*, vol. *24*(6): 733-751

Useem, M. (1982) "Classwide rationality in the politics of managers and directors of large corporations in the United States and Great Britain", *Administrative Science Quarterly*, vol. *27*(2): 199-226

Wang, P., Robins, G., Pattison, P., & Lazega, E. (2013) "Exponential random graph models for multilevel networks", *Social Networks*, vol. *35*(1): 96-115

Wasserman, S., & Pattison, P. (1996) "Logit models and logistic regressions for social networks: i. An introduction to markov graphs and p*", *Psychometrica*, vol. *61*(3): 401-425

Wasserman, S., Katherine, F. (1994) *Social Network Analysis - Methods and Application*, Cambridge University Press

Woo, E.-S., & Koh, H. C. (2001) "Factors associated with auditor changes: a Singapore study", *Accounting and Business Research*, vol. *31*(2): 133-144

Zeitlin, M. (1974) "Corporate ownership and control: The large corporation and the capitalist class", *American Journal of Sociology*, vol. *79*(5): 1073-1119

Zuckermann, E. W. (1999) "The categorical imperative: Securities analysts and the illegitimacy discount", *The American Journal of Sociology*, vol. 104: 1398-1438

3

Impact of the IFRS on the disclosure of income tax figures by Romanian listed companies

Costel Istrate[a,1]

[a]*Alexandru Ioan Cuza University of Iaşi, România*

Abstract: The transition to IFRS in Romania, in the separate financial statements (in 2012) led to the application of new rules in the accounting for income tax. We found significant differences between accounting and taxable income, which can suggest a trend towards more de facto disconnection between accounting and taxation. Deferred tax liabilities are more present than deferred tax assets in the listed companies' balance sheet, even if the weight of these liabilities is less important that the weight of the deferred tax assets. The effective tax rate (calculated in three ways: with total tax, current tax and cash paid tax) is, in most cases, higher that the Romanian statutory rate. As expected and consistent with several previous studies, fixed assets are the main source of temporary differences and, thus, of deferred tax assets and liabilities. The main contribution of the paper consists in filling a gap in the literature on the impact of the IFRS in Romania, in the special topics concerning income taxes (current and deferred), in the measure of the difference between net accounting income and taxable income, as well as in calculating and interpreting the effective tax rate for the Romanian listed companies.

Keywords: transition to IFRS, deferred taxation, effective tax rate, Romanian listed companies

[1] *Corresponding authors*: Department of Accounting, Management Information Systems and Statistics, Alexandru Ioan Cuza University of Iaşi, Faculty of Economics and Business Administration, Bd. Carol 1, No. 22, 700505, Iaşi, România, e-mail address: istrate@uaic.ro

1. Introduction

The relations between accounting and taxation have often been approached from the point of view of the gap between net income and taxable income. Many studies analyze the differences between income measurement accounting criteria and fiscal criteria and they notice the existence of a more or less important disconnection between accounting and taxation. These differences are an important point to take into account when classifying accounting systems (Gee *et al.*, 2010; Nobes, 2011; Kvaal & Nobes, 2013; Hellman *et al.*, 2015) and they allow one to construct an alternative measure of income (Graham *et al.*, 2012) or of companies' aggressiveness in managing accounting income and/or to evade taxes. Accounting standards themselves can take into account this gap between net income and taxable income. In the case of companies listed on a financial market, the users' needs for information are such that regulators have been determined to set complex and detailed rules for the recognition and the presentation of income taxes, as well as for current income tax or deferred income taxes.

In the accounting recognition of income tax, the simplest solution would be to limit oneself to take into account only current tax for the fiscal year); this would lead to a expense and a liability whose values would be taken as such in tax returns filled in by each individual entity. This is the only solution featured in the accounting for individual companies in many European countries. On the contrary, in the case of more sophisticated accounting regulations – such as IFRS, as well as US GAAP and other standards applicable to listed companies – the recognition of the current tax is not enough; the latter is complemented by deferred taxes. In order to justify the obligation to account deferred taxes, IAS 12 reminds that "if it is probable that recovery or settlement [of an asset, respectively, of a liability] will make the future tax payments larger (smaller) they would be if such recovery or settlement were to have no tax consequences, the [...] standard requires an entity to recognize deferred tax liabilities (assets), with certain limited exceptions". Another justification proposed by IAS 12 for the recognition of all (current and deferred) taxes on income consists in a characteristic feature of accrual accounting – the tax consequences of transactions and other events must be recognized in the same way as the transactions and the events themselves. These arguments used by IAS 12 are strongly supported by general accounting principles and by the guidelines imposed in IASB's *Conceptual Framework of Financial Reporting*. This does not prevent initial accounting recognition and the settlement of deferred taxes from making book-keeping more costly and more complex. At the same time, users encounter more difficulties in comprehending certain essential financial information, such as net income or comprehensive income.

The 34th European directive (European Parliament, 2013) does not mention deferred tax, except in the case of information to be disclosed in notes by medium and large-size companies and by public interest entities – "when a provision for deferred tax is recognised in the balance sheet, the deferred tax balances at the end of the fiscal year, and the movement in those balances during the financial year" must be disclosed. Therefore, this applies only to one category of companies and to only one provision, which is a liability disclosed in a particular manner.

Since 1994, Romanian Accounting Standards (RAS) have been following European directives more or less faithfully. Except for the period 2001-2005 - and only for certain large companies which had to apply standards harmonized with IAS and with European directives – the RAS do not mention deferred tax and therefore, the obligations of Romanian companies were limited to the recognition of current taxes.

In the early 2000s, as a result of pressures from international financial bodies (the World Bank and the IMF), the Romanian standard-setter tried to introduce the International Accounting Standards (IAS) for certain companies. This orientation towards IAS (which have become IFRS) was all the more powerful since Romania wanted to become a member of the EU and so, it had to adjust to the new requirements for the European financial reporting rules (Regulation 1606/2002). Thus, beginning with 2007, IFRS were going to be applied only in the consolidated financial statements of listed entities and in certain other companies (in the latter case, generally, they were to be applied on a voluntary basis). Given that the Regulation 1606/2002 allows member states to extend the obligation of the enforcement of IFRS, beginning with 2012, the Romanian authorities imposed the use of IFRS in the individual accounting of companies listed on a regulated market and in the individual accounting of other entities (especially banks, irrespective of whether they are listed or not). This is how IFRS were introduced in the current accounting practice of several dozens of Romanian firms. This is also how Romanian accountants (re)discovered deferred taxes.

On the other hand, Romanian accounting after 1990 (the beginning of the modern market economy in Romania) was built on bases which connected it strongly with taxation. Istrate (2009: 25-26), Istrate (2011), Fekete *et al.*. (2012), Păunescu (2015) notice that since the 1990s, the connection between accounting and taxation (especially in the case of income tax) has been very tight, both *de jure* and *de facto,* and that the *de jure* disconnection which started in the 2000s (especially beginning with 2004) has not always been consistently followed *de facto.* Even the application of IFRS does not always ensure the disconnection between accounting and taxation at the level allowed by current Romanian accounting and fiscal regulations. This *de facto* connection is the result of choices made by companies in the sense of simplifying their accounting; often, a fiscally accepted accounting option is preserved so as to limit tax adjustments when calculating income tax. Despite these states of fact, which are very frequent in the accounting practices of Romanian firms, the application of IFRS and their implementation by foreign shareholders of certain large Romanian companies, have contributed to the fact that, gradually, the *de facto* disconnection between accounting and taxation would become more and more visible. In the case of listed companies, this disconnection leads to accounting values which often differ from the fiscal values of certain assets and liabilities and thus, to the emergence of deferred taxes.

To our knowledge, the impact of the IFRS on accounting figures of Romanian listed companies, concerning income taxes, has not been studied so far.

The study, which is essentially descriptive, aims to identify the impact of IFRS on the disclosure of information on income tax in the financial statements of Romanian companies listed on the Bucharest Stock Exchange (BSE). Apart from the emergence of deferred taxes (liabilities and assets in the balance sheet, expenses/revenues in the income statement), we have measured the differences between net income and taxable income, reconstituted starting from the tax expense and the statutory tax rate: these differences are very important – they often go beyond 50% and, on average, IFRS have led to their augmentation. In the balance sheets, the deferred tax assets appear less frequently than deferred tax liabilities, but liabilities are much more significant in terms of weight in total assets. In the income statement, deferred taxes are recognized in almost two thirds of the listed companies – a negative deferred tax expense is recognized much more frequently than a pozitive one. In the notes, only two thirds of the listed companies give a clear image of how the effective tax rate comes close to the statutory tax rate and the items proposed to describe these differences are quite general. We have also calculated the effective tax rate which does not change radically with the application of IFRS.

Our paper fills a gap in the literature on the impact of the IFRS on the income taxes of Romanian listed companies. The main contributions of the papers are:
- we found an empirical confirmation of the increasing disconnection between accounting and taxation for the listed companies applying IFRS – the differences between net income and reconstituted taxable income are significant;
- the effective tax rate (ETR) calculated for Romanian listed companies emphasis a very particular situation: ETR is systematically and significantly higher than the statutory rate, in contrast to the situation in many other European or non-European countries;

- our result could be compared with the situation in other countries as to obtain an image of the relationship between accounting and taxation at the EU level or, more realistically, at the level of Central and Eastern European countries.

The following sections of this article provide a literature review, the description of our methodology and of the used sample, the main results and our conclusions.

2. Literature review

The analysis of the relation between accounting and taxation refers mainly to the income tax: the accounting and fiscal rules to measure income, the differences between net income and taxable income, and starting from that, the study of the more or less important connection between accounting and taxation. One can add here the impact of differences between accounting and taxation on the quality of earnings reported by listed companies, the impact of deferred taxes on accounting figures, the relation between taxes and the financial market prices, the influence of obligations for the financial recognition of the relation with fiscal audits, the relation between these differences and the financial auditor's opinion ... The differences between accounting and taxation are due to at least two factors (Hanlon & Heitzman, 2010): the different objectives of accounting and taxation and the "aggressiveness" in managing the income or of the taxable income, so as to reach certain objectives.

In this study, we shall start with a review of the literature on the relation between accounting and taxation in Romania, followed by the main results reported in the literature on the IFRS impact on income tax, the obligations established by IAS 12 to disclose taxes and the role of deferred taxes.

2.1 The relationship between taxation and accounting in Romania

The 1990s witnessed the emergence of the market economy in Romania. Istrate (2011) retraces the evolution of the relation between accounting and taxation between the 1990s and 2011 and notices that, in the beginning, there was a strong connection between them and in time, fiscal authorities became aware of the fact that the objectives of taxation do not necessarily converge with those of accounting. After a first stage of almost total alignment between accounting and taxation - Filip and Raffournier (2010) notice that net income and taxable income are strongly connected - successive reforms, both in accounting (under the influence of the IFRS) and in public finance, have led to the current situation which is characterized by a *de jure* disconnection between accounting and taxation but which, in practice, is accompanied by numerous situations of *de facto* connection (Fekete *et al.*, 2012; Păunescu, 2015; Deaconu & Cuzdriorean, 2016). The first stage in the application of IAS in Romania (2000 - 2005) was characterized by partial conformity with IAS - the connections between accounting and taxation remained strong (Filip & Raffournier, 2010; Ionașcu *et al.*, 2014). By interviewing persons directly involved in the enforcement of IFRS in Romania, Albu and Albu (2012) found that the transition to IFRS was going to lead to extra costs, including for reasons that had to do with obligations to supply fiscal information that begins to differ from accounting information.

2.2 Impact of the IFRS on some accounting numbers: tax expense, tax assets and/or liabilities

In Europe, the compulsory application of IFRS starting with 2005, has determined IAS 12 *Income Tax* to be applied by a large number of companies (in certain countries, similar standards were in force before this date, for certain entities). In fact, even though the initial obligation to enforce IFRS referred only to the consolidated financial statements of listed groups, certain member states chose to extend their application to other situations: the individual accounting of listed companies, consolidated and/or individual statements of non-listed companies (Table 1).

In general, the introduction of IFRS has generated important changes in the accounting – taxation relation: Chen and Gavious (2015) review several studies which document an augmentation of disparities between accounting and taxation in certain countries which adopt IFRS; this allows decision-makers to put in place complicated fiscal mechanisms, with minimal effects on net income. Guggiola (2010) notices that a tight relation between accounting and taxation is often a limit to the full adoption of IFRS.

Table 1. Use of options provided by IAS Regulation (1606/2002), in July 2014

Application of IFRS in the individual accounting of listed companies	Application of IFRS in the consolidated accounting of non-listed companies	Application of IFRS in the individual accounting of non-listed companies
14 countries impose it	16 countries impose it	12 countries impose it
8 countries permit it	12 countries permit it	10 countries permit it
6 countries do not permit it	no country forbidden it	6 countries do not permit it

(*Source:* http://ec.europa.eu/finance/accounting/docs/legal_framework/20140718-ias-use-of-options_en.pdf)

Kvaal and Nobes (2013) study how companies from five different countries in terms of their position in the classification of accounting systems enforce the information disclosure rules imposed by IAS 12. The goal of Kvaal and Nobes' study (2013) is to see if the enforcement of IFRS leads, in different countries, to similar disclosures concerning income taxes, and if listed companies disclose sufficient information for the analysis. Kvaal and Nobes' conclusion (2013) is that, for the five countries which they study (Australia, France, Germany, Spain and Great Britain), despite the generalized application of IFRS, there remain systematic differences in how they report income tax information.

The adoption of IFRS has led to the increase of the total fiscal expense of companies in all EU member countries (between +3.3% and +10.1%) by enlarging the taxable basis (Haverals, 2007). Gee *et al.* (2010) find that, for a country where the relation between accounting and taxation was very tight – Germany – the enforcement of IFRS is materialized in the significant reduction of fiscal influence on IFRS accounting practices, especially for large groups.

Chen and Gavious (2015) notice a significant decrease of conformity between accounting and taxation with the enforcement of IFRS, but they find that the flexibility thus introduced for the manipulation of net and taxable incomes can be counter-balanced by a better management of taxes by fiscal authorities.

For the case of the United Kingdom and with IFRS information, Abdul Wahab and Holland (2015) find that on average, net income surpasses taxable income for the years 2005-2010, except for the year 2009.

2.3 Rules for the financial presentation of income tax

According to IAS 12, completed by other standards, the calculation of current and deferred taxes should be materialized in the disclosure of information, such as:

- in the balance sheet: current tax assets and liabilities, deferred tax assets and liabilities (the latter in non-current elements);
- in the income statement: the tax expense or income connected to the accounting income generated by current operations; income from discontinued operations must be entered in a single line in the income statement, net of tax (IFRS 5);
- in the cash-flow statement; paid income tax must be disclosed separately, in operational cash flows (IAS 7);
- in notes: the elements of the tax expense/income (current tax, deferred tax, adjustments concerning the previous fiscal years or rate changes etc.); the total amount of taxes directly recognized in equity; an explanation (reconciliation) of the relation between tax expense and pre-tax income;

the amount of temporary deductible differences, fiscal losses and tax credits for which the liability of deferred tax has not been recognized etc.

A further obligation concerning the disclosure of tax-related information is mentioned in IFRS 8 *Operational sectors* – the tax expense or income by each identified sector. Leung and Verriest (2015) notice that the decision to recognize income taxes by sector may be influenced by the tendency of company management to hide tax sources, so as to avoid too much fiscal transparency.

2.4 The role of deferred taxes

The recognition of deferred tax liabilities is allowed only to the extent that "it is probable that the entity will have sufficient taxable profit relating to the same taxation authority and the same taxable entity, in the same period as the reversal of the deductible temporary difference (or during periods into which a tax loss arising from the deferred tax asset can be carried back or forward)". This rule imposed by IAS 12 highlights the observance of the accounting principle of the conservatism – a gain is recognized as such only if it is estimated that it will be realized. This is not exactly the historical meaning of the accounting conservatism (which does not accept the recognition of probable gains), but the IFRS are not reputed for their orientation towards the classical interpretation which forbids all over-evaluation of assets *et al.*1 under-evaluation of liabilities[1]. Thus, accounting research is oriented towards the measure of the prudence with which entities approach deferred taxes, that is the scope of the accounting recognition of deferred tax liabilities. Hellman (2008) finds that by the affordances that it provides for the accounting recognition of deferred tax liabilities, IAS 12 leads to more opportunities for *temporary conservatism* and reduces *consistent conservatism*[2]. Azmi and Mahzan (2009) notice that Malaysia is characterized by a high degree of prudence in enforcing IAS 12.

The impact of taxes on declared income was analyzed including from the point of view of affordances for earnings management. Dhaliwal *et al.* (2004) argue that the tax expense is very complex; this complexity offers the possibility to plan the effective tax rate and the estimation of the tax expense supposes significant latitude, due to tax contingencies, to provisions/depreciations, and to tax concessions. Graham *et al.* (2012) propose three approaches to income tax in accounting research: earning management, the association between the differences accounting – taxation and the characteristic features of incomes, value relevance of tax information.

Raedy *et al.* (2011) find that for investors, the detailed presentation of differences between net income and taxable income does not have much more influence than the global presentation of these differences.

3. Methodology and sample

Our analysis is grounded in the IFRS accounting figures published by Romanian companies listed on the Bucharest Stock Exchange – BSE – from 2011 to 2014, but we shall also analyze certain information from the pre-IFRS period (2007-2011: RAS – Romanian accounting Standards). The information become from individual financial statements. We took 2007 as the starting year – the first year when Romania was part of the EU. The RAS applicable in 2007 were in force in 2006 as well, but the available data are more comprehensive beginning with 2007. The year 2011 features twice because for this financial year we have RAS figures (2011 RAS financial statements) and IFRS figures (comparative figures published in IFRS 2012 financial statements). During these years, there were between 78 and 89 companies listed on the BSE. We have finally obtained figures for 75 observations by year, after eliminating companies for which financial statements for all years were not available. The sample comprises 375 RAS observations and 300 IFRS observations. Among these 75 companies, there are 11 operating in the financial sector; in our calculations and interpretations, we shall take them into account. The data were collected manually from financial statements published by listed companies on their websites or on the BSE's website.

We have collected the following information which comes from several parts of financial statements:
- from the balance sheet: total assets, deferred tax liabilities, deferred tax assets;
- from the income statement: income before tax, total tax expense (distributed in current tax and deferred tax), net income, the explicit recognition of the deferred tax expense in the income statement;
- from the cash flow statement: income tax paid;
- from the notes: the disclosure of information on current tax and deferred tax accounting policies, the presence of a specific note for the description of the total tax expense, the presence of a statement of the reconciliation between statutory tax rate and effective tax rate, the form of such a reconciliation, the disclosure of the effective tax rate, the explanation of the difference between theoretical tax and the tax presented in the income statement (especially the number of items and their nature), the presence of a note which analyses deferred tax liabilities and assets and the items presented in this note.

The choice for these variables was strongly influenced by previous studies, Raedy *et al.* (2011), Poterba *et al.* (2011), Ebrahim and Fattah (2015) and especially Kvaal and Nobes (2013).

Starting from our collected data, we have calculated simple indicators, such as:
- the effective tax rate (ETR 1): the total tax expense reported in the income statement divided by income before tax;
- the effective tax rate (ETR 2), retaining the current tax expense (for the IFRS periods), so as to ensure a comparison with the pre-IFRS period;
- the effective tax rate (ETR 3), retaining the income tax paid;
- the difference between income before tax (which is featured in the income statement) and the taxable income reconstituted by dividing the tax expense by the legal tax expense;
- the weight of deferred tax liabilities and assets in the total sum from the balance sheet.

In RAS, obligations to disclose tax information were quite limited:
- there was no obligation for the distinct disclosure of tax assets in the balance sheet, but in the notes;
- in the income statements, there was a single line – the financial year's tax expense;
- in the notes, companies used to supply information on the passage from net income to taxable income, most often on the simplified model of the tax return form.

Since before the IFRS, the accounting of Romanian listed companies did not recognize deferred taxes, we could expect the IFRS to influence significantly the effective taxation rate.

4. Results

We shall present the main results of our study descriptively. The five steps of our presentation bear on the differences between income before tax and reconstituted taxable income, the disclosure and the weight of deferred taxes in the total assets, the disclosure and the sign (expense or income) of deferred taxes in the income statement, the calculation and analysis of actual effective tax rates and, finally, the disclosure in the notes of other tax information.

4.1 Differences between income before tax and taxable income

The income before tax (IBT) is in the income statement, while taxable income (TI) is reconstituted starting from the tax expense, divided by the legal tax rate[3] (Lev & Nissim, 2004; Hanlon, 2005; Donohoe, 2015; Abdul Wahab & Holland, 2015). During our study period (2007-2014), the legal tax rate in Romania was stable, 16%. In a short period of time (April 2009 – September 2010), companies whose calculated tax was lower than thresholds established by law had to pay a minimum tax depending on their total revenues. This made certain highly unprofitable companies declare current tax, which led to reconstituted tax incomes that stood very far apart from net incomes. On the other hand, among the 675 observations, there are 96 (14.22%) for which the total tax expense is zero – we consider that, in these cases, taxable income is zero or negative and that it is not necessary to be considered when calculating the effective tax rate and differences between accounting income and taxable income. Nevertheless, we have only eliminated 75 of these 96 observations, because for the other 21, accounting income is positive and the gap in relation to taxable income can be explained by important specific elements (reported tax losses, various tax deductions, tax credits). Table 2 features the results of our calculations, first for the entire sample and by separating the two types of differences (IBT>TI vs. IBT<TI); then we eliminated the companies that had paid only the minimum tax in 2009 and 2010. The percentages are obtained in relation to IBT. To make comparable the pre-IFRS periods with IFRS figures, we have done the calculations again (for the IFRS periods) by taking into account only current tax.

Table 2. Evolution in the differences between income before tax (IBT) and the taxable income (TI), for the Romanian listed companies

Year	Differences between IBT and TI, based on current tax expense						Differences between IBT and TI, based on total tax expense (starting with 2011 IFRS)					
	IBT>TI		IBT<TI		Total (absolute values)		IBT>TI		IBT<TI		Total (absolute values)	
	N	%	N	%	N	%	N	%	N	%	N	%
2007 RAS	38	39.70	30	45.24	68	42.15						
2008 RAS	34	46.61	29	55.65	63	50.77						
2009 RAS	27	42.34	47	76.23	74	63.86	The numbers are the same as in the current tax situations – there was not deferred taxation in RAS					
2009 RAS**	21	30.58	34	69.53	55	54.66						
2010 RAS	21	39.75	53	83.06	74	70.77						
2010 RAS**	16	27.64	39	74.77	55	61.06						
2011 RAS	19	43.26	38	59.76	57	54.26						
2011 IFRS	25	39.34	41	63.92	66	54.61	29	33.67	37	64.54	66	50.97
2012 IFRS*	22	40.19	44	72.35	66	61.63	30	45.68	37	58.02	67	52.49

Year	Differences between IBT and TI, based on current tax expense						Differences between IBT and TI, based on total tax expense (starting with 2011 IFRS)					
	IBT>TI		IBT<TI		Total (absolute values)		IBT>TI		IBT<TI		Total (absolute values)	
	N	%	N	%	N	%	N	%	N	%	N	%
2013 IFRS*	22	40.31	46	79.07	68	66.53	28	50.81	40	84.50	68	70.63
2014 IFRS	16	54.03	47	62.39	63	60.27	30	78.49	33	59.90	63	68.75

*Outliers are winsorized at the 5th and, respectively 95th percentiles (Ghosh & Vogt, 2012).
** For 2009 and 2010, the indicators are calculated after the eliminations of observations with a negative net income and a minimum tax paid.

The differences between IBT and TI that we can notice in Table 2 (based on current tax) seem very important for all the years taken into account, both in RAS and in IFRS. If for the period 2007-2011 (RAS) there are two years (2007 and 2008) with more companies having an IBT higher than the TI, for all the other years, the observations with a TI higher than the IBT are many more numerous; there are so many specific elements (taxable reintegration) which lead to current taxes that are higher than calculated taxes based on IBT only. At the same time, the scope of differences in the case in which IBT<TI is, however, much more important than in the situation when IBT>TI. Taking into account deferred taxes does not change much the tendency, but the gap between the IBT>TI and IBT<TI observations diminishes considerably and, in 2014, there is even a more important average value in IBT>TI than in the case of IBT<TI. These results will then be completed by the calculation of the effective tax rates.

The situations in which TI is higher than IBT, with important and significant differences, can point to a low income quality (Lev & Nissim, 2004; Hanlon et al., 2012; Chen & Gavious, 2015). In fact, the level of taxable income is used as a reference in the analysis of the quality of the income of listed entities (Graham et al., 2012). Hanlon (2005) states that entities with significant differences between TI and IT come to disclose less persistent incomes than the other entities. On the other hand, IBT which is higher than TI can be a measure of the manipulation of earnings so as to show better performance (Hanlon & Heitzman, 2010).

4.2 Deferred taxes in the balance sheet

The size and the type of operations of listed companies are such that it is very likely that there would emerge situations in which the book value of certain elements of the balance sheet (assets and liabilities) become different from their tax base. Temporary imposable and deductible differences emerge if tax rules differ from accounting rules in the evaluation of assets and liabilities, amortization, depreciations, the spreading in time of certain expenses and/or revenues. IAS 12 imposes the compensation of liabilities and assets issuing from deferred taxes if certain conditions are met (the existence of a legally enforceable right to compensate for current tax liabilities and assets and the existence of a same fiscal authority that levies these taxes). Thus, in principle, an entity that has tax assets and liabilities only in relation with a single fiscal authority will recognize either a deferred tax liability or a deferred tax asset in its balance sheet. This is the case of the majority (more than 90%) of Romanian companies which apply the IFRS in their individual accounting – they have to pay income tax to a single Romanian tax authority, so they compensate for deferred tax liabilities and assets, so that in the individual IFRS balance sheets one encounters, quite frequently, either a liability or an asset (Table 3).

Deferred tax assets are the most frequent – they can be encountered in more than half of the observations (58.67%) while liabilities are recognized only in 19.33% cases. But the weight of assets is highly superior to that of liabilities: 4.52% on average versus 2.74%, respectively. This could suggest that in the income statement, deferred tax net income are recognized more frequently, on average, than deferred tax net expenses. If we calculate again after eliminating financial companies, the results are similar: a slight increase in the weight of liabilities and a very slight decrease of the weight of deferred tax assets.

Table 3. Deferred tax assets and liabilities in the balance sheets of Romanians listed companies

Year	Total observations	Deferred tax assets in the balance sheet		Deferred tax liabilities in the balance sheet		Deferred tax assets and liabilities in the balance sheet	
		N	% in total assets	N	% in total assets	N	% in total assets
2011 IFRS	75	13	4.51%	42	2.91%	5	9.38% et 2.63%
2012 IFRS	75	11	5.81%	47	2.58%	5	10.43% et 2.54%
2013 IFRS	75	15	4.61%	43	2.90%	5	12.44% et 2.89%
2014 IFRS	75	19	3.70%	44	5.59%	8	7.28% et 2.75%
Total	**300**	**58**	**4.52%**	**176**	**2.74%**	**23**	**8.54% et 2.71%**

4.3 Deferred tax expense/income in the income statement

In IFRS, tax expense (or income) comprises current tax and deferred tax. The existence of deferred taxes can have a significant influence on the total amount of the tax expense and on the net income of the fiscal year. For the IFRS period 2011-2014, among the 300 observations in our sample, there are 196 which show deferred taxes in the income statement: 69 cases of net deferred tax expense and 127 cases of net deferred tax income (Table 4). In 54 situations deferred taxes are the only ones which are featured – current tax is zero.

A few other observations on the information supplied in Table 4:

- almost one third of the Romanian listed companies recognize losses in IFRS (more precisely 30.66%), while the proportion of unprofitable companies in RAS (2007-2011) is of only 18.93%; it is true that the periods are not necessarily comparable (even though in RAS one could notice the immediate effects of the 2008 crisis) – this confirms (and extends, with data for several fiscal years), the results of Săcărin (2014) and Istrate (2014) who noticed that the transition to IFRS in 2012 led to a strong decrease in net income for the comparative year 2011;
- the proportion of companies that recognized a current tax (that is an immediate tax liability) is almost the same (68.67%) as the one of beneficiary companies, while before the IFRS, the weight of companies paying annual tax comes to 85.33% (78.13% after the elimination of unprofitable companies that paid the flat tax);
- deferred taxes are recognized in 196 observations out of 300 (65.33%) – for the other companies, either there were no temporary differences, or deductible differences are compensated with taxable differences, or there were no restatements to apply to initial tax liabilities/assets;
- since the first application of IFRS (2011 restated), most companies reach a net deferred tax income, that is probably due to the existence of temporary deductible differences which are higher than taxable differences and/or to they come to recognize fiscal losses; we can notice here a proof of optimism among many companies: for 39 observations, the net deferred tax income is accompanied by fiscal loss for the financial year – the respective companies estimate that their future incomes can allow them to settle these assets.

Table 4. Deferred tax expense/income in the income statement of Romanian listed companies

Year	Total observations		Total tax expense in the income statement**	Current tax expense in the income statement**	Deferred tax in the income statement, from which**		
					Total	Net expense	Net income
2007-2011 RAS	Total, from which	375	320	320*	n.a.	n.a.	n.a.
	IBT > 0	304	287	287	n.a.	n.a.	n.a.
	IBT < 0	71	33	33*	n.a.	n.a.	n.a.
2011 IFRS	Total, from which	75	64	54	45	18	27
	IBT > 0	53	51	49	34	15	19
	IBT < 0	22	13	5	11	3	8

Year	Total observations	Total tax expense in the income statement**	Current tax expense in the income statement**	Deferred tax in the income statement, from which**		
				Total	Net expense	Net income
2012 IFRS	Total, from which	75	66	52	52	18	34
	IBT > 0	51	50	48	37	16	21
	IBT < 0	24	16	4	15	2	13
2013 IFRS	Total, from which	75	67	48	54	21	33
	IBT > 0	52	51	46	39	16	23
	IBT < 0	23	16	2	15	5	10
2014 IFRS	Total, from which	75	63	52	45	12	33
	IBT > 0	52	52	50	35	10	25
	IBT < 0	23	11	2	10	2	8
Total	Total, from which	300	260	206	196	69	127
	IBT > 0	208	204	193	145	57	88
	IBT < 0	92	56	13	51	12	39

*From which 27 companies paying the flat tax in 2009 and 2010
** All data represent number of companies.

4.4 Reconciliation of the statutory tax rate and the effective tax rate

IAS 12 imposes the disclosure of a reconciliation between the expense or the net tax income and the income before tax of the financial year. Beginning with 2012, we have to expect that Romanian listed companies disclose such information in notes. In fact, among the 300 valid IFRS observations, this picture of a reconciliation is present in 193 cases (64.33%), the legal tax rate (16% for the entire period) in 160 cases (53.33%), while the effective rate is featured in only 15 cases (2.5%). The elements which explain the difference between legal rate and effective tax rate are, most frequently, recognized in compliance with the outline of tax return. In the 184 cases where we found explanations on the passage from legal rate to effective tax expense, there are between 1 and 8 items (Table 5). The most frequent are very general elements such as *non-deductible expenses*, *non-imposable revenues*, which do not reveal much about the detailed causes of the difference between net income and taxable income. The structure of the information recognized in this note is such that it was impossible for us to differentiate between temporary and permanent differences. We must also recall that even for one and the same company, the format of the recognition in the notes is not similar from one year to another, there are significant differences in recognition between companies, which means that the frequency of the recognition of items must be approached with caution.

Table 5. Items disclosed in the reconciliation of the effective tax expense and the statutory tax expense, by the Romanians listed companies

Items	Frequency
1. Non-deductibles expenses	162
2. Non-imposable revenues	159
3. Sponsoring	68
4. Elements assimilated to taxable revenues	60
5. Deductions related to legal reserves	59
6. Temporary differences	51
7. Others elements*	42
8. Fiscal losses	41
9. Tax credits	25
10. Elements assimilated to deductible expenses	23
11. Tax reductions or tax exemptions	22
12. Accounting depreciation different from fiscal depreciation	16
13. Restatements for the transition to IFRS	13
14. Revaluation of fixed assets	12
15. Impairments	9
16. Special tax rules for dividends	8
17. Provisions	7
18. Fines	6

*Raedy et al (2011) found that the items *Others* is the most present between the 22+19= 41 items identified in the financial statements of more than 600 American companies in the 1993-2007 period.

Some other information required by IAS 12 is the separation of tax expense in current tax expense and deferred tax expense/income. In most observations (231 out of 300), we notice a preference for this separation in the notes - only 61 entities having chosen to do it directly in the income statement.

IAS 12 rules impose the calculation of the effective tax rate (ETR) by considering total tax expense and income before tax, if it is positive (ETR 1). The figures calculated for the observations in our sample are presented in Table 6. The legal rate is 16% for the entire analyzed period. In order to better grasp the impact of differences between accounting and taxation concerning income measurement and to ensure a cross-sectional comparability throughout the studied period, we have chosen to present two other indicators, simultaneously: the effective tax rate calculated on the basis of the current tax expense – ETR 2 – and the effective tax rate calculated starting from the income tax paid during the fiscal year (ETR 3). These three effective tax rates are used by Donohoe (2015) who, in order to calculate them, cumulates data for three fiscal years and eliminates observations with a negative income. Dyreng *et al.* (2008) cumulate taxes paid on periods going up to 10 years so as to compare them with cumulated income for the same period, so as to obtain more suggestive results in the identification and measure of tax evasion. The cumulus can be explained easily when we compare ETR 1 or ETR 2 with ETR 3 – in fact, part of the tax is paid in the fiscal year following the one in which income was obtained and so cumulated figures can be more representative. In a first panel in Table 6, we shall calculate by year, and in the second and third panel, we present indicators obtained after the aggregation of tax expenses and incomes for 5 fiscal years in RAS and for 4 fiscal years in IFRS. For ETR 3, the information concerning tax paid comes from cash-flow statements; we eliminated all observations for which this information was not available or for which there was no income tax paid. For the same indicator, when there was paid tax and negative income, we chose to calculate by taking income in its absolute value.

The first commentary on the indicators calculated in Table 6 have to do with the fact that the annual effective tax rate for beneficiary companies is higher than the legal Romanian rate of 16%, except for ETR 1 in 2007 RAS and ETR 3 in 2011 IFRS and in data cumulated in RAS. This can lead us to believe that fiscal rules are very constraining in what concerns the deductibility of recognized expenses and/or that listed Romanian companies are not very involved in fiscal optimization operations that could decrease total tax expense concerning income tax. In fact, if we compare these indicators with the situation in the United States, for instance, we notice a very net difference – GAO (2013) finds an effective tax rate for American companies far behind the legal rate, while for EU countries, the effective tax rates (for the non-financial sector) are, in general, lower than legal rates (EU, 2015, p. 146).

In panels 2 and 3 from Table 6, we have cumulated income before tax, the (total and current) tax expense and the tax paid by each listed company, for 5 and, respectively, 4 fiscal years. Given the compensations between fiscal years, the slightly delayed tax payment and the gradual elimination of temporary differences, we believe that the results obtained starting from these cumulated data are more robust than those in panel 1 in Table 6. In fact, the differences noticed between annual ETRs and cumulated ETRs, by considering only income before taxes (annual, respectively cumulated) are almost null for ETR 1 and ETR 2. The situation of ETR 3 is slightly contrasted and it is due probably to the fact that the respective companies have not paid the tax that they have declared.

In an initial sample we kept 11 companies whose activities are essentially financial. In order to consider the specific features of the financial sector (like most studies), we have recalculated by eliminating financial companies: the vast majority of average effective tax rates are slightly higher than those calculated for the entire sample, which can suggest that non-financial companies have less affordances to manage taxable income. However, the differences are not significant.

Table 6. Effective tax rate for Romanian listed companies

Year	Observations	ETR 1	ETR 2	ETR 3	
				N	%
Panel 1 – By year, IBT > 0					
2007 RAS	68	15.74%	15.74%	38	20.71%
2008 RAS	61	16.83%	16.83%	38	19.44%
2009 RAS	60	19.22%	19.22%	48	17.25%
2010 RAS	58	22.06%	22.06%	53	16.03%
2011 RAS	57	20.53%	20.53%	46	16.84%
Total RAS	**304**	**18.75%**	**18.75%**	**223**	**17.80%**
2011 IFRS	53	17.41%	17.64%	46	15.93%
2012 IFRS	51	16.96%	18.02%	48	18.48%
2013 IFRS	52	19.36%	20.01%	39	21.07%
2014 IFRS	52	17.59%	19.27%	42	19.78%
Total IFRS	**208**	**17.83%**	**18.73%**	**175**	**18.70%**
Panel 2 – Cumulated data for 5 years (RAS) and 4 years (IFRS) – total observations					
2007-2011 RAS	375 :5=75	12.31%	11.37%	75	7.56%
2011-2014 IFRS	300 :4=75	12.30%	10.62%	75	8.88%
Panel 3 – Cumulated data for 5 years (RAS) and 4 years (IFRS) –observations with IBT > 0					
2007-2011 NCR	55	19.26%	18.91%	46	15.57%
2011-2014 IFRS	48	16.98%	18.64%	42	16.91%
Outliers were winsorized at the 5th and 95th percentile.					

To compare these results with those of other Romanian companies, we have used data published by companies listed on an alternative market hosted by the BVB as well – the AeRo Component – launched in the early 2015 and on which listed companies are generally small-sized. Since this market (AeRo) is not considered regulated, companies listed on it are not bound to enforce IFRS – they contend themselves with RAS and so they only publish information on current tax. For the fiscal years 2010-2014, we could obtain 769 valid observations (positive income before tax and tax expense): 127 for 2010, 169 for 2011, 159 for 2012, 152 for 2013 and 162 for 2014. The effective tax rate (ETR 2) is decreasing (from 25.47% in 2010 to 18.73% in 2014), but the average for the five fiscal years is 20.73%, very close to the average of companies listed on the regulated market. When we recalculate with data cumulated for 5 RAS fiscal years (2010-2014), we obtained 23.55% by retaining only positive cumulated income (versus 11.16% for all 259 observations).

4.5 Disclosure on temporary differences sources

IAS 12 also imposes the disclosure of the main sources of temporary differences that led to the emergence of deferred tax liabilities and assets. We must first point out that, for the Romanian listed companies, in only 160 observations (out of 300) can one find such information in the notes. In Table 7, we have centralized the main elements stated by the Romanian listed companies which have enforced IFRS in their individual accounting.

Table 7. Assets and liabilities generating temporary differences and deferred income tax for the Romanian listed companies

Item	Frequency
Non-current assets	145
Receivables	82
Provisions	69
Financial instruments	59
Inventories	52
Pensions obligations	38
Tax loses	35
Other liabilities	28
Investment properties	17
Prepaid expenses	14
Legal reserves	8
Prepaid revenues	6
IFRS restatements	6
Constructions contracts	6
Tax credits	6
Loans	4
Biological assets	1

Fixed assets are the main source of temporal differences, mainly because of depreciation methods, of cost components, of revaluation and impairment rules. For the other elements of the assets and liabilities that are featured in Table 7, the sources of temporary differences come mainly from accounting evaluation rules which are not always fiscally recognized (depreciations, the use of fair value in accounting, the accounting recognition of certain provisions that are not recognized fiscally).

5. Conclusion

The passage to IFRS in Europe has generated numerous studies on their effects in terms of the information reported in financial statements. Lyle *et al.* (2008) find, in the responses received from persons involved in the transition to the IFRS (preparers, auditors and users), that these standards contribute to more credibility and reliability in financial statements, but they increase the complexity of financial reporting, which makes the process of the elaboration and analysis of accounting and financial information more difficult. In fact, complexity is a recurrent issue in studies on the impact of IFRS (Stent *et al.*, 2015). We agree with the authors who state that part of this complexity comes from very complex rules for the recognition of deferred taxes.

Our study aims to identify the main consequences of the transition to IFRS of Romanian listed companies, on the disclosure of information concerning taxes on benefits. We have retained in our sample the individual financial statements of 75 entities from a period which starts in 2007 (the year when Romania joined the EU) and ends in 2014 (the last year for which there are available data); in total, there are 375 observations with figures according to Romanian accounting standards and 300 observations according to IFRS; for the year 2011 there are two series of numbers in RAS (taken from financial statements from 2011) and in IFRS (taken from financial statements from 2012 – the first in IFRS).

Several interesting conclusions can be drawn from our descriptive analysis. First, the reconstitution of taxable income, starting from the tax expense, leads to very important differences between this taxable income and the accounting income before tax, both in RAS and in IFRS. These figures can testify to the significant gap between accounting rules and tax rules, which confirms, to a certain extent, an evolution towards an increasingly more important *de facto* disconnection between accounting and taxation. At the same time, following the literature, we can argue that these differences signal the low quality of the accounting income. Second, the enforcement of IFRS beginning with 2012 has led to the emergence, in the balance sheets of Romanian listed companies, of deferred tax liabilities and/or assets. There are more companies which recognize assets, but the weight of these assets, on average, is less important that the weight of liabilities. Third, the deferred tax expenses/incomes are present in more than 65% of the companies in our sample; the effective tax rate calculated starting from figures published in the profit and loss account is systematically higher than the legal rate of 16% in Romania, for the three formulas that we have used (by retaining, successively, the total tax expense, the current tax expense and the paid tax). Finally, the information supplied in the notes on the sources of deferred taxes allows us to notice that non-current assets are the main elements that generate temporary differences.

The results of the paper could be compared with the situation in other countries as to obtain an image of the relationship between accounting and taxation at the EU level or, at least, at the level of Central and Eastern European countries.

Our study has several limitations. First, it is essentially descriptive. Second, the sample is narrow – we could extend it to companies listed on other East-European markets. Also, we have not connected tax information disclosure to variables such as industry, company size, the ownership (including the presence of the State as a shareholder), the composition of the board, the audit quality and the audit cost, the presence in tax heavens. All these limitations can represent just as many directions for future research. It would be equally possible to analyze the evolution of the direction of differences between accounting income and taxable income for each company (positive and/or negative differences).

Acknowledgement

Earlier versions of this paper were presented to the 37th Congrès of AFC, Clermont-Ferrand 2016 and to the 11th AMIS Conference, Bucharest 2016. Many thanks to the anonymous reviewers of the two conferences and to the participants who comment the paper and contribute to its improvement.

References

Abdul Wahab, N. S. & Holland, K. (2015) "The persistence of book-tax differences", *The Accounting Review*, vol. 47, no. 4: 339-350.

Albu, N. & Albu, C. N. (2012) "IFRS in an emerging economy: lessons from Romania", *Australian Accounting Review*, vol. 22, no. 4: 341-352

Azmi, A. A. C. & Mahzan, N. (2009) "Recognition of Deferred Tax Assets Practices and Conservatism", *Journal of Accounting Perspectives*, vol. 2, no. 1: 22-35

Chen, E. & Gavious, I. (2015) "The roles of book-tax conformity and tax enforcement in regulating tax reporting behaviour following International Financial Reporting Standards adoption", *Accounting and Finance*, available on-line at http://onlinelibrary.wiley.com /doi/10.1111/acfi.12172/epdf

Deaconu, A. & Cuzdriorean, D. D. (2016) "On the tax-accounting linkage in the European emerging context" *Journal of Accounting in Emerging Economies*, vol. 6, no. 3 : 206 - 231

Dhaliwal, D. S., Gleason, C. A. & Mills, L. F. (2004) "Last-chance earnings management: using the tax expense to meet analysts' forecasts", *Contemporary Accounting Research*, vol. 21, no. 2: 431-459

Donohoe, M. P. (2015) "The economic effects of financial derivatives on corporate tax avoidance", *Journal of Accounting and Economics*, vol. 59, no.1: 1-24

Dyreng, S. D., Hanlon, M. & Maydew, E. L. (2008) "Long-run corporate tax avoidance", *The Accounting Review*, vol. 83, no. 1: 61-82

Ebrahim, A. & Fattah, T. A. (2015) "Corporate governance and initial compliance with IFRS in emerging markets: The case of income tax accounting in Egypt", *Journal of International Accounting, Auditing and Taxation*, vol. 24, no. 1: 46-60

EU (2015) Taxation Trends in the European Union. Publication Office of the European Union, available on-line on http://ec.europa.eu/taxation_customs/ resources/documents/ taxation/gen_info/economic _analysis/tax_structures /2015/report.pdf, [30th of Decembre 2015]

European Parliament (2013) Directive 2013/34/EU of the European Parliament and of the Council of 26 June 2013 on the annual financial statements, consolidated financial statements and related reports of certain types of undertakings, amending Directive 2006/43/EC of the European Parliament and of the Council and repealing Council Directives 78/660/EEC and 83/349/EEC, available on-line at http://eur-lex.europa.eu/legal-content/EN/TXT/HTML/?uri=CELEX:32013L 0034&from=EN, [15th April 2015]

Fekete, S., Cuzdriorean-Vladu, D. D. & Albu, C. N., Albu, N. (2012) "Is SMEs accounting influenced by taxation? Some empirical evidence from Romania", *African Journal of Business Management*, vol. 6, no. 6: 2318-2331

Filip, A. & Raffournier, B. (2010) "The value relevance of earnings in a transition economy: the case of Romania", *The International Journal of Accounting*, vol. 45, no. 1: 77-103

GAO (2013) "Corporate Income Tax – Effective Tax Rates Can Differ Significantly from the Statutory Rate. Report to Congressional Requesters", available on-line on http://www.gao.gov/assets/660/654957.pdf [28th Decembre 2015]

Gee, M., Haller, A. & Nobes, C. (2010) "The influence of tax on IFRS consolidated statements: the convergence of Germany and the UK", *Accounting in Europe*, vol. 7, no. 1: 97-122

Ghosh, D. & Vogt, A. (2012) "Outliers: An evaluation of methodologies", *JSM – Section on Survey Research Methods*, available on-line at https://www.amstat.org/sections/srms/proceedings/y2012/files/30406872402.pdf [15 December 2015]

Graham, J. R., Raedy, J. S. & Shackelford, D. A. (2012) "Research in accounting for income taxes", *Journal of Accounting and Economics*, vol. 53, no. 1-2: 412-434

Guggiola, G. (2010) "IFRS adoption in the E.U., accounting harmonization and market efficiency: A review", *International Business & Economics Research Journal*, vol. 9, no. 12: 99-112

Hanlon, M. (2005) "The persistence and pricing of earnings, accruals, and cash-flows when firms have large book-tax differences", *The Accounting Review*, vol. 80, no. 1: 137-166

Hanlon, M. & Heitzman, S. (2010) "A review of tax research", *Journal of Accounting and Economics*, vol. 50, no. 2-3: 127-178

Hanlon, M., Krishnan, G. V. & Mills, L. F. (2012) "Audit fees and book-tax differences", *The Journal of American Taxation Association*, vol. 34, no. 1: 55-86

Haverals, J. (2007) "IAS/IFRS in Belgium: quantitative analysis of the impact on the tax burden of companies", *Journal of International Accounting, Auditing and Taxation*, vol. 16, no. 1: 69-89

Hellman, N. (2008) "Accounting conservatism under IFRS", *Accounting in Europe*, vol. 5, no. 2: 71-100

Hellman, N., Gray, S. J., Morris, R. D. & Haller, A. (2015) "The persistence of international accounting differences as measured on transition to IFRS", *Accounting and Business Research*, vol. 45, no. 2: 166-195

Ionaşcu, M, Ionaşcu, I., Săcărin, M. & Minu, M. (2014) "IFRS adoption in developing countries: the case of Romania", *Accounting and Management Information Systems*, vol. 13, no. 2: 311-350

Istrate, C. (2009) *Contabilitatea nu-i doar pentru contabili! (Accounting is not only for accountants!)*, Bucharest: Universul Juridic

Istrate, C. (2011) "Evolutions in the accounting-taxation (dis)connection in Romania, after 1990", *Review of Economics and Business Studies*, vol. 4, no. 2: 43-62

Istrate, C. (2014) "Impact of IFRS on the accounting numbers of Romanian listed companies", *Accounting and Management Information Systems*, vol. 13, no. 3: 466-491

Kvaal, E. & Nobes, C. (2013) "International variation in tax disclosure", *Accounting in Europe*, vol. 10, no. 2: 241-273

Leung, E. & Verriest, A. (2015) "The impact of IFRS 8 on geographical segment information", *Journal of Business Finance & Accounting*, vol. 42, no. 3-4: 273-309

Lev, B. & Nissim, D. (2004) "Taxable income, future earnings, and equity values", *The Accounting Review*, vol. 79. no. 4: 1039-1074

Lyle, N., Stevens, C., Tophoff, V. & Mallett, R. (2008) "Financial Reporting Supply Chain: Current Perspectives and Directions", IFAC, New York, available on-line at https://www.iaasb.org/system/files/publications/files/financial-reporting-supply.pdf, [26th Decembre 2015]

Nobes, C. (2011) "IFRS practices and the persistence of accounting system classification", *Abacus*, vol. 47, no. 3: 267-283

Păunescu, M. (2015) "Revenue recognition and measurement. accounting principles vs. tax rules for Romanian entities", *Audit Financiar*, vol. 13, no. 1: 81-90

Poterba, J., Rao, N. & Seidman, J. (2011) "Deferred tax positions and incentives for corporate behavior around corporate tax changes", *National Tax Journal*, vol. 64, no. 1: 27-58

Raedy, J., Seidman, J. & Shackelford, D. (2011) "Is there information in the tax footnote?", available on-line on http://www.insead.edu/facultyresearch/areas/accounting/events/documents/Raedy_Seidman_Shackelford_02022011x.pdf [accessed at 10th December 2015]

Săcărin, M. (2014) "Impactul adoptării pentru prima oară a IFRS de către societăţile nefinanciare cotate la Bursa de Valori Bucureşti", *Audit Financiar*, vol. 12, no. 1: 46-54

Stent, W., Bradbury, M. E., Hooks, J. (2015) "Insights into accounting choice from the adoption timing of International Financial Reporting Standards", *Accounting and Finance* (http://onlinelibrary.wiley.com/doi/10.1111/acfi.12145/pdf)

Notes

[1] In fact, in the current conceptual framework of the IASB, the qualitative characteristic of prudence is not featured explicitly any more, which leaves the door open for the accounting recognition of probable gains. IFRS take advantage of this and they allow or impose the recognition of such revenues in a large number of cases (investment properties, biological assets and agricultural produce, financial instruments). Hellman (2008) notices that in many Western countries, before the arrival of the IFRS (and especially of IAS 12), deferred tax asset, which corresponded to a reported fiscal loss, was not recognized.

[2] In explaining the two forms of conservatism, Hellman (2008) argues that *temporary conservatism* consists in the temporary application of the prudence principle, that is changes in accounting estimates which lead to the temporary reduction of equity; *consistent conservatism* is the choice of the accounting method which leads to the lowest evaluation of equity.

[3] This formula is not perfect, due to differences coming from fiscal credits, tax cuts and other elements which do not impact net or fiscal products and charges.

4

Timeliness of corporate reporting in developing economies

Ömer Faruk Güleç [a,1]

[a] *Hacettepe University, Turkey*

Abstract: This paper empirically investigates the effects of both firm and audit - specific factors on the timeliness of financial reporting practices of firms listed on Borsa Istanbul using panel data methodology. This study employs a data set containing annual data from 150 non-financial Turkish listed companies in Borsa Istanbul between the years 2009 – 2014 to document their reporting behaviors. Descriptive analysis indicates that average reporting time is 69 days for the whole sample and 62 days and 74 days for individual and consolidated financial statements respectively. In line with prior studies, firm size, dividend per share, auditor type and good news (income), unsurprisingly, has a significant negative impact on timeliness behavior of sample firms. In addition, financial statement type (individual and consolidated financial statements) also has a significant effect on reporting time. On the other hand price to book ratio and leverage of firms have no significant impact as hypothesized. Examining the reporting behavior of emerging markets contribute to the literature through comparing with the developed countries and indicating the factors which have impact on timeliness. The outcomes of research also provide some insights to the interested parties and regulatory bodies to evaluate the preparation of financial statements in terms of timeliness.

Keywords: Timeliness of corporate reporting, Reporting delay, Emerging countries, Regulation, Borsa Istanbul

[1] *Corresponding author*: Business Administration Department, Hacettepe University Faculty of Economics & Administrative Sciences 06800 Ankara; ; Email address: omerfarukgulec@hacettepe.edu.tr

1. Introduction

Reporting is a way of companies' communication through divulging any financial or nonfinancial information with the annual reports to a wide range of users. In particular, financial statements play a major role for the parties with the different purposes in decision making. High-quality and useful accounting information require qualitative characteristics, such as the relevance of information, comparability, reliability and understandability. Timeliness is one of the main determinants of financial reporting quality and transparency of which attributed to the corporate governance principles. Timeliness is a crucial element of adequate disclosure and important characteristics of financial statements (Dyer & McHugh, 1975). Thus, timeliness of corporate financial reporting is a significant facet of effective communication associated with the other features of financial reporting.

Timely reporting mitigates the adverse effects of insider trading activities and aids to build trustworthy environment in capital markets. It is a known fact that companies in emerging countries are prone to disclose less information than developed ones. In the absence of strict regulations and transparency, information asymmetry comes out, and one effective way to impede these adverse impacts is to be in prompt about annual reports (Ashton et al., 1989). Therefore, reporting on time is crucial to lessen the effect of poor conditions related to investor rights in emerging capital markets and inhibit the insider trading.

Timeliness has received much attention due to the number of institutional and foreign investors and investment funds increase. It has become a critical issue more than ever due to the changes in the economy, technology, expectations and business practices (Owusu-Ansah & Leventis, 2006). Hence, regulatory bodies (Capital Markets Board), laws (Turkish Commercial Code) or professionals preparing the financial statements place importance to the deadline times and reporting delays. Publication period of annual reports for either separate or consolidated financial statements are shortened for annual statements but remain same for interim periods in Turkish Commercial Code.

This paper discusses the determinants of reporting behavior of companies under the light of disclosure theories. Factors or motivations that affect publishing financial statements earlier or later within a regulatory deadline are explored in a detailed manner. This study aims to identify the period of the timing of issuance of financial statements listed on Borsa Istanbul and clarify the main factors on the timeliness of financial reporting. Examining the timeliness of reporting on Borsa Istanbul is an interesting issue for several reasons. First, BIST is an emerging market that is relatively less regulated and needs to be more institutionalized. Secondly, trading volume, foreign ownership, and companies that went public are increasing. Therefore, timeliness of financial reporting catches the attention of players in the markets. Finally, to integrate to the Euro Zone and to comply with International Financial Reporting Standards (IFRS), timeliness examination for Borsa Istanbul has a vital importance. First motivation for studying the timeliness is policy based. Examining the factors which have impact on timeliness might aid to regulatory bodies and other. The outcome of the research would provide a valuable input to the interested parties. Timely reporting in emerging markets is of particular importance since the information asymmetry and reporting lag is much longer in comparison to developed countries. Therefore, analyzing Turkish capital markets in terms of timeliness will provide some insights to the preparers and users of financial statements.

The remainder of the paper is structured as follows. In the next section, the historical background and regulatory framework of timeliness are discussed. In section 3, the most relevant literature is. Next sections proceed with research design, empirical findings and conclusion.

2. Regulatory framework

Law of Capital Market and Turkish Commercial Code are the regulatory sources for the reporting and these codes force the companies to publish their financial statement within a regulatory deadline. Turkish Commercial Code (Article 409) requires that shareholders should hold the general assembly within three months following the end of each financial year. Since balance sheet and meeting agenda of the company needs to be prepared three weeks before the assembly, publication time of financial reporting has been changed by Capital Markets Board. Communiqué on Principles of financial reporting which states the arrangements on financial reporting procedures published by Capital Markets Board of Turkey in the official gazette on 13.06.2013.

According to the Article 10 related to disclosure of financial reports expresses that firms which are not obliged to prepare consolidated financial statements have to report within 60 days and firms which are obliged to prepare consolidated financial statements have to report within 70 days following the end of their accounting periods. For the interim reports, 30 days and 40 days is given as a regulatory deadline for individual and consolidated financial statements respectively. Also, if the interim reports are the subject of the independent audit, ten extra days is added to the deadline. Additional time is dependent on the presence of valid reasons and applied by the application of the responsible manager from financial reporting committee or other committees.

Disclosing of financial statements needs to take place in the most reputable website of the firm for at least five years. According to the Capital Markets Board.

Communiqué on Principles of financial reporting, most reputable web-site term is used when a firm has more than one web-site. Since this study covers the period between 2009 and 2014, the mandatory deadline is different for the previous years for 2009, 2010, 2011 and 2012. According to the Communiqué published in 2003, individual and consolidated financial statements have to be published ten weeks and fourteen weeks of the financial year – end respectively. Therefore, this difference is handled in the empirical analysis and descriptive statistics separately. The deadlines for individual and consolidated financial statements are given chronologically below in Table 1.

Table 1. Regulatory deadline for financial statements

Types of Financial Statements	Annual Period		Interim Period	
	Individual	Consolidated	Individual	Consolidated
Since 2013	60 Days	70 Days	30 Days	40 Days
Before 2013	10 Weeks	14 Weeks	4 Weeks	6 Weeks

* Weekly term has changed into daily term in Turkish Commercial Code (2013)

3. Literature review

Studies on the timeliness of financial reporting mainly stress on two aspects of variables that are firm-specific factors measured directly from financial statements or corporate governance variables attained from annual reports or websites of companies.

Dyer and McHugh (1975) is the first study to try to examine the timeliness from the perspective of auditors and preparers of financial statements through using questionnaires for Australian firms. They subdivide the lags into four periods starting with auditor examination and ending with printing or publishing time to analyze the delays in a deeply manner. Firm size, profitability and financial year – end are the primary corporate based variables to measure the timeliness in reports.

Lawrence (1983) and Whittred and Zimmer (1984) document the relation between the financially distressed firms and reporting delays. According to the results, companies which are the candidates of bankruptcy issue their annual reports or auditor reports much later than the other companies. Atiase et al. (1989) discuss the issue of price reaction to the issuance of financial statements timing through controlling the firm size and bad news effect. They employ a multivariate model that measures how reporting delay influences the price reactions in larger or smaller firms. They conclude that due to size effect, market reaction is limited for larger companies. On the other hand, reporting delay or early publishing has a significant impact on price reactions for smaller firms especially with bad news announcement. Soltani (2002) underlines the audit qualification and implies that audit reporting delays on individual reporting are more affected from the quality of auditor than consolidated annual reporting. This paper also finds the regulatory deadline 180 days superfluous at least for listed companies which caused encouraging results for French context.

Leventis and Weetman (2004) is a milestone study which applies an empirical model in Athens Stock Exchange for the year 1997 and emphasizes the delays in not only for financial statements but also for audit reports. This study combines the theories with the surrogate variables to explain timeliness of financial reporting with a different view. Trading volume, industry concentration ratio or gross plant property and equipment variables are some factors used in the timeliness of financial reporting for the first time to the best of our knowledge. Trading volume is used to prove that whether companies have higher trading volume publish their financial statements earlier to decrease information costs. Dogan *et al.* (2007) analyze the timeliness of reporting with an aspect of good news vs. bad news through calculating the return on asset and return on equity and states that firms divulge net income report earlier. According to their results, size and gearing of the firm are also related to the timeliness of financial reporting.

El-Masry *et al.* (2008a) and El-Masry *et al.* (2008b) mainly focus on the association between the timeliness of reporting and corporate governance characteristics of firms. Both studies employ a model which takes a snapshot to the websites of companies to measure the timeliness of corporate internet reporting. In addition to firm specific variables such as liquidity, firm size, profitability, they also use corporate governance variables for the purpose of disclosing what factors have more impact on the timeliness of financial reporting. McGee (2008) is one of the best studies that gives insights about corporate governance and timeliness of financial reporting with different countries applications and comparisons. He examines 20 countries, such as USA, Russia, China, etc. and results that timeliness is related to countries' specific factors as well as firm characteristics.

Aktas and Kargin (2008) explore the association between the timeliness feature and profitability of the company and come up with the result that higher positive earnings per share is effective and have a significant effect on early reporting. Lee *et al.* (2008) compare the multinational and domestic companies with regards to timeliness and document that multinational firms' reporting lag is shorter even though their audit delay is longer because of the complexity of accounting transactions. Moreover, companies disclose bad news and net loss and high leverage are associated with reporting delays, but firms audited by big 4 and larger companies report earlier. Turel

(2010) focuses on reporting lead time with firm and auditor specific determinants for the Turkish listed firms. She examines 211 non-financial companies with five different hypothesis related to size, industry, the sign of income, auditor type and opinion. According to the results, 59% of the firms publishing individual financial statements and 66% of the firms publishing consolidated financial statements prepare their reporting earlier than the regulatory deadline. In addition, while firms with positive income publish financial statements earlier, companies audited by big four report later. Size is not statistically significant. Akle (2011) investigates the period between 1998 and 2007 for the companies listed on the Egyptian stock exchange. Average days of financial reporting gradually decreases over the years and application of corporate governance principles effectively helps to reduce the timing of issuance notably in the financial sector.

Iyoha (2012) studies the impact of firm attributes on the timeliness of financial reports in Nigeria. With the panel data analysis and 61 companies between the periods 1999 – 2008, the paper concludes that the age of the company has a significant impact on timeliness. In addition, sectors are found significantly different regarding timeliness. Specifically, the banking sector is the fastest one to publish financial statements earlier. Other firm-specific variables such as profitability, size or financial year end do not have any significant impact on early reporting.

Al-Shwiyat (2013) examines the Amman Stock Exchange with 120 sample companies with several factors such as company's age, return on assets, return on equities, dividends and earnings per share. 111 days is the average reporting time which is a long period when comparing to the other developing countries. While the leverage and the firm size have significant positive impact on timeliness, earnings per share ratio has a significant negative relationship. Vuran and Adiloğlu (2013) research 178 companies for 2009 to analyze timeliness with many firm-specific variables. They separate the financial statements according to type of financial statement as a consolidated or individual and examine the current ratio, ROA, CFO, interest expense, size and sign of income.

4. Research design

4.1. Sample selection

The sample of this study includes 150 non-financial firms listed on Borsa Istanbul. In this paper, timeliness of financial reporting is handled by the firms listed on Borsa Istanbul during the period 2009 - 2014. All the companies included in the sample fulfill the following two criteria. Firstly, they are all listed on the market since 2009 and none of them was expelled during the period 2009 - 2014. Five companies whose year-end is other than 31 December were excluded from the sample. The analysis consists of a total 900 firm- year observations from the financial statements of firms using Thomson Reuters Eikon database and Public Disclosure Platform. Since the financial statements of the banking sector and insurance companies are differ in many ways, non – financial companies were chosen as our sample. It is also consistent with the previous studies such as Ismail and Chandler (2005) and Owusu-Ansah and Leventis (2006).

Table 2. Sample firms

Non-Financial Firms Listed on BIST for 2009	192
Firms Have Missing Data and Outliers	-37
Firms Have Different Financial Year -End	-5
Firms Available For Analysis	150
Total firm-year observations	900

4.2. Hypothesis development

Several company attributes or corporate governance characteristics have been analyzed in previous timeliness studies to clarify which factors have more impact on reporting timely. In this study, seven firm-specific factors determined to analyze the timeliness of financial reporting on Borsa Istanbul. These are company size, auditor type, income, leverage, financial statement type, price to book ratio and dividend per share.

4.2.1. Firm size

Firm size is a widely used variable in timeliness of reporting literature and mixed results (positive or negative relations) presented in the empirical analysis. Studies come up with the positive relationship between the reporting lead time and firm size suggest that larger firms are subject to more transactions and accounting department deals with more complex accounting issues. On the other hand, most of the studies find a negative correlation for the size variable. Arguments which support this hypothesis start with the idea that having more resources and established accounting department and staff or having sophisticated accounting systems lead larger firms to report earlier (Owusu-Ansah, 2000). Since larger firms' internal control systems provide effective process to auditors, auditing mechanism spends less time while assessing the accounting information in larger firms (Dyer & McHugh, 1975).

Moreover, larger companies have more followers, particularly financial analysts or investors heavily rely on the timeliness of financial reporting (Leventis & Weetman,

2004). Firm size is a significant indicator of proving larger firms are followed by many investors than small companies. Therefore, larger companies are in the spotlight with regards to punctuality of financial reporting. Total assets is used dichotomously to measure the firm size and to display the negative relationship in the model for the first hypothesis. Firm-year observations are classified into three categories and assigned to small, medium and large firms in terms of their total assets value.

H1: Firm size is negatively associated with reporting lead time.

4.2.2. Auditor type

Auditor type is a common determinant in many papers that clarifies the relationship between the companies' financial statements audited by internationally known auditing firms (Big Four) and the duration from the financial year-end to first issue date. Many models split the sample with a dichotomous variable to introduce the model of those audited by Big 4 and audited by local firms. Al-Ajmi (2008) used to term auditee's size to evaluate the agency costs and concludes that larger firms are audited by larger or reputable auditors to mitigate the agency cost. Clatworthy and Peel (2010) and Hashim *et al.* (2013) argue that auditing by Big 4 helps to decrease the duration of reporting since their resources and experience is qualified enough than the other firms. Ahmed (2003) studies the auditor type with the other variables such as audit fee and international linkage due to the lack of big 4 or 5 in the sample countries. In order to introduce the dummy variable for auditor type and eliminate the subjectivity, auditor fee, auditor size and existence of international linkage are used to categorize to auditors regards to big or small. In this paper, Big 4 is used to analyze the relationship between auditor type and timeliness.

H2: Auditor type is negatively associated with reporting lead time.

4.2.3. Good news vs. bad news (income)

The profitability of a company, in other words, reporting net income or loss has significant effects on timely reporting as mentioned in previous studies. Signaling theory suggests that more profitable firms disclose more information and abide by the deadline through reporting earlier (Ismail & Chandler, 2005). On the other hand, management with bad news avoids publishing earlier to cover up the losses and reduce the adverse effects. From this point of view, companies tend to report positive news earlier than unfavorable ones which are held by many researchers to link with disclosure theories (Milgrom, 1981).

Haw *et al.* (2000), Owusu and Ansah (2000) and Whittred and Zimmer (1984) also states that publishing of financial statements earlier is related to favorableness of news. It is a well-known fact that managers are eager to disclose any positive information as soon as possible when comparing the negative news. They might withhold unfavorable news through hoping to receive any positive news to compensate the effects of negative results (Givoly & Palmon, 1982). Thus, share prices might be gradually less affected during this discretionary created time.

Good news vs. bad news are measured with different variables on the timeliness of financial reporting such as annual change in profitability, the examination of remarks or comments in the audit reports, return on equity or return on assets. In this study, return on assets is used to measure the profitability of the firms.

H3: Profitability (Good news) is negatively associated with reporting lead time.

4.2.4. Leverage

Gearing or in other words, leverage refers to use debt to finance the operations. Trade – off theory suggests that larger firms tend to be highly geared and it resulted that firms prefer debt financing are supposed to publish their financial statements earlier for the purpose of credibility (El-Masry Abdelsalam *et al.*, 2008). On the other hand, Abdullah (2006) and Carslaw and Kaplan (1991) claim that high leverage is positively associated with timeliness because auditor check over on highly leveraged firms takes too much time. They also provide that high leverage refers to the financial distress and firms under pressure might withhold the financial statements for a while to reduce the adverse effects as mentioned earlier. Leverage is measured as total debts over total assets.

H4: Leverage (gearing) is positively associated with reporting lead time.

4.2.5. Financial statement type

Leventis and Weetman (2004) analyze the reporting practices of individual companies rather than group companies due to the fact that group companies are subject to different regulations and variables used in their model are much complicated to measure for the group companies. Soltani (2002) examines group and non-group companies with regards to presenting annual accounts to France authorities. Because consolidated and separate financial statements have different characteristics and deadlines, they need to be evaluated differently.

H4: There is an association between the financial statement type and timeliness of financial reporting.

4.2.6. Price to book ratio and dividend per share

In order to measure the market effectiveness in the model, two variables are added. Firms with high dividend yield tend to report financial statements earlier in conjunction with the signaling theory (Abdulla, 1996). There is no hypothesis developed for the price to book ratio to the best our knowledge. However, it might be considered that firms with higher price to book ratio are prone to report earlier because of the price performance of the firm (Fama & French 1995).

H5: Price to book ratio is negatively associated with reporting lead time.

H6: Dividend per Share is negatively associated with reporting lead time.

4.3. Model specification

Panel data analysis offers a combination of regression and time series data type. It includes both cross-sectional and time series dimensions for each individual. This makes it possible to study a dynamic aspect of the problem (Frees, 2004).
A panel data regression model with k variables displayed as:

$$Y_{it} = \beta_{1it} + \beta_{2it}X_{2it} + \beta_{3it}X_{3it} + \cdots + \beta_{nit}X_{nit} + u_{it} \qquad (1)$$

In the model I;1,2,....,n shows cross section and T= 1,2,....,n shows time periods. Also, u_{it} is assumed to be zero mean and constant variance. There are more parameters predicted than observations. Therefore model cannot be predicted in this form and it should be reconstructed. In order to do that, there have to be some assumptions made to have the models known as fixed effects and random effects. Firstly, we assume all regression coefficients are equal to common units; then model can be shown;

$$Y_{it} = \beta_1 + \beta_2X_{2it} + \beta_3X_{3it} + \cdots + \beta_nX_{nit} + u_{it} \qquad (2)$$

β_1 is a common intercept for all units and $\beta_2, \ldots, \beta_k$ parameters are common marginal effects of each explanatory variables. In other words, β parameters show no difference between units and times. This model is also known as fixed effects model. Random effects model is the different form of fixed effects model regarding intercept. Random effects intercept term is modeled as $\beta_1 = \overline{\beta}1 + \mu_i$ and the model is shown as β_1. In order to present which model is superior, Hausman test is the analysis of the different models.

$$Y_{it} = (\overline{\beta}1\mu_i) + \beta_2X_{2it} + \beta_3X_{3it} + \cdots + \beta_nX_{nit} + u_{it} \qquad (3)$$
$$Y_{it} = \overline{\beta}1 + \sum_{n=2}^{N} \beta nX_{nit} + (u_{it} + \mu_i) \qquad (4)$$

4.3.1. Reporting lead time model

$Lead\ Time_{it} = \beta_1 + \beta_2Size_{it} + \beta_3Leverage_{it} + \beta_4Income_{it} + \beta_5PTB_{it} + \beta_6DPS_{it} + \beta_7Fin.Stat.Type_{it} + \beta_8A.Type_{it} + u_{it}$

Reporting lead time is measured through calculating the number of days between the financial year end of the companies (31 December) and the first publication date which is on Public Disclosure Platform. Public Disclosure Platform (PDP) is an electronic system through where all notifications, news and financial information of companies are published mandatorily. The system covers over 600 companies and 3000 users all over Turkey. PDP is a platform where all users have a chance to access accurate and fair information in prompt about listed companies at low costs through the website. In the past studies such as Leventis and Weetman (2004), discretionary delays, particularly in audit reports delays, handled and measured as the dependent variable. However, because of regulations of the timing of reporting financial statements in Turkey, publishing of audit reports and financial statements happen simultaneously.

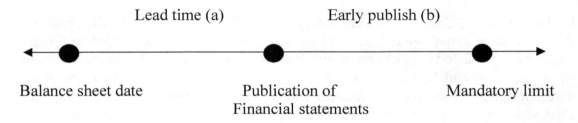

Table 3. Independent variables

Variables	Definition	Expected sign
Firm Size	Total Assets Dummy Variable (3 Category) (Large, Medium, Small)	-
Leverage	Financial Leverage Ratio	+
Income	Return On Assets	-
PTB	Price to Book Ratio	-
DPS	Dividend per Share	+
Financial Statement Type	Dummy Variable (Consolidated or Individual)	+
Auditor Type	Dummy Variable (Big 4 vs. Local Auditors)	+

All companies publish their financial statements within the mandatory deadline, except special permissions from Capital Markets Board. The fear of being influenced by the market participants negatively or any punishment that might take place from the regulatory authorities play a role in reporting timely for the companies. Although all companies meet the regulatory deadline, there is a huge difference between the issue of financial statements and the end of the financial year. In this paper, individual and consolidated financial statements examined separately with the purpose of presenting the actual situation in a better way. Intervals for publishing and the yearly information is given tables below for both types of financial statement.

Table 4. Reporting lead time for individual financial statements

Interval (Firm-year)	2013 - 2014		Interval (Firm-year)	2009 - 2012	
	Perc.	Cum.Perc.		Perc.	Cum.Perc.
0-40 days	3%	3%	0-40 days	2%	2%
41-50 days	16%	19%	41-50 days	11%	13%
51-59 days	28%	**47%**	51-59 days	16%	29%
Regulatory limit 60 days	**53%**	100%	60-69 days	25%	**54%**
			Regulatory limit 70 days	**46%**	100%

Table 4 displays the lead time for separate financial statements within the regulatory deadline in different periods. The regulatory deadline was 70 days (10 weeks) between the years 2009 – 2012 and %54 percent of sample published early and % 46 percent of the sample on very last day. However, for the last years, 2013 and 2014, the percentage of publishing early decreased to % 47 percent because of the ten days reduction in deadline. Publishing separate financial statements earlier than 40 days is generally uncommon. Turkish firms which prepare separate financial statements are mostly eager to publish their financial statements on the last day. Yearly information is given in figure 1 below, and it states that early publishing rate decreases in connection with the regulatory deadline decreases from 70 days to 60 days.

Figure 1. Reporting lead time for individual financial statements

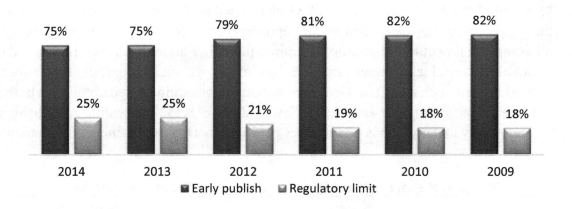

Table 5. Reporting lead time for consolidated financial statements

Interval (Firm-year)	2013 - 2014		Interval (Firm-year)	2009 - 2012	
	Perc.	Cum.Perc.		Perc.	Cum.Perc.
0-50 days	9%	9%	0-60 days	16%	16%
51-60 days	22%	31%	61-70 days	21%	37%
61-69 days	43%	**74%**	71-80 days	14%	51%
Regulatory limit 70 days	**26%**	100%	81-90 days	12%	63%
			91-100 days	25%	**87%**
			Regulatory limit 101 days (14 weeks)	**13%**	100%

Early publishing rate also decreased for consolidated financial statements since the decrease in the number of days for group companies is almost a month. However, firms prepare consolidated financial statements are likely to publish earlier when the interval's first lines examined. It denotes that almost %35 – 40 percent of sample publish just as separate financial statements report. Figure 2 proves that early publishing fluctuates more than individual financial statements in different years.

Figure 2. Reporting lead time for consolidated financial statements

Early publish   Regulatory limit

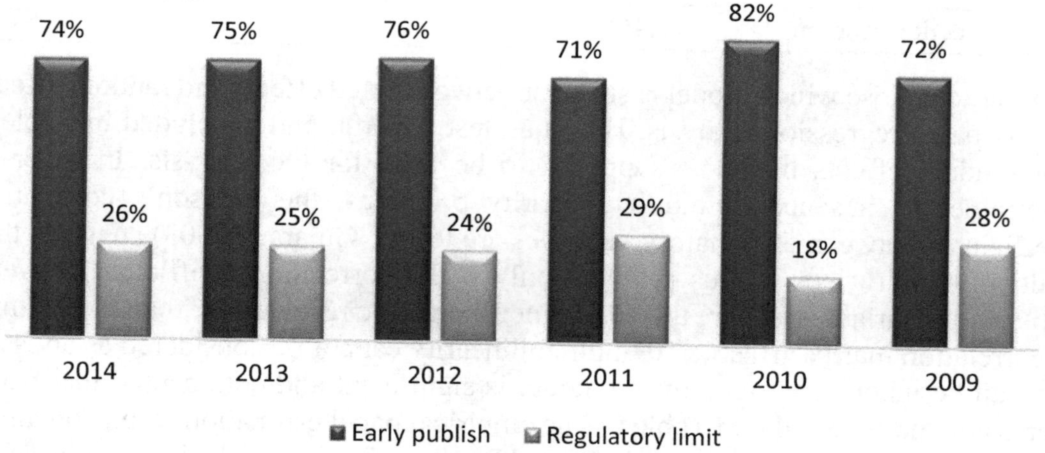

4.4. Research findings

Descriptive statistics for dependent and independent variables are given in Table 6. According to the results, an average day of publishing financial statements is 69 days, and in addition, it is 62 days for individual financial statements and 74 days for consolidated financial statements. Maximum and minimum days are 130 days and 30 days respectively. According to the Communiqué, in presence of reasonable causes and reasons acceptable by the Board (CMB), an additional time may be granted to entities for public disclosure of interim and annual financial reports.

Table 6. Descriptive statistics for variables

	Mean	Median	Maximum	Minimum	Standard Deviation
Lead time	69	68	130	30	16
Roa	3.80	3.68	38.25	-35.66	9.11
Leverage	0.48	0.47	1.70	0.02	0.24
Ptb	9.98	5.02	162.60	0.11	13.91
Dps	0.31	0.00	16.42	0.00	1.06
Large firms	0.33	0.00	1.00	0.00	0.47
Medium firms	0.34	0.00	1.00	0.00	0.47
Small firms	0.32	0.00	1.00	0.00	0.47
Auditor	0.65	1.00	1.00	0.00	0.48
Fin. type	0.59	1.00	1.00	0.00	0.49

Table 7. Hausman test result

	Chi-Sq. Statistic	Chi-Sq. Degree of Freedom	Probability
Cross-section random	13.461	8	0.097

In order to choose which model is superior between fixed effects and random effects for the panel regression analysis, Hausman test was run and concluded in Table 7 that random effects model is supposed to be used for the analysis. In order to determine the absence of multicollinearity problems, the Pearson's correlation coefficients between explanatory variables are tested. Gujarati (2003) suggests that multicollinearity is a serious problem only if the correlation coefficient between explanatory variables is more than 0.8. Since there is no result above than these limits in correlation matrix in Table 10, multicollinearity cannot be considered as an issue and can be ignored. F value of the model is significant and commented that panel regression model is valid in Table 9. The empirical panel estimation results obtained from OLS model, Fixed Effects Model and Random Effects Model is given in Table 9. The results presented in Table 9 shows that except for leverage and price to book ratio, all variables are significant and the explanation power of the model is %14.37.

Company size shown as total assets with dichotomous variables constituted the first hypothesis is confirmed when table 9 results examined. According to the results, there is a statistically significant negative association between the firm size and timeliness of financial reporting. It conforms to previous studies such as Leventis and Weetman (2004) or Owusu and Ansah (2000). Larger firms are more likely to report earlier than the small firms due to the fact that larger firms have more sources and more motivations to be time sensitive.

Auditor type represented dichotomously as Big 4 or local has a 5% significant negative impact on timely reporting as expected. Many studies such as Garsombke (1981) or Ahmed (2003) reached the same results that audit delay or reporting delay is both lesser for the firms audited by Big 4. It is assumed that international audit firms are more experienced which makes them audit more effectively and efficiently with more sources promptly. Davies and Whittred (1980), Givoly and Palmon (1982) and Owusu and Ansah (2000) are the other studies which concentrate on the association between the auditor type (size) and timely reporting and hypothesized the negative correlation as in this study.

Income factor which is the most stressed determinant in reporting studies via good vs. bad news is also discussed in this study. Good news is likely to released very quickly because disclosing income needs less examination perceived positive motivation for both investors and management (Haw *et al.*, 2000). On the other hand, firms financially unhealthy are inclined to delay the announcement of bad news to mitigate the adverse effects (Al-Ajmi, 2008). Management incentives related to internal reporting hypothesis is another motivation to hide the bad news for a while as well.

Different measurements are used to analyze the income factor in timeliness such as the change in profitability in Givoly and Palmon (1982) or Haw *et al.* (2000), the level of profitability (Dyer & McHugh, 1975), sales growth as revenue changes in (Ismail & Chandler, 2005). Abdulla (1996) and Al-Ajmi (2008) use more than one variable to measure the good news-bad news effect in timeliness in particular dividend per share in addition to other common measurements. Thus, return on asset and dividend per share variables are used to investigate the effect of profitability on reporting lag. According to the results in Table 9, both variables have a negative impact and 10% significant and proves that profitability of a company or paying high dividends are essential motivations of issuing financial statements earlier.

Capital structure of a company is another facet of timeliness studies. Firms that have higher gearing might experience the possibility of failure and bankruptcy and are expected to delay the issuance (Carslaw & Kaplan, 1991). Although many studies find positive relationship such as Abdulla (1996), Carslaw and Kaplan (1991) or Owusu and Ansah (2000), there is another view supports the negative correlation. It suggests that firms having high debt to asset ratio might demand experienced auditors to compensate the suspicions of third parties and it leads to early publishing (Al-Ajmi, 2008). Even though the results display positive association, gearing has not a significant impact on the timeliness of financial reporting.

Since the examination of group companies and separate financial statements have different requirements of publishing, dichotomous variable is used to determine the effects of financial statement type and it is a substantial issue needs to be considered in the analysis. Price to book ratio is the last variable explored and to the best knowledge, there is no hypothesis found on the timeliness of financial reporting. However, in order to elaborate the market performance of firms with regards to timeliness, price to book ratio is considered as a good measurement. Yet, there is no significant relation even the negative coefficient found.

Table 8. Hypothesis results

H1: Firm Size	Negative relation (Accepted)
H2: Leverage	Not significant (Rejected)
H3: Income	Negative relation (Accepted)
H4: Price to Book	Not significant (Rejected)
H5: Dividend per Share	Negative relation (Accepted)
H6: Financial Statement Type	Accepted
H7: Auditor Type	Negative relation (Accepted)

Table 9. Panel regression results

Dependent Variable: Lead Time (Number of days)	ORDINARY LEAST SQUARE		FIXED EFFECTS MODEL		RANDOM EFFECTS MODEL	
	Coefficient	Probability	Coefficient	Probability	Coefficient	Probability
Income (ROA)	-0.152	0.015	-0.108	0.1130	-0.113	0.068*
Leverage	6.008	0.006	-2.757	0.5551	3.123	0.299
Price to Book (PTB)	-0.008	0.452	-0.023	0.1114	-0.017	0.171
Dividend per Share (DPS)	-1.318	0.005	-0.457	0.4086	-0.832	0.08*
Firm Size (Large)	-4.1	0.000	-8.737	0.0000	-6.171	0.000***
Firm Size (Medium)	6.817	0.000	14.165	0.0000	-3.384	0.029**
Firm Size (Small)	2.717	0.025	5.428	0.0171	9.556	0.000***
Auditor Type	-3.960	0.000	-3.514	0.1290	-3.549	0.019**
Financial Statement Type	1.41	0.000	1.33	0.0000	14.363	0.000***
Constant	62.379	0.000	67.104	0.0000	63.569	0.000***
R- Squared	0.236		0.627		0.144	
Prob. (F-Statistics)	0.000***		0.000***		0.000***	
Durbin-Watson Statistics	0.98		1.645		1.407	

***, **, * %1, %5, %10 respectively

Table 10. Correlation matrix

	Lead time	ROA	Leverage	PTB	DPS	Large	Medium	Small	Auditor	Fin. type
Lead time	1 ---									
ROA	-0.21 0.000***	1 ---								
Leverage	0.18 0.000***	-0.43 0.000***	1 ---							
PTB	-0.04 0.2073	0.01 0.9301	-0.03 0.445	1 ---						
DPS	-0.16 0.000***	0.31 0.000***	-0.13 0.000***	-0.03 0.43	1 ---					
Large	-0.06 0.061*	0.17 0.000***	0.12 0.000***	-0.01 0.695	0.08 0.014**	1 ---				
Medium	-0.02 0.542	0.07 0.029**	-0.16 0.000***	0.06 0.09*	0.05 0.142	-0.51 0.000***	1 ---			
Small	0.08 0.012**	-0.25 0.000***	0.04 0.21	-0.04 0.182	-0.13 0.000***	-0.49 0.000***	-0.5 0.000***	1 ---		
Auditor	-0.15 0.000***	0.13 0.000***	0.04 0.264	-0.02 0.47	0.14 0.000***	0.34 0.000***	-0.05 0.099*	-0.28 0.000***	1 ---	
Fin. type	0.36 0.000***	-0.01 0.891	0.12 0.000***	-0.05 0.151	0.02 0.64	0.34 0.000***	-0.05 0.116	-0.29 0.000***	0.11 0.000***	1 ---

*** , ** , *   %1, %5, %10 respectively

5. Concluding remarks

One measure of the quality of financial reporting under the concept of transparency is timeliness of financial reporting in addition to the other concepts such as accuracy, consistency, appropriateness, clarity and convenience (Al-Ajmi, 2008). Thus, it is an important intrinsic characteristic and an essential element of information relevance suggested by major standard setters over the years (Clatworthy & Peel, 2010).

This study empirically aims to investigate the association between timeliness of annual financial reporting and both firm-specific and audit related factors for the 150 non-financial companies listed on Borsa Istanbul for the period 2009 to 2014. Descriptive analysis indicates that average reporting time is 69 days for the whole sample and 62 days and 74 days for individual and consolidated financial statements respectively. The deadline for reporting used to be 10 weeks and 14 weeks for individual and consolidated financial statements and it was reduced in 2013 to 60 days and 70 days for both types respectively.

In line with prior studies, firm size, dividend per share, auditor type and good news (income), unsurprisingly, has a significant negative impact on timeliness behavior of sample firms. Also, financial statement type has a significant effect. On the other hand price to book ratio and leverage of firms have no significant impact as hypothesized. Although these conclusions are consistent with previous studies, findings of the study may not be generalized due to the limitations of not only it includes non-financial firms but also the period it covers. Future studies may concentrate on financial firms and larger period to justify the results with different variables. Corporate governance features or cross country examinations might also be included in the studies to analyze the timeliness in a comprehensive manner and to increase the robustness of the subject.

References

Aktas, R. & Kargin, M. (2008) "Timeliness of Reporting and the Quality of Financial Information", *International Research Journal of Finance and Economics*, vol. 31(5):1450-2887

Abdulla, J. (1996) "The timeliness of Bahraini annual reports", *Advances in International Accounting,* vol. 9: 73-88

Abdullah, S.-N. (2006) "Board composition, audit committee and timeliness of corporate financial reports in Malaysia", *Corporate Ownership and Control,* vol. 4(2): 33-45

Adiloğlu, V. A. (2013) "Is Timeliness of Corporate Financial Reporting Related to Accounting Variables? Evidence From Istanbul Stock Exchange", *International Journal of Business and Social Science,* vol. 4(6)

Ahmed, K. (2003) "The timeliness of corporate reporting: A comparative study of South Asia", *Advances in International Accounting,* vol. 16: 17-43

Akle, Y. H. (2011) "The relationship between corporate governance and financial reporting timeliness for companies listed on Egyptian Stock Exchange: An empirical study", *Internal Auditing and Risk Management,* vol. 2(22): 81-90

Al-Ajmi, J. (2008) "Audit and reporting delays: Evidence from an emerging market", *Advances in Accounting,* vol. 24(2): 217-226

Al-Shwiyat, Z. M. M. (2013) "Affecting factors on the timing of the issuance of annual financial reports. Empirical study on the Jordanian public shareholding companies", *European Scientific Journal,* vol. 9(22)

Ashton, R. H., Graul, P. R. & Newton, J. D. (1989) "Audit delay and the timeliness of corporate reporting", *Contemporary Accounting Research,* vol. 5(2): 657-673

Atiase, R. K., Bamber, L. S. & Tse, S. (1989) "Timeliness of financial reporting, the firm size effect, and stock price reactions to annual earnings announcements", *Contemporary Accounting Research,* vol. 5(2): 526-552

Carslaw, C. A. & Kaplan, S. E. (1991) "An examination of audit delay: Further evidence from New Zealand", *Accounting and Business Research,* vol. 22(85): 21-32

Clatworthy, M. A. & Peel, M. J. (2010) "Does corporate governance influence the timeliness of financial reporting? Evidence from UK private companies", Paper presented at the HEC Accounting And Management Control Department Research Seminar

Davies, B. & Whittred, G. P. (1980) "The association between selected corporate: Attributes and timeliness in corporate reporting: Further analysis", *Abacus,* vol. 16(1): 48-60

Dogan, M., Coskun, E. & Celik, O. (2007) "Is timing of financial reporting related to firm performance? An examination on ISE listed companies", *International Research Journal of Finance and Economics,* vol. 12: 220-233

Dyer, J. C. & McHugh, A. J. (1975) "The timeliness of the Australian annual report", *Journal of Accounting Research,* vol. 13: 204-219

El-Masry, A., Abdelsalam, O. & El-Masry, A. (2008) "The impact of board independence and ownership structure on the timeliness of corporate internet reporting of Irish-listed companies", *Managerial Finance,* vol. 34(12): 907-918

El-Masry, A., Ezat, A. & El-Masry, A. (2008) "The impact of corporate governance on the timeliness of corporate internet reporting by Egyptian listed companies", *Managerial Finance,* vol. 34(12): 848-867

Fama E.F. & French K.R (1995) "Size and book to market factors in earnings and returns", *The Journal of Finance*, vol. 50(1): 131-155

Frees, E. W. (2004) *Longitudinal and panel data: analysis and applications in the social sciences*, Cambridge University Press

Givoly, D. & Palmon, D. (1982) "Timeliness of annual earnings announcements: Some empirical evidence", *Accounting Review*, vol. 57(3): 486-508

Gujarati, D. N. (2003) *Basic Econometrics*, New York: McGraw-Hill

Hashim, F., Hashim, F. & Jambari, A. R. (2013) "Relationship between corporate attributes and timeliness in corporate reporting: Malaysian evidence", *Jurnal Teknologi*, vol. 64(2)

Haw, I. M., Qi, D. & Wu, W. (2000) "Timeliness of Annual report releases and market reaction to earnings announcements in an emerging capital market: The case of China", *Journal of International Financial Management and Accounting*, vol. 11(2): 108-131

Ismail, K. & Chandler, R. (2005) "Disclosure in the quarterly reports of Malaysian companies", *Financial Reporting, Regulation and Governance*, vol. 4(1): 1-26

Iyoha, F. (2012) "Company attributes and the timeliness of financial reporting in Nigeria", *Business Intelligence Journal*, vol. 5(1): 41-49

Lawrence, E. C. (1983) "Reporting delays for failed firms", *Journal Of Accounting Research*, vol. 21(2): 606-610

Lee, H. Y., Mande, V. & Son, M. (2008) "A comparison of reporting lags of multinational and domestic firms", *Journal of International Financial Management and Accounting*, vol. 19(1): 28-56

Leventis, S. & Weetman, P. (2004) "Timeliness of financial reporting: applicability of disclosure theories in an emerging capital market", *Accounting and Business Research*, vol. 34(1): 43-56

McGee, R. W. (2008) "Corporate governance in transition economies", *Corporate Governance in Transition Economies*, Springer, pp. 3-20

Milgrom, P. R. (1981) "Good news and bad news: Representation theorems and applications", *The Bell Journal of Economics*, vol. 12(2): 380-391

Owusu-Ansah, S. (2000) "Timeliness of corporate financial reporting in emerging capital markets: Empirical evidence from the Zimbabwe Stock Exchange", *Accounting and Business Research*, vol. 30(3): 241-254

Owusu-Ansah, S. and Leventis, S. (2006) "Timeliness of corporate annual financial reporting in Greece", *European Accounting Review*, vol. 15(2): 273-287

Soltani, B. (2002) "Timeliness of corporate and audit reports: Some empirical evidence in the French context", *The International Journal of Accounting*, vol. 37(2): 215-246

Turel, A. (2010) "Timeliness of financial reporting in emerging capital markets: Evidence from Turkey", *Istanbul University Journal of the School of Business Administration*, vol. 39: 227-240

Whittred, G. & Zimmer, I. (1984) "Timeliness of financial reporting and financial distress", *Accounting Review*, vol. 59(2): 287-295

5

Corporate governance, audit committee and the internet reporting of strategic information by UAE non-financial listed firms

Mostafa Kamal Hassan [a1]

[a] *University of Sharjah and on leave from Alexandria University, Egypt*

Abstract: The study examines the effect of internal governance mechanisms on the Internet Reporting of Strategic Information (IRSI) in an emerging market economy, the United Arab Emirates (UAE) It relies on the agency theory and the innovation diffusion theory to generate testable hypotheses and augment the explanation behind the empirical results. The study applies a multiple regression on a sample of 37 non-financial firms listed on Abu Dhabi and Dubai financial markets to test the association between audit committee, independent non-executive directors, frequency of board meetings, type of external auditor and IRSI while controlling for firm size, level of risk, firm complexity and firm profitability. The empirical findings show that IRSI is positively and significantly associated with audit committee quality, firm size, level of risk and firm complexity. The findings also show that IRSI is negatively and significantly correlated with the frequency of board of directors meetings. These empirical findings assist UAE regulators and international business community with insights concerned with governance-IRSI relationship. The findings also reveal that board directors and members in audit committee may contribute to the diffusion of innovative disclosure practices such as IRSI. The study is one of few studies that combine the agency theory and innovation diffusion theory to examine the relationship between internal governance mechanisms, particularly audit committee, and the IRSI in an emerging market economy such as the UAE.

Keywords: audit committee, governance, agency theory, innovation diffusion theory, online reporting, "strategy" disclosure, UAE

[1] *Corresponding author*: Mostafa Kamal Hassan, Associate Professor in Accounting, Department of Accounting, College of Business Administration, University of Sharjah, and on leave from Alexandria University, Egypt, Sharjah, UAE, PO Box 27272, E-mail: mhassan@sharjah.ac.ae.

1. Introduction

Despite the existence of several studies that examine internet reporting in different Western and European countries (e.g. Debreceny *et al.*, 2002 in the USA; Abdelsalam *et al.*, 2007 in the UK; Marston, 2003 in Japan; Marston & Polei, 2004 in Germany; Oyelere *et al.*, 2003 in New Zealand; Xiao *et al.*, 2004 in China; Boubaker *et al.*, 2011 in France): few studies paid attention to the internet reporting of strategic information (Santema & Rijt, 2001; Santema *et al.*, 2005; García-Sanchez *et al.*, 2011) In the context of emerging economies, some studies investigate the internet reporting in Gulf and Middle East countries such as (Hussainey & Al-Nodel, 2008 in Saudi Arabia; Ezat & El-Masry, 2008 in Egypt; Al-Htaybat, 2011 in Jordan; Oyelere & Kuruppu, 2012 in the UAE) Yet there is a paucity of research that examines the internet reporting of strategic information in emerging market economies such as the UAE. In the context this shortage, this paper, assesses the extent to which UAE non-financial listed firms voluntarily communicate strategic information over the internet and, second, examines the influence of internal governance mechanisms and other firm-specific characteristics on the extent of that disclosure.

This study contributes to the existing literature on corporate communication using online reporting (e.g. Xiao, *et al.*, 2004; Capriotti & Moreno, 2007; García-Sanchez *et al.*, 2011; Hashim *et al.*, 2014) Xiao *et al.* (2004) investigated the relationship between corporate characteristics and the online reporting of the content of annual reports for a sample of Chinese firms. Capriotti and Moreno (2007) examined the presence and the organization of corporate responsibility on the websites of firms listed on Spanish stock market. These studies do not underscore the communication of strategy related information over the internet. They also overlook the influence of corporate governance on the online reporting. In filling this gap, García-Sanchez *et al.* (2011) and Hashim *et al.* (2014) examined the association between corporate governance and IRSI for samples of Spanish firms and Malaysian firms respectively. Yet both studies do not examine the effect of the audit committee on the IRSI as the case of the current study. In the context of the UAE, Oyelere and Kuruppu (2012) explored whether UAE firms operate websites to communicate financial information to different stakeholders. Hence, the influence of audit committee, as one of governance mechanisms, on the online reporting in emerging economies is under researched, the matter that makes the issue of corporate governance and the IRSI worth an examination in the UAE.

Furthermore, many of internet reporting studies rely on the economic-based theories – such as agency theory, signaling theory and political cost theory – to examine the association between internet reporting and firm-specific characteristics such as firm size, profitability and leverage (e.g. Craven & Marston, 1999; Ettredge *et al.*, 2002; Debreceny *et al.*, 2002; Oyelere *et al.*, 2003) This study utilizes a multi-theoretic perspective to study the association between internal governance mechanisms, firm-specific characteristics and the IRSI in UAE. The study uses a complementary perspective that cross-fertilizes ideas from economic-based theories, known as Positive Accounting Theory (PAT) and innovation diffusion theory. The use of such a multi-theoretic approach is recommendable to explain the empirical findings in an emerging market economy such as the UAE.

The UAE provides an appropriate context to this study for several reasons. First, the UAE enacted a corporate governance code that mandatorily requires the formation of audit committees (ACs) that follow world-wide AC "best practice" (2007 amended 2009) Second, the UAE has pumped huge investment in the Information Technology (IT) infrastructure whereby the country is ranked as the 24 of 142 countries in IT developments (The Global Information Technology Report 2010-2011 Report; World forum, 2011) Therefore, it is worth examining the association between various dimensions of governance and the IRSI in UAE. Finally, the study findings are in the interest of the UAE policymakers and regulators as well as other countries, especially the Gulf Cooperation Council and Middle East countries because they share similar social, political and economic contexts.

The study is organized in seven sections. After this introduction, section two defines the Internet Reporting of Strategic Information (IRSI) Section three discusses the study theoretical framework. Section four presents the UAE institutional context. Section five discusses the hypotheses development. Section six discusses the study methodology. Section seven discusses and explains the empirical findings, before the conclusion section.

2. Internet Reporting of Strategic Information (IRSI)

IRSI is defined as the integration of technology, especially the internet, in the reporting activities related to the firm's strategies, policies, plans, market position, products and customers (Santema et al., 2005; Garcıa-Sanchez et al., 2011) Most firms make significant investments on their websites to: 1) improve the communication with investors; 2) publish information on timely basis, 3) enable information users to obtain complete information and consequently, 4) enhance investors' judgment and decision-making process (Debreceny et al., 2002; Marston, 2003; Marston & Polei, 2004; Oyelere et al., 2003; Xiao et al., 2004) Owing to these benefits, the IRSI is becoming an important corporate practice (Ibid.) The IRSI reduces agency costs expressed in preventing managers from using their discretion to pursue their own interests. Yet it may lead to significant competitive disadvantages since the firm may disclose what it intends to do in the future. (Lim et al., 2007)

Although there is no definitive framework for the IRSI, several scholars indicated elements of what they termed as "strategy" related information. For example, Lim *et al.*, (2007) argue that non-financial information, such as corporation's missions, visions, goals, outcomes, types of customers, different markets and products, is the most notable type of information when the firm managers communicate with the firm stakeholders. Corporate managers' ultimate goal of publishing this type of "strategic" information is to distinguish their corporations from their competitors (Santema & Van de Rijt, 2001) Likewise, the AICPA reports underlying themes encourage the firm managers to disclose information about their firms' plans, opportunities, strategies, and other non-financial measures of key business processes in an attempt to align firms' annual reports with the needs of the financial reports' users (AICPA, 1994; The Jenkins Committee Report published in 1994) Corporate managers are encouraged to supply what Santema *et al.* (2005, p. 35) define as "strategy disclosure" "*The revelation of information an organization decides to share with its stakeholders on the strategy it is pursuing and going to pursue in the future*". Hence, the IRSI is a special type of voluntary disclosure that a firm may use to disseminate information about its future plans and strategic goals.

"Strategic" related information can be published through the firm's annual reports or the firm's websites. Although the importance the firm's annual report as means of information disclosure has been well documented in the academic literature (Hassan, 2008; 2012; 2014): Lodhia *et al.* (2004) argue that technological developments together with the emergence of network communication undermined the traditional annual report disclosure communication. This is because the annual reports disclosure has become less timely, less interactive and less accessible in comparison to internet reporting. Accordingly, internet reporting, and the IRSI is no exception, has become a powerful force to evolve traditional disclosure because it is expected to provide a remedy for the recent principal problems of printed annual reports. (Xiao *et al.*, 2002; Jones & Xiao, 2003)

3. Theoretical framework

The economic-based theories suggest that accounting disclosure, and the IRSI is no exception, is likely to reduce cost of capital, reduce information asymmetry and highlight (signal) certain information to stakeholders (Healy & Palepu, 2001; Gallego-Alvarez *et al.*, 2008; Cormier *et al.*, 2005; Lim *et al.*, 2007; Boubaker *et al.*, 2012) Corporate managers are likely to disclose "strategy" information over the internet when the benefits of that disclosure exceed its total costs. Reducing information asymmetry is another motive behind the disclosure of strategic information (Lim *et al.*, 2007; Gallego-Alvarez *et al.*, 2008; Boubaker *et al.*, 2012) Managers disclose strategic information over the internet to reduce the information asymmetry between informed and uninformed investors and consequently enhance their firms communication processes (Gallego-Alvarez et al., 2008; 2011; Garcia-Sanchez et al., 2011) Corporate managers also use the IRSI to make different stakeholders aware of their managerial ability (Healy and Palepu, 2001; Chalmers and Godfrey, 2004) The provision of "strategy" related information on the firm website not only signals a good corporate image but also avoid misevaluation of the management actions. According to signaling theory, the IRSI is one of the means for corporate managers to distinguish themselves and their firms from others on dimensions such as quality, performance and expected future expansion (Gallego-Alvarez et al., 2008; 2011; Garcia-Sanchez et al., 2011; Boubaker et al., 2012)

Lodhia et al., (2004) argue that technological developments together with the emergence of network communication undermined the traditional annual report disclosure communication. This is because the annual reports disclosure has become less timely, less interactive and less accessible in comparison to internet reporting. Accordingly, internet reporting has become a powerful force to evolve traditional disclosure because it is expected to provide a remedy for the recent principal problems of printed corporate reporting (Xiao et al., 2002; Jones & Xiao, 2003) In the context of IRSI, these benefits are contrasted to the competitive disadvantages because firms may disclose what they intend to do in the future (Lim et al., 2007) These unique features of the IRSI not only render the costs and benefits of adopting this type of disclosure uncertain but also suggest that the adoption of this technology-based innovation involves complex tradeoffs beyond the economic factors introduced under the banner of economic-based theories. Consequently, the literature on the innovation diffusion theory can enrich the explanation behind the extent of the disclosure of "strategic" information over the internet.

The innovation diffusion theory complements economic-based theories explanations of accounting disclosure by highlighting the role of agents in the diffusion of the IRSI. The diffusion of IRSI is defined as a process by which information about that technological-based reporting is communicated across different companies over time. Diffusion occurs when people possessing the knowledge about that technological-based disclosure moves from one specific social context - usually a firm- to another firm (Bao & Bao, 1989: 304; BjØrnenak, 1997: 4) Some of the organizational members may have the knowledge about a certain accounting innovation and diffuse (i.e. share) this information with other organizational members. (Hussein, 1981) The firm's auditor, the independent non-executive directors and regulators are different groups that contribute in the diffusion of an innovation such as the IRSI (Clarke et al., 1999) BjØrnenak (1997) argues that these groups are defined as change agents. These agents' main role is to promote for new ideas such as the IRSI.

Carpenter and Feroz (2001) argue that firms adopt some practices, like the IRSI, because of social pressures exist in the society through the firm stakeholders such as auditors, regulators and innovation change agents. Accordingly, firms' managers comply with these pressures in order to obtain social legitimacy (Touron, 2005; Hassan, 2008) DiMaggio and Powell (1983) argue that innovation is diffused through coercive, normative and mimetic isomorphic mechanisms. Coercive isomorphism is illustrated by the influence of the state or government agencies on firms through the enactment of legislation. It is the process by which a firm is pressured by powerful external organizations, such as the government and providers of capital, to adopt an innovation irrespective of its benefit to the firm. Normative isomorphism stems primarily from the professions. The professional associations' rule of conduct exerts pressure to adopt certain practices, like the IRSI, across different firms operating in the same field. Finally, mimetic isomorphism reflects the desire to mirror others' practices that are recognized as both successful and worthy adopting.

4. The UAE institutional context

The UAE is one of six countries constituting the Arabian Gulf region (i.e. Bahrain, Oman, Qatar, Saudi Arabia, UAE and Kuwait) The country is a member of Gulf Confederation Council (GCC) and geographically located in the western region of Asia. Like other Gulf region counties, the UAE's major economic resource is crude oil, which constitutes almost 10% of the world's reserves (Aljifri & Khasharmeh, 2006) Although Gulf region countries share similar characteristics in terms of culture, customs, religion and language, they are not homogeneous in terms of their levels of corporate governance and institutional developments (Baydoun *et al.*, 2013; Shehata, 2015) Each country has its unique mixture of intra-country specific legal, economic, social and political institutions (Hassan, 2008; 2014) Each country has its uniqueness and the UAE is no exception. The UAE has witnessed a remarkable socio- economic growth over the last few years and therefore, the country has become a key focus for personal and institutional investors (Obay, 2009)

The UAE actively established commercial partnerships with Western and European countries in order to benchmark international best practices in different fields. It maintained a strategy of "marketing the country as an attractive destination for business as well as residence" (Irvine, 2008; Hassan, 2014) As an emerging capital market with ambitious plans to be recognised internationally, the UAE engaged in huge developments in various sectors. One aspect of these developments is that the UAE has mobilized the country different sectors to apply the latest Information Technology (IT) The country officials consider that IT is an essential element for a repaid development and for benchmarking international best practices. For example, the government funded Dubai Internet City which is a free trade zone created specifically for e-commerce. The UAE government also funded Dubai Silicon Oasis which is a free trade zone and integrated technology park (The Global Information Technology Report 2010-2011 Report). These projects have ranked the UAE as the 24 of 142 countries. (World Forum, 2011)

The UAE also established Information Communication and Technology (ICT). Fund by mid of 2005. The underlying aim of that fund is to use advanced communication technology in promoting a culture of entrepreneurship. The Fund's key objective is to strengthen the UAE global leadership position through IT-based investing ideas that contribute to the intellectual growth of the sector. (UAE ICT Fund Report, 2011) These technological developments were executed concurrently with the country institutional developments related to the adoption of proper corporate governance standards. (Hassan, 2012; 2014)

As part of the UAE strategy towards harmonizing the country governance practices with that of international best practices, the country established the Hawakama (Governance) Institute in 2006 in association with a number of international agencies such as Organization of Economic Cooperation and Development (OECD) (Baydoun et al., 2013) Since that time, the UAE has attempted to develop its regulatory environment while harmonizing different national legislations and guidelines with the requirements of international best practices of corporate governance (Hassan, 2012) In early 2007, the country successfully aligned its legal and statutorily requirements with international best practices of governance under the banner of the UAE code of corporate governance (ES&CMA decision R/32 of 2007) This code comprehensively refines and delineates elements of corporate governance fragmentally introduced by the UAE Corporation Act of 1984, the UAE central bank guidelines and the ES&CMA decision no. 3 of 2000 concerning transparency and disclosure.

Similar to other GCC countries (Baydoun et al., 2013; Shehata, 2015): The UAE code outlines specific and detailed corporate governance requirements that corporations must comply with in order to meet what the code states "institutional governance discipline criteria". The code also requires listed corporations to prepare, as an integral part of annual reports, a governance report. This report should outline, as the code states, information about board of directors' duties, composition, structure, and the selection process of directors. The report should also include information about board committees, internal control systems, directors' remuneration, risk management, shareholders rights and rules governing the appointment and discharging of the external auditors. (Hassan, 2012) The UAE sat a timeframe to implement and enforce its code of governance across the UAE listed corporations. The country specified a transitional period until May 2010 in which all listed UAE corporations must comply with the code of governance requirements otherwise penalties are charged in case of non-compliance

(ES&CMA decision no 518 of 2009). The UAE code is, therefore, the strictest one across Gulf region countries since it uses comply/penalize approach while other GCC countries apply comply/explain approach. (Shehata, 2015)

In 2009, the UAE amended its code of governance in the light of practical problems encountered during the transition period. One of these problems is that most of Gulf corporations, and UAE corporations are no exception, are highly controlled by a few controlling shareholders or dominated by family ownership (Baydoun, *et al.*, 2013). Therefore, there is a rarely any separation between the ownership and management. This particular institutional characteristic undermines the importance of monitoring and controlling via non-executive directors. Compared to Western and European countries wherein diverse shareholders exists and consequently managers-owners conflict of interest is resolved via monitoring and controlling mechanisms such as non-executive and independent directors, the Gulf region institutional feature mobilizes corporations to overlook that issue due to the high level of family ownership and consequently the lack of conflict of interest between ownership and management. (Baydoun, *et al.*, 2013)

Another major problem facing the implementation of corporate governance codes in GCC countries is the underdevelopment of capital markets in these countries (Hassan and El-Kelish, 2012; Shehata, 2015) Despite the importance of capital markets as an external governance mechanism leading to enhancing wealth creation for shareholders and improving the control over the management opportunistic behaviour, GCC countries capital markets are still in their early stages. Compared to other GCC countries, the UAE has three capital markets: the Abu Dhabi Stock Market (ADX): Dubai Financial Market (DFM) and the Dubai International Financial Stock Exchange (DIFX) currently known as NASDAC Dubai (Oyelere & Kuruppu, 2012; Hassan & El-Keslish, 2012; Shehata, 2015).

The Emirates Securities and Commodities Market Authority (ES&CMA) regulate both the ADX and the DFM, yet the DIFX has a separate and independent regulator – the Dubai Financial Services Authority (DFSA). The ES&CMA enforces the application of best governance practices on all listed non-financial companies, yet DFSA enforces the compliance with principles of good governance on the financial sector, mainly - banks, insurance companies, asset management and investment companies (www.dfsa.ae). The existence of three capital markets is a sign of progressive market operations, yet investors can observe that the ES&CMA did not pass a formal code governing the takeover processes, the matter that may expose distressed non-financial firms to pressures from rivals to merge together – i.e. hostile takeover. By contrast, there is a takeover code which applies to listed firms on the NASDAC Dubai (Hassan & El-Kelish, 2012).

Although GCC countries codes of governance are similar (Shehata, 2015): the survey results by Boydoun *et al.* (2013) show variations in practicing these codes across GCC countries. Boydoun *et al.* (2013) surveyed the practice of corporate governance underlying principles of: 1) shareholder rights and obligations, 2) internal processes including board composition, reward system and board committees and 3) transparency including disclosure and external audit. The survey shows that the UAE earned the highest score in terms of shareholder rights and obligations, yet it scored lower, the third, in terms of internal process and transparency.

Like other GCC countries, one of the key aspects of the UAE code is that it pays attention to the composition of the board of directors. In addition to separating the chairman role from the CEO role, the UAE code states that the majority of board members must be non-executive directors, one third of the board members must be independent directors; and the remainder of the board may be executive members (UAE corporate governance code, 2009). In the UAE, finding qualified, experienced independent and/or non-executive directors is a major issue because of the small population of potential directors, the matter that makes it difficult to find an individual who is genuinely independent and significantly contributes to governance processes. (Baydoun *et al.*, 2013: 17) Nevertheless, both independent directors and non-executive directors can be working in other firms and therefore they may possess the knowledge about new innovations such as the IRSI. Accordingly, they can act as change agents promoting for new ideas.

The UAE code defines both the non-executive directors and independent directors. The non-executive director is a director who is not dedicated on a full time basis to the management of the firm or does not receive a monthly or annual salary from the firm. The independent director is a director who neither himself/herself, his/her spouse nor first-degree relative is a member of the executive management of the firm during the last two years or has a relationship that creates financial deals with the firm, parent firm, sister firm or allied firm during the last two years if the total amount of these transactions exceeds 5% of the paid-up capital of the firm or five millions Dirhams – i.e. UAE currency. Compared to other GCC countries except Bahrain, one of the unique feature of UAE code is that it defines material business relationship for board member independency in financial terms whereas most GCC countries require independence of board members in terms of being former employees or senior managers. (Shehata, 2015: 328)

The UAE code also stipulates that the board of directors shall form an audit committee consisting of non-executive board members, provided that majority of the committee's members shall be independent members. The Committee shall consist of at least three members, of whom a member shall be an expert in accounting affairs. The code requests that the audit committee shall meet at least once on a quarterly basis or whenever necessary. Like other GCC countries, the

UAE code delineates audit committee duties in terms of monitoring the integrity of the financial statements, the effectiveness of the internal control function, the appointment of external auditor and overseeing the risk management systems. (Shehata, 2015)

This study examines the effect of internal governance mechanisms on the IRSI and has faced several challenges. One of these challenges is that it examines the governance-IRSI association for a sample of annual reports published by December 2010, a few months after the completion of the UAE specified transitional period (i.e. May 2010). The matter that had some implications in achieving a coherent set of data related to the classification of independent directors and non-executive directors. Reading the UAE firms' corporate governance report shows that some firms reported three categories of board members: non-executive, independent and executive directors. While other firms reported two categories: executive and independent non-executive directors, since the independent directors can also be non-executive directors according to the UAE code. Some firms reported the following categories of board members: independent non-executive, executive and independent directors. This inconsistency may lead to financial statement users' confusion and casts doubt on the quality of published information particularly it is hard to think of a situation in which an independent director is not a non-executive one.

Since the study underlying assumption is that both independent and non-executive directors have connections with other firms and can act as change agents promoting for new ideas such as the IRSI, the use of independent non-executive directors as a category seemed appropriate since it fits with the study objectives and helps in creating a coherent set of data for statistical analysis. Nevertheless, one must recognize that the quality of governance information published in the UAE firms' annual reports has improved compared to the quality of information published during the transition period to enforce the UAE code of governance. (see Hassan, 2012)

Another challenge is the operationalization of the audit committee as an internal governance mechanism. This is because the UAE adopted a comply/penalize approach to enforces its code of governance. Under this a stringent approach the examination of a single characteristic of audit committee such as the composition or independence may not be adequate since the possibility of variation across firms is low. Therefore, the study operationalizes the audit committee though developing an audit committee quality index which will explain later in section 6.2.

5. Hypotheses development

Independent non-executive directors

The literature well documents that board members' independence is an important element in monitoring the corporate financial accounting process. (Klein, 2002; Hanniffa & Cooke, 2005; Garcia-Sanchez et al., 2011) For example, Beasley (1996) provides evidence that the proportion of independent directors is positively related to the board's ability to influence disclosure decisions. Chen and Jaggi (2000) find a positive relationship between the proportion of independent non-executive directors and the firm disclosure by Hong Kong listed firms. Ajinkya et al. (2005: 371) provide evidence on the positive relation between board independence and level of disclosure. Cheng and Courtenay (2006) provide further evidence that firms with a higher proportion of independent non-executive directors have significantly higher levels of voluntary disclosure than those firms with balanced boards. Xiao et al. (2004) also conclude that online reporting is positively associated with the proportion of independent non-executive directors. The innovation diffusion theory also supports such an expectation by seeing independent non-executive directors as change agents. Since those directors would be working in other firms and may have prior experience of IRSI, they can suggest the adoption of the IRSI. Therefore, the study hypothesizes:

H1: The extent of IRSI is positively associated with the proportion of independent non-executive directors on the board.

Board meetings

According to agency theory, the frequency of board meetings is expected to have a positive effect on the strategic disclosure (Garcia-Sanchez, 2011) Frequent meetings provide a meaningful forum of communication. Therefore, corporate directors and managers would be having a sufficient time to exchange ideas and discuss issues of strategic nature. Garcia-Sanchez et al. (2011: 478) argue that active boards are those who meet most frequently in order to fulfill their duties. Lipton and Lorsch (1992) argue that frequent meetings signal the vigilance of the board whereby more time is devoted for consultation and the implementation of the corporate strategy. The innovation disunion theory also supports such an expectation. Since one third of the board members must be independent directors (UAE code of governance, 2009): the more frequent board meetings will lead to better chances for those independent directors to promote for new ideas such as the IRSI. Therefore, the study hypothesizes:

H2: The extent of IRSI is positively associated with the frequency of the board of directors' meetings.

The type of auditor

Big audit firms are expected to maintain more independent auditing service and more strict in complying with audit standards than smaller audit firms (DeAngelo, 1981; Malone*et al.*, 1993) Since big audit firms have greater incentives to demand higher quality disclosure, corporations appoint these firms in an attempt to signal their desires to abide by the demand of higher quality disclosure (Healy & Palepu, 2001) Several studies provide empirical evidence confirming that the level of disclosure is positively related to firms employing big audit firms (Inchausti, 1997; Klein, 2002) Likewise, Xiao *et al.* (2004) and Debreceny *et al.* (2002) argue that compared to domestic auditors, large auditors especially the Big 4 international audit firms are more likely to facilitate the diffusion of innovative practice such as the IRSI. They add that auditors' reputation provides creditability of that type of reporting. Extending this line of reasoning to the IRSI, the study hypothesizes:

H3: The extent of IRSI is greater among firms audited by the Big-4 audit firms than by non-Big4 audit firms.

Audit Committee Quality

Barua *et al.* (2010) argue that the audit committee (AC) enhances the reporting processes and reduces information asymmetries between management and stakeholders. Li *et al.* (2012) add that AC plays an important role in enhancing the board of directors' effectiveness in monitoring the firm management. Empirical evidence suggests that the AC composition has a positive effect on the quality of disclosure. For example, the existence of independent members and financial experts in the AC is found to be positively associated with the perceived financial reporting quality (Jamil and Nelson, 2003; Ika *et al.* 2012) Prior literature also suggests that AC characteristics influences the committee's ability to effectively execute its duties (Abbott *et al.*, 2003; Carcello & Neal, 2003; Kelton & Yang, 2008) Li *et al.* (2012) argue that independent ACs are more likely to be free from management influence and therefore these committees ensure the quality and credibility of the reporting process. Likewise, accounting experts have also been associated with higher quality financial reporting (Barua *et al.*, 2010) Kelton and Yang (2008) find a positive association between a more diligent AC (measured by size, frequency of meetings, independence, number of members with financial expertise) and internet reporting.

Since the majority AC members are likely to be independent directors (UAE code of governance 2009): the innovation diffusion theory also supports Audit Committee Quality (ACQ)-IRSI positive relationship. The existence of those independent directors in the AC is expected to facilitate the diffusion of innovative practice such as the IRSI since those directors may have prior knowledge of IRSI from working in other firms. In line with the international trend, the UAE code (2009) instates a regime wherein listed firms must form diligent and vigilant ACs that apply, what Rainsbury *et al.* (2008) call, "best practices AC". The UAE code of corporate governance sets principles of AC "best practices". These principles state that ACs should: 1) comprise of non-executive directors, 2) have a majority of independent directors, and (3) have a member who is an accounting expert. As part of these best practices, the code requests AC to hold a minimum of four meetings a year and be comprised of at least three members. Therefore, the study hypothesizes that:

H4: *The extent of IRSI is positively associated with the firm AC quality.*

6. Methodology

6.1 Sample

The study relies on a sample of 37 non-financial firms listed on Dubai and Abu Dhabi financial markets for the year ending December 31 2010. Despite being a small sample size, this sample represents 88 percent of UAE non-financial listed firms. Due to the weak websites, and insufficient published information on these websites, some firms were removed. To achieve the study objectives, data was collected from three main sources: 1) firms' websites, 2) firms' annual reports published by the end of 2010, and 3) firms' corporate governance reports published by the end of 2010. Firms' websites were checked against the IRSI index (appendix 1) which was crafted solely to measure the variation in that type of disclosure across UAE non-financial listed firms. The website of each firm was printed and checked against the IRSI index over a period spanning over May 2011 - August 2011. The underlying point, here, is that both board members and members of AC discuss, recommend and make decisions regarding the IRSI during 2010, yet the results of their discussions are put into effect on later dates. In other words, there will be a time lag between directors' recommendations and the implementation of these recommendations. Accordingly, board members and ACs perform their tasks during 2010 but the effect of their recommendations is expected to be during 2011.

6.2 Research design and variables measurements

The study applies a cross-sectional regression analysis. It tests the relationship between the IRSI, as a dependent variable, and two sets of independent variables: first, AC quality variables, board independence variables and, second, firm-specific characteristics variables. The following subsections discuss how the study's variables are measured.

6.2.1 The dependent variable: the IRSI index

The study uses content analysis to craft an index that quantifies the qualitative IRSI disclosure. It codifies firms' websites textual information into different categories recommended by prior studies. The study undertakes an extensive review of prior studies to craft an IRSI index and to develop a list of IRSI index items (i.e. sentences) (Santema et al., 2005; García-Sanchez et al., 2011; Padia & Yasseen, 2011; Santema & Van de Rijt, 2001; Hashim et al., 2014) Although, the use of sentence, as a unit of analysis, is reliable than using word, such a use was supported by examining the thematic content of each sentence since the same idea of a strategic disclosure item may be described using different sentences (Hasseldine et al., 2005; Hassan, 2014) Then the total number of sentences (i.e. items) is used to quantify the disclosure volume. The index is crafted solely for the purpose of measuring differences in IRSI levels across listed non-financial firms. In other words, the index is a yardstick to measure the level of "strategy disclosure". Appendix 1 outlines the IRSI items.

Following to the review of prior studies, 11 items were determined and checked against firms' websites. This checking process modified the index's items while harmonizing the index with the UAE context. The modification processes led to: first, eliminating some items (2 items) and, second, adding new items (6 items) accordingly, the maximum score includes 15 items. The added six items are: 1) published in firms' websites, 2) "strategy" related items and 3) broadly scored by prior studies that indirectly addressed the issue of strategy disclosure (White, 1996; Depoers, 2000; Petersen & Plenborg, 2006; Lim et al., 2007; Gallego Álvarez et al., 2008; 2011) The matter which establishes a credibility and reliability of the IRSI disclosure index since it is being developed after looking at numerous previous studies in various countries while considering the UAE context. (see Appendix 1)

The inclusion/exclusion of an item in the maximum score is based on the ground that it is disclosed by at least two firms in the sample. In other words, an item that is not disclosed by all firms, or only by one firm, is excluded from the expected score. Therefore the inclusion of the six items, scored during checking process, seems appropriate an approach to harmonize the IRSI on index-based prior studies with the UAE context. The IRSI index coincides with other studies that quantify the extent of voluntary disclosure. (e.g. Barako et al., 2006; Hassan, 2009; 2012)

One of the important issues during crafting the IRSI index is whether some items should be weighted more heavily (i.e. important) than others. In accounting research, both weighted and un-weighted disclosure indexes are used (e.g. Hassan; 2009; 2012) On the one hand, the use of weighted disclosure index has been criticized because it involves a bias towards a particular user group. On the other hand, the un-weighted index, known as dichotomous scores where 0 is awarded for non-disclosed items and 1 is awarded for disclosed items, has been criticized on its assumption that all index items have equal importance. Nevertheless, various studies argue that the use of un-weighted or weighted indices do not significantly affect the results and considered as highly subjective (Al-Razeen & Karbhari, 2004; Alsaeed, 2006; Lopes & Rodrigues, 2007) For the purpose of this study the un-weighted index was chosen. This is because the study does not focus on one particular user group but rather all users of the IRSI. Therefore, there is no need to confer different importance levels to the disclosure items. The contents of each firm's website are compared to the items listed in Appendix 1 and coded as 1 if thematically disclosed or 0 if not disclosed.

6.2.2 The statistical model and independent variables

The relationship between independent variables, i.e. ACQ, board independence, firm-specific variables, and the IRSI is tested through the model presented below:

$$IRSI index = \beta_0 + \beta_1 INED + \beta_2 BODMeeting + \beta_3 AUD + \beta_4 ACQ + \beta_5 SIZE$$
$$+ \beta_6 OrgCom + \beta_7 RISK + \beta_8 profitability$$

The study relies on prior studies to measure ACQ, board independence and firm-specific characteristics variables (e.g. Gul & Leung, 2004; Haniffa & Cooke 2002, 2005; Cerbioni & Parbonetti, 2007; Li et al., 2008; 2012; Cheng & Courtenay, 2006; Kelton & Yang, 2008; Garcia-Sanchez et al., 2011; Gallego-Alvarez et al., 2008; 2011; Cormier et al., 2005; Lim et al., 2007; Boubaker et al., 2012; Xiao et al., 2004; Chen & Jaggi, 2000; Hashim et al., 2014) Table 1 summarizes the definition, measurement, source of information and predicted sign of all variables utilized in this study. Some of governance variables were not considered because of data unavailability. For example the information about managerial ownership, ownership diffusion/concentration and the presence of shareholder representative on the board was not easy to score. This confirms Baydoun et al., (2013: 17) survey results which found that UAE scores less in in disclosure relating to ownership interests in comparison to other GCC countries.

Although board the size is one of the governance mechanisms, it was not incorporated in the study original regression model for two reasons. First, the board size has been considered in using the percentage of independent non-executive directors divided to the board size to measure the board independency. Second, the study pays close attention to examine the association between change agents promoting new ideas, such as the IRSI, through their connections with other firms and the extent of that disclosure. Therefore, the original regression model incudes outside directors, external auditor and the audit committee (wherein the majority are outside directors) as change agent promoting new ideas such as the IRSI.

Nevertheless, the study incorporates board size in a robustness test in order to corroborate the empirical findings as shown in section 7.4

Table 1. Variables definition and measurement

Variables	Predicted sign	Measurement	Sources of information
Dependent variable The Internet Reporting of Strategic Information (IRSI)		Un-weighted Index	Firms' websites
Independent variables Independent Non-Executive Directors (INED)	+	% of INED to Total # of Board of Directors	Governance Report
Board Meetings (BOD Meetings)	+	Total # of board meeting per year	Governance Report
External Auditor (AUD)	+	Dummy variables: 1 if the auditor is a Big 4 and 0 otherwise	Governance Report
Audit Committee Quality (ACQ)	+	ACQ score (see below)	Governance Report
Control variables Firm size (SIZE)	+	Logarithm of the total assets	Annual reports
Firm Complexity (Complexity)	+	Total # of products	Firms' websites
Risk (Risk)	+	Total debt divided to total assets	Annual reports
Profitability (Return on Assets) (ROA)	+/-	Net Income divided to Total Assets	Annual reports
Robustness test Board Size (BOD Size)	+/-	Total # of Board of Directors	Governance Report

6.2.2.1 Audit Committee Quality Measurement

By mid of 2007, the UAE security market passed a corporate governance code that mandatory requires the formation of ACs that apply best practice. The UAE adopts the US model in which corporate governance rules are mandatory applied. The country does not adopt the UK "comply or explain' approach to corporate governance. This mandatory requirement reduces the likelihood of greater variation in corporate governance structure and practices by UAE listed firms. In this context, the examination of a single characteristic of AC such as the composition or independence may not be adequate to assess the quality of an AC. Therefore, the study utilizes a number of criteria to develop ACQ index. This approach seems an appropriate one to apply because of the UAE stringent corporate governance requirements.

The UAE code of governance states that ACs should: 1) comprise of non-executive directors whereby the majority of these directors are classified as independent directors, 2) have a member who is an accounting expert, 3) AC should hold a minimum of four meetings a year and 4) AC should be comprised of at least three members. The code compels listed firms to form diligent ACs that apply what Rainsbury et al., (2008; 2009) call "best practices" AC. Following Rainsbury et al. (2008, 2009) approach, the study relies on the UAE corporate governance principles of "best practices" AC to craft an index that captures ACQ. Therefore the study investigates ACs quality expressed in terms of: 1) the existence of non-executive directors, 2) the percentage of independent directors, 3) the existence of members with accounting expertise, 4) the frequency of meetings and 5) the size of the AC. The ACQ index, therefore, identifies different measures that are consistent with the UAE code of governance.

The first ACQ measure is the existence of NED. As discussed earlier, the UAE firms' corporate governance report shows that some firms reported three categories of AC members: non-executive, independent and independent non-executive, while other firms reported two categories: independent and independent non-executive directors. The study assigns the value of 1 if the AC composition clearly includes and states the category of non-executive director or 0 otherwise. In other words, the study assigns a value of 0 if the firm reported the AC is comprised of independent directors only. The study applied a stringent approach to score this item because the more categories of directors the AC include the better the decisions it takes (Rainsbury et al., 2008, 2009)

The second AC quality measure is AC independence. In this regard, the index assigns a value of 1 if 51% of the AC members or more is independent directors and 0 otherwise. The third ACQ measure is the existence of accounting expertise. The index assigns a value of 1 if the audit committee includes a member who posses accounting expertise or 0 otherwise. One of the underlying issue, here, is the definition of "accounting expertise" (DeFond et al., 2005; Davidson et al., 2004; Naiker & Sharma, 2009; Barua et al., 2010) Barua et al., (2010) argue that accounting expertise is a controversial issue since some scholars conflates between "auditing expertise" and "financial expertise". Rainsbury et al., (2009) add that the term "financial/accounting expertise" can be broadly or narrowly interpreted. They argue that the SOX Act adopts a broad definition to avoid the exclusion of qualified presidents and chief executive officers, with non-accounting background, to be appointed as experts. In line with the UAE code of governance, the study adopts a narrow definition of accounting expertise. This is because of a lack of consistency in the disclosures of directors' backgrounds in firms' corporate governance reports in the UAE. Therefore, the ACQ index assigns a value of 1 if the AC includes a member with accounting background or 0 otherwise.

The fourth ACQ measure is the frequency of AC meetings. Several studies argue that more diligent ACs appear to have frequent meetings (Abbott *et al.*, 2003, Barua *et al.* 2010) Kelton and Yang (2008) found a positive association between the number of audit committee meetings and internet reporting. Li *et al.*, (2012) argue that ACs that meet more frequently would have more time to perform the role of monitoring the corporate reporting process efficiently. They add that adequate meeting time by the ACs sends a signal of the committee's intention to remain informed and vigilant. In line with Barua *et al.* (2010): the study uses the number of AC meetings per year as a proxy for the diligence of the AC. Furthermore, more meetings facilitate the diffusion of IRSI since meetings enable a thorough discussion of innovative ideas such as IRSI. In this regard, the UAE code of governance states that "AC shall meet at least once on a quarterly basis". Since more meetings means more vigilant and diligent ACs and the UAE firms' ACs are required to hold a minimum of four meetings a year, the ACQ index assigns a value of 1 if the number of meetings is more than four and 0 otherwise.

The fifth ACQ measure is the size of AC. Bédard *et al.* (2004) argue that the larger the AC, the more likely it resolves potential problems in the financial reporting process because it is likely to provide diversity of expertise ensuring effective monitoring. One can argue that since AC is mostly comprised of outsiders (independents and NED) directors with diverse views, knowledge and expertise of due to their prior experiences in different firms, they may benchmark best practices such as the IRSI to the firm where they sit on its AC. In other words, ACs members may act as change agents in the diffusion process of IRSI across different firms. The UAE code of governance states that "AC shall consist of at least three members". Since the UAE firms' ACs are required to be compromised of three members, the ACQ index assigns a value of 1 if the number of AC members is more than three and 0 otherwise.

6.2.2.2 Firm-specific characteristics measurements

Prior studies provided extensive empirical work articulating firm-specific characteristics to the extent of internet reporting (e.g. Cerbioni & Parbonetti, 2007; Cheng & Courtenay, 2006; Hanifia & Cooke, 2002; Kelton & Yang, 2008; Garcia-Sanchez *et al.*, 2011; Gallego-Alvarez *et al.*, 2008; 2011; Boubaker *et al.*, 2012; Xiao *et al.*, 2004) Building on these studies, the study measures firms-specific variables such as firm size (SIZE): complexity (Complexity): risk (Risk): and profitability (ROA).

Size: Lopes and Rodrigues (2007: 32) argue that larger firms are expected to have economics of scale and therefore additional disclosure is less costly in comparison to smaller ones. Watts and Zimmerman (1978) argue that larger firms have higher information asymmetry between managers and shareholders. Therefore, larger firms are likely to disclose more information to reduce agency costs related to information asymmetry. Following this line of reasoning, several studies provided evidence supporting the influence of the firm size on the level of disclosure on the internet (e.g. Oyelere *et al.*, 2003; Marston & Polei, 2004; Ashbaugh *et al.*, 1999; Craven & Marston, 1999; Pirchegger & Wagenhofer, 1999; Ettredge *et al.*, 2002; Xiao *et al.*, 2004; Gallego-Alvarez *et al.*, 2008) Accordingly, the paper controls for the firm size since IRSI-firm size might be positively correlated.

Organization complexity: Bushman *et al.*, (2004) argue that firms, with diversified locations and diversified products, are likely to have more activities. They add that these firms are more complex and therefore more information disclosure is necessary in order to encourage potential investors to make investment decisions. Complex firms need to disclose more strategic information since nondisclosure could signal bad news that adversely affect the firm's share price. Likewise, Hanifia and Cooke (2002) argue that the firm complexity may explain the variation in level of disclosure. The firm complexity has different dimensions including geographical locations, geographical concentrations, number of production lines, type of the industry and number of products (Bushman *et al.*, 2004; Hanifia & Cooke, 2002) For example, Gallego-Alvarez *et al.*, (2011) test firm complexity-online reporting relationship for a sample of Spanish universities. They measured complexity by the number of faculties. Their underlying assumption is that more complex universities will disclose a larger level of information on their websites compared to less complex universities. Extending that line of reasoning to IRSI, encourages to control for organizational complexity since IRSI and organizational complexity might be positively correlated.

Level of Risk: Several empirical studies suggest that higher leverage levels lead to higher agency costs, therefore high levels of disclosure can be used to reduce these costs (Lopes & Rodrigues, 2007; Hassan, 2009; Gallego-Alvarez *et al.*, 2008; Garcıa-Sanchez *et al.*, 2011) One can argue, therefore, that firms with higher levels of risk will disclose greater amounts of strategic information because corporate managers are willing to explain how they will manage their corporations' debt levels. The literature also suggests corporate managers have personal interest to disclose strategic information in order to signal to wider stakeholders how they efficiently prepare the required resources to pay for debts (Debreceny *et al.*, 2002; Boubaker *et al.*, 2012) In this regard, Garcıa-Sanchez *et al.* (2011) add that the disclosure of strategic information may signal or, as they claim, directs investors to the corporation's strengths. Based on the above, we control for the effect of firm leverage on IRSI.

Profitability: One of the possible motives that drive corporate managers to supply strategic information over the internet is to reduce cost of capital. Profitable firms have the incentive to distinguish themselves from less successful ones in order to raise capital at the lowest possible cost (Kelton and Yang, 2008; Gallego-Alvarez *et al.*, 2008; 2011; Garcıa-Sanchez *et al.*, 2011; Boubaker *et al.*, 2012) One way to achieve this is through internet reporting (Marston & Polei, 2004) According to signaling theory, investors generally perceive the absence or poorly disclosed information as an indication of "bad news" about the corporation. Nevertheless, some empirical studies found no association between the firm's profitability and internet reporting (Ashbaugh *et al.*, 1999; Ettredge *et al.*, 2002; Oyelere *et al.*, 2003) Because of the inconclusiveness of empirical findings, the paper controls for the firm profitability.

7. Results and discussion

7.1 Descriptive statistics

Table 2 summarizes the frequency level for each item of strategic information disclosure among listed UAE non-financial firms. Table 3 presents descriptive statistics of the model variables[1]. It shows that the IRSI index has a mean value of 7.45 which indicates that on average UAE non-financial firms tend to disclose 7 items out of 15 items (or 47%) of strategic information. Compared to Spanish firms' average of (25%) (Garcıa-Sanchez *et al.*, 2011): the UAE non-financial firms' amount of IRSI is quite moderate like Malaysian firms (Hashim *et al.*, 2014)

Table 2. Frequency level for each strategic disclosure item

Strategic Disclosure Items	No. of firms disclosing	Percentage (%) of firms disclosing	Item rank
1. Objectives, mission and company's philosophy	22	59.46	4
2. Strategic alliances	11	29.73	13
3. Strategic position of company in its sector (leader,2nd.etc)	21	56.76	5
4. Company strategic planning (projects of expansion into other markets, products, regions)	20	54.05	7
5. Company annual planning/ performance against targets/graphs	16	43.24	10
6. Description of the competition context	19	51.35	8
7. Risk Control and management - Governance	27	72.97	2
8. Information on risks (financial, commercial, technical)/	14	37.84	11
9. Information on production processes	12	32.43	12
10. Strategic Business Unit –deleted	1	02.70	16
11. Weakness and Threats –deleted	1	02.70	16

Strategic Disclosure Items	No. of firms disclosing	Percentage (%) of firms disclosing	Item rank
12. Information on quality certification - added	29	78.38	1
13. Information on cost effective strategy -added	10	27.03	14
14. Information on innovative approaches - added	10	27.03	14
15. Health, Safety and Environment Strategy -added	21	56.76	5
16. Strategy towards workforces and their benefits -added	18	48.65	9
17. The firm's customer groups– added	26	70.27	3

Table 2 shows that the highest frequency level for "quality certification" with 29 firms (87.38%) have disclosed the item on the internet. The second place of high frequency item is "risk control and management – governance" with 27 firms (72.97%) followed with the item "the firm customer groups" with 26 firms (70.27%) The item of "objectives, mission and company's philosophy" scored the fourth in rank with 22 firms (59.36%) disclosing this item. Yet this item is the highest disclosed item by Spanish firms (García-Sanchez *et al.*, 2011) and Malaysian firms (Hashim *et al.*, 2014) "Strategic positon of the company" and "health, safety and environment strategy" disclosure items scored the same level and therefore ranked as fifth with 21 firms (56.76%) disclosing these items. Yet the former item is the second most frequently disclosed item by Spanish firms (García-Sanchez *et al.*, 2011) and the lowest disclosed item by Malaysian firms (Hashim *et al.*, 2014).

Table 2 shows that items commonly disclosed are as follow: "company strategic planning" with 20 firms (54.05%): "description of competitive context" with 19 (51.35%): "strategy towards the workforce" with 18 firms (48.65%): "company annual planning" with 16 firms (43.24%) and "information on different risks" with 14 firms (37.84%) Like Spanish firms (García-Sanchez *et al.*, 2011): the UAE non-financial firms have a moderate disclosure of "company strategic planning" item, yet the extent of disclosing this item is inconsistent with the Malaysian case which reported that time as the least disclosed one (Hashim *et al.*, 2014) The "company annual planning" item was the least disclosed one by the Spanish firms (7.7%) and Malaysian firms (29.07%) (García-Sanchez *et al.*, 2011; Hashim *et al.*, 2014): yet 43 percent of UAE non-financial firms disclose such an item.

Both the "information on risks" and "description of competitive context" items are disclosed more by UAE firms in comparison to Spanish firms (García-Sanchez *et al.*, 2011): yet they are less disclosed by UAE firms in comparison to Malaysian firms (Hashim *et al.*, 2013) Table 2 also shows that the lower disclosed items are "information on production processes" with 12 firms (32.43%): "strategic alliance" with 11 firms (29.73%) and "information in cost effectiveness and innovation strategy" with 10 firms (27.03%) The least disclosed items are "strategic business unit" and "weakness and threats" with 1 firm (02.70%) each and therefore there were removed from the IRSI index.

Table 3. Descriptive Statistics of all variables

	N	Range	Minimum	Maximum	Mean	Std. Deviation
IRSI	37	12.00	2.00	14.00	7.4595	3.19370
% INDED	36	0.55556	0.33333	0.88889	0.6565617	0.18149
BoD Meetings	35	5.000	4.000	9.000	6.05714	1.23534
AUD	37	1	0	1	0.78	0.417
ACQ Score	37	5.00	0.00	5.00	2.7297	1.12172
Size (Log of Assets)	37	7.66912	17.80824	25.47736	21.6372522	1.65014
Complexity (# Products)	33	20.00	1.00	21.00	5.6364	4.70915
Risk (Debt to Assets)	37	0.82980	0.03890	0.86870	0.4125054	0.21379
Profitability	37	0.536665	-.288588	0.248077	0.04478365	0.07916
BOD Size	37	12	5	17	7.97297	2.386146

Table 3 shows that the ACQ index has a mean value of 2.73 which indicates that on average UAE non-financial firms tend to have reasonable "best practices" ACs by end of 2010. The following percentages of firms in the sample were given the following scores for ACQ measures: 0 (2.7% per cent); 1 (8.1 per cent); 2 (32.43 per cent); 3 (32.43 per cent); 4 (19.92 per cent); and 5 (5.4 per cent) According to the underlying assumption of the crafted ACQ index, the ACs comply with the UAE code basic requirements which are mandatorily required and, at the same time, voluntarily exceed these requirements. ACs voluntarily practice 2.7 measures out of 5 measures of ACQ described earlier in section 6.2. Table 4 summarizes the frequency level for each ACQ measure among listed UAE non-financial firms.

Table 4.Frequency level for each ACQ item

ACQ items	No. of firms practicing	% of firms practicing
The existence of NED	26	0.70
51% of or more of AC members are independent	33	0.89
The existence of an accounting expertise	19	0.51
Held more than four meetings per the year	13	0.35
Comprised of more than three members	10	0.27

Table 4 reports a similar pattern of ACQ measures found in the Australian firms by end of 2001 (Baxter, 2010) The cause behind this similarity is that the year 2001 was a time period in which there was no mandatory audit committee regulation in Australia other than the requirement to disclose the existence or otherwise of an audit committee. Accordingly, Baxter (2010) study examined the voluntary adoption of ACQ measures by Australian firms. Although the UAE applies a stringent approach regulating every aspect of ACQ measures, the crafted ACQ index underlying assumption is to score the ACQ measure if it is voluntarily practiced beyond the basic mandatory requirements.

Table 4. Pearson Correlations among all variables

	IRSI	% INED	BOD Meet	AUD	ACQ Score	Log of TA	# Products	Risk DA	Profitability	BOD Size
IRSI	1									
% INED	0.004	1								
BOD Meetings	0.007	0.022	1							
AUD	-0.048	0.016	0.111	1						
ACQ Score	0.284	0.068	0.021	-0.069	1					
Size (Log of Assets)	0.499**	0.166	0.099	0.347*	0.177	1				
Complexity (# Products)	0.387*	-0.218	0.173	0.062	0.078	0.145	1			
Risk (Debt to Assets)	0.485**	0.155	0.066	0.084	-0.22	0.441**	0.246	1		
Profitability	-0.109	0.205	0.019	0.024	0.016	-0.25	0.217	-0.087	1	
BOD Size (Robustness)	0.366*	-0.074	0.144	0.329*	0.142	0.320	0.159	0.093	-0.079	1

* Correlation is significant at the 0.05 level (2-tailed)
** Correlation is significant at the 0.01 level (2 tailed)

7.2 Assessing the validity of the model

Table 3 shows that the IRSI index and explanatory independent variables have considerable dispersion in the scores, as represented by the minimum, maximum, and the standard deviation. Yet some variables were not reported by firms and therefore the number of observations of these variables is less than the study sample of 37 firms. Since the model incorporates different explanatory independent variables, it is of importance to check the existence of multicollinearity (Alsaeed, 2006; Barako et al. 2006; Oliveira et al., 2006, Hassan 2009).

Two different approaches are used to test the existence of the multicollinearity problem; first, the correlation matrix; second, the variance inflation factor (VIF). (Mangena & Tauringana, 2007; Hassan, 2009) The correlation matrix provides an idea of the relationship between explanatory variables. Although, there is no agreement among researchers regarding the cut-off correlation percentage, scholars suggest that correlation greater than 70% may create the multicollinearity problem and therefore considered harmful. (Alsaeed, 2006; Mangena & Tauringana, 2007) Table 5 presents Pearson correlation coefficients among the independent variables.

Table 5 shows that the multicollinearity problem does not exist among the model independent variables and therefore regression analysis can be applied with confidence. Nevertheless, Field (2000) suggests that even when the correlations between the independent variables are not very high, some degree of multicollinearity can still exist. Therefore, the paper uses Variance Inflation Factor (VIF) as another effective means to test multicollinearity among variables. The paper computes the VIF for each independent variable as shown in table 6.

Although there is no hard rule about what VIF value at which to multi-collinearity causes a problem, scholars suggest the VIF of 10 is a good value at which to worry (Naser et al., 2006; Alsaeed, 2006) The VIFs should not exceed the critical value of 10 (Field, 2000) The largest VIF factor observed for the full models was 2.142 (SIZE) and the VIFs of all other independent variables are below 2.00. In line with prior studies, VIF results support the lack of presence of multi-collinearity in the regression models (e.g. Ho & Wong, 2001; Naser et al. 2006; Mangena & Tauringana, 2007) Therefore, the regression analysis results can be interpreted with a greater degree of confidence.

Furthermore, Table 6 shows Durbin-Watson statistic for the regression model. This statistic is used to test the non-existence of autocorrelation (i.e. the assumption of independent errors) Field (2000) suggests that Durbin-Watson value which is less than 1 or greater than 3 should pose a problem. He adds that the closer to 2 the value is the better the model. Therefore, Durbin-Watson values, shown in Table 6, are acceptable and consequently the problem of autocorrelation is not significant.

7.3 Multiple regression results

Table 6 present multiple regression model results. Table 6 shows that %INED, BOD meetings, AUD, ACQ, Firm Size, Number of Products, Risk and Profitability explain 50.3% of the variation IRSI (F = 4.675, Sig. = 0.002) These results imply that independent variables explain 50 percent of the variation in IRSI at significant level of 0.05. Below is a discussion and comments on the multiple regression results.

Table 6. Model Coefficients +

	Predicted sign	β	Std. Error	Beta	t	Sig.	VIF
(Constant)		-10.778	6.090		-1.770	0.091	
% INED	+	-1.812	2.795	-0.103	-0.648	0.524	1.471
BOD Meetings	+	-1.212	.477	-0.419	-2.542	0.019**	1.590
AUD	+	-1.011	1.036	-0.141	-0.976	0.340	1.228
ACQ	+	1.083	.452	0.353	2.397	0.026**	1.269
Firm Size	+	0.994	.351	0.543	2.834	0.010**	2.142
Complexity	+	0.188	.102	0.283	1.839	0.080*	1.379
Risk	+	5.144	2.327	0.351	2.211	0.038**	1.469
Profitability	+/-	-2.441	6.068	-0.063	-0.402	0.692	1.420

Predicted sign	β	Std. Error	Beta	t	Sig.	VIF
F-statistics				4.675		
Sig.				0.002**		
Durbin-Watson				1.785		
R²				0.640		
Adjusted R²				0.503		
N				37		

1. **Level of significant is 0.05.
2. * Level of significant is 0.10.
3. + Dependent variable is IRSI.

Table 6 shows that frequency of board of directors meetings (BOD Meetings): ACQ, firm size (Size) and firm risk (Risk) are statistically significant with IRSI at a level of 0.05. It also shows that firm complexity (Complexity) is statistically significant with IRSI at a level of 0.10. As predicted, the regression model significant variables are positively correlated IRSI except for frequency of board of directors meetings (BOD Meetings) accordingly, the empirical findings support H4. The empirical findings document a significant BOD meetings-IRDI relationship yet in an opposite direction to the study prediction. Table 6 also shows that board independence (%INED): auditor type (AUD): and firm profitability (ROA) are not statistically significant with IRSI at a level of 0.05.

The (%INED) result contradicts with prior studies that document a significant positive relationship between the proportion of independent non-executive directors and firms' disclosure quality (Xiao et al., 2004; Cheng & Courtenay, 2006) Yet this result is consistent with other studies that find no relationship between level of disclosures and independent non-executive directors (Cullen & Christopher, 2002; Ho & Wong, 2001; Haniffa & Cooke, 2002; 2005; Hashim et al., 2014) Therefore one can suggest that INEDs may not be able to exert sufficient influence to enforce or diffuse a better IRSI. They either lack the superior information possessed by inside directors or they are under time constraints as a result of multi-directorship as independent outside director appointments. Furthermore, outside directors are usually part timers and it is more difficult for them to understand the complexities of the firm where they site as INED. The non-significant impact of independent non-executive directors on the IRSI can also be attributable to their less concern with voluntary disclosure such as IRSI compared to their concern with mandatory disclosure (Hashim et al., 2014)

The corporate profitability (ROA) is not statistically significant. This result is consistent Xiao et al. (2004) and Boubaker et al. (2012) findings. Xiao et al. (2004, 2014) conclude that the ROA-Online reporting non-significant association is a reflection to the lack of emphasis on accounting-based performance or because of the existence of earning management behavior in China. One can suggest the same in the UAE since firms' profitability has no influence on the IRSI. Another possible explanation is that the IRSI is driven by the competitiveness among firms operating in the same industry, therefore profitable firms are reluctant to publish information, on their websites, describing future plans, strategies and market position. This reluctance is simply to avoid revealing information that may encourage other rival firms to enter into the market (García-Sanchez et al., 2011)

The (AUD) result contradicts with prior studies' findings that confirm a relationship between high profile auditing firms and high levels of disclosures (Xaio et al., 2004; Chalmers & Godfrey, 2004; Kelton & Yang, 2008; Boubaker et al., 2012) One possible explanation here is that big audit firms do not offer a guarantee against the information published on corporations' websites. Another explanation is that auditors only take notice of legal and professional matters/responsibilities specified in their code of conducts and laws. Since IRSI is not an issue subject to external auditors checking and verification, external auditors do not influence that type of disclosure. A further explanation for this result can be the way in which the internet reporting was defined. Both Xiao et al. (2004) and Kelton and Yang (2008) describe internet reporting in terms of the content and presentation while this study describes internet reporting in terms of an index that capture "strategy" disclosure over the internet.

Unexpectedly, the frequency of board of directors meetings (BOD Meetings) is negatively correlated with IRSI at level of 0.05. This is inconsistent with what the study had envisioned earlier at the hypothesis formulation and with Hashim et al., (2014) study which shows no association between board meetings and IRSI for a sample of Malaysian firms. Nonetheless, result is consistent with García-Sanchez et al. (2011) study that shows a BOD Meetings-IRSI negative association for a sample of Spanish firms. One of the possible explanations for this unexpected result can be that BOD suggests limited disclosure that can cause competitive disadvantages or negative response in stock prices. In this sense, an active BOD which meets frequently opposes disclosing strategic information that may impair the competitive position of the firm if known by the firm rivals. In contrast to Gallego-Alvarez et al., (2011): the empirical findings show that the firm complexity (Complexity) is positively associated with the IRSI at level of 0.05.

As predicted, the Audit Committee Quality (ACQ) is a significant variable influencing IRSI at level of 0.05%. On the one hand, the audit committee may play a monitoring role encouraging the corporate management to produce financial information on the internet. On the other hand, the AC may become change agents disseminating knowledge about IRSI. Due to their multi-directors membership in different corporations, they may diffuse ideas about IRSI across firms. The significant relationship between ACQ and IRSI may also be interpreted as the existence of AC in UAE is not for window dressing, i.e. ritualistic, but is effective in enhancing the firm image in terms of transparency. One can argue that the AC's role is not only about the financial reporting process, but it extends to the reporting of non-financial information including IRSI.

In accordance with the predict direction, firm size (Size) is found significantly correlated to IRSI at level of 0.05. Size-IRSI relationship result agrees with prior literature that suggests a size-disclosure significant relationship (e.g. Oyelere et al., 2003; Marston & Polei, 2004; Ashbaugh et al., 1999; Craven & Marston, 1999; Ettredge et al., 2002; Xiao et al., 2004; Gallego-Alvarez et al., 2008; Boubaker et al., 2012) There are several reasons to explain these results. First, managers of larger firms utilize IRSI to attract demotic investors and foreign investments. They are also willing to explain the size of their firms and consequently avoid political sensitivity either nationally or internationally.

Second, large firms benefit from economies of scale and therefore for them it is less costly to supplement traditional financial information reported in annual reports with IRSI. In accordance with the predict direction, firm risk is found significantly correlated to IRSI at level of 0.05. This result is consistent with Garcıa-Sanchez et al., (2011): yet it disagrees with Gul and Leung (2004): Oyelere (2003) and Alvarez et al. (2008)

7.4 Robustness test

The regression model, reported in table 6, excludes the board size (BOD Size) as one of the governance variables. Table 6 governance variables were chosen because they are aligned with the study underlying assumption that outside directors and external auditor can act as change agents promoting for new ideas such as IRSI while enhancing the monitoring capability of the board. Since executive directors may act as non-executive ones in other firms, they may bring new ideas from the firms in which they serve as non-executive directors. In order to address that issue and to corroborate the regression results, the study ran a multiple regression test while adding the board size.

The regression results, presented in Table 7, show similar results to the original model results, presented in table 6, except that the firm complexity (Complexity) becomes insignificant and the audit committee quality (ACQ) becomes significant at level of 0.10. Consistent with prior studies (Ezat & El-Masry, 2008 (Egypt); Garcıa-Sanchez et al., 2011 (Spain); Hashim et al., 2014 (Malaysia)): table 7 shows that the board size (BOD Size) has a significant positive association with IRSI at a level of 0.10. The robustness test, to large extent, substantiates the original regression model results.

Table 7. Model Coefficients +

	β	Std. Error	Beta	t	Sig.	VIF
(Constant)	-9.429	5.807		-1.624	.120	
% INED	-1.251	2.661	-0.071	-0.470	0.643	1.490
BOD Meetings	-1.004	0.465	-.348	-2.161	.043**	1.687
AUD	-1.342	0.996	-.188	-1.347	0.193	1.268
ACQ	0.832	0.448	.271	1.855	.078*	1.396
Firm Size	0.783	0.351	.427	2.231	.037*	2.393
Complexity	0.151	0.099	.227	1.529	0.142	1.438
Risk	5.348	2.204	.365	2.427	0.025	1.473
Profitability	-2.496	5.741	-.064	-.435	0.668	1.420
BOD Size	0.358	0.193	.278	1.861	.077*	1.460
F-statistics				5.028		
Sig.				0.001**		
Durbin-Watson				1.811		
R^2				0.694		
Adjusted R^2				0.556		
N				37		

**Level of significant is 0.05.
* Level of significant is 0.10.
+ Dependent variable is IRSI.

8. Conclusion

The study examines internal governance mechanisms impact on corporate transparency expressed in terms of the IRSI. It examines the influence of audit committee, board independence and firm-specific characteristics on the IRSI a special type of voluntary disclosure that a firm may use to disseminate information about its strategies, policies, plans, market position, products and customers. The study findings highlight that UAE non-financial firms publish strategic information over the internet. The mean average of the UAE non-financial firms disclosure of strategy related information is 47% which is higher than Spanish firms (mean = 25%) (Garcıa-Sanchez et al., 2011) and close to the Malaysian firms (mean = 50.1%) (Hashim et al., 2014) The UAE non-financial firms seem to use IRSI to obtain a competitive position while avoiding competitive disadvantages.

In order to obtain a competitive position, the most frequently items being disclosed are "quality certification", "risk control and management – governance", "the firm customer groups" "objectives, mission and company's philosophy", "strategic positon of the company" and "health, safety and environment strategy". The disclosure of these items encourages domestic and international investors to invest on the UAE because it helps investors' financial analysts to make informed decisions. It also assists different stakeholders because they are able to identify the uniqueness or the strength elements of the firm. Hence, the UAE non-financial firms utilize IRSI as an opportunity to promote themselves and disseminate information to stakeholders beyond those information published in regulated annual reports.

In order to avoid competitive disadvantages, the UAE non-financial firms disclose other strategy related information at lower level. Some of these items are moderately disclosed such as "company strategic planning", "description of competitive context", "strategy towards the workforce" "company annual planning" and "information on different risks" while other items are less frequently disclosed such as "information on production processes", "strategic alliance" and "information in cost effectiveness and innovation strategies". The UAE firms seem to consider these items as having high privacy level in order to compete in the challenging business environment and minimize the risk of competitive disadvantages.

The study findings highlight whether the UAE listed non-financial firms transformation towards the establishment of "best practice" AC is ritualistic or otherwise. In this regard, Baydoun et al. (2013: 15) highlight that although the UAE code of governance includes a provision relating to audit committee, a fundamental concern is the gap between the law and the actual practice. Baydoun et al. (2013: 15) reinforce their idea by quoting the Dubai Chamber of Commerce and Industry survey results which state that "awareness of corporate responsibility of governance at management levels is high [...] however, it becomes increasingly apparent that companies are saying one thing and doing another" (DCCI, 2006, p. 10 cited in Baydoun, 2013: 15) The paper results show that most of UAE listed non-financial firms have Audit Committees that apply "best practices" in alignment with the UAE code of governance requirements.

Nevertheless, interpreting the study results in the light of Baydoun et al. (2013) findings raises questions about the management position regarding their firms' alignment with the UAE code of governance. In this regard, Trabelsi et al. (2004) argue that the management position can be either opportunistic or ritualistic. They add that opportunistic position involves an active role of managers in their attempt to seek specific advantages and consequently reap benefits of applying new practices. To recall, the establishment of AC seems to legitimate the UAE to international best practices introduced by international governance institutions such as OECD. The active role of managers can also be expressed in terms of their role as change agents diffusing knowledge about innovative disclosure practices such as IRSI.

In contrast, ritualistic position describes manages uncritical adherence to prescribed regulations. Accordingly, the role of managers is passive since they just comply with rules without necessary believe in the importance of these rules. In other words, managers comply with the code of governance requirements, particularly the formation of ACs, without necessarily believe in the role of these ACs. To claim that the UAE listed non-financial firms' ritualistically form ACs requires a more in-depth investigation that relies on case-based studies of individual firms. This investigation goes beyond the scope of the current paper and therefore represents an area of future research.

The study is expected to add value to researchers, practitioners and policymakers in UAE. For researchers, the study extends on previous internet reporting studies by examining the influence of audit committee quality on the IRSI which is becoming a critical matter in the UAE. For practitioners, the study is concerned with one of the most critical aspects of corporate governance, i.e. AC, and therefore it highlights aspects of internal governance that is in the interest of both investing community and accountancy profession. One of these aspects is multi-directorship issue in which a board member is becoming increasingly busy and therefore spends insufficient time on board work to be properly informed on firm matters and prepare for board discussions. Likewise, Baydoun *et al.* (2013) highlight the difficulty of finding genuinely independent directors in small countries, such as the UAE, which in turn prevents from making a significant contribution to corporate governance. Future research is recommended to explore these issues further.

The OECD Principles of Corporate Governance underscores the importance of internet to disseminate information (Oyelere & Kuruppu, 2012) Therefore, regulatory agencies and policymakers in the UAE need to develop a regulatory framework that encourages internet reporting while regulate the form and content of this reporting. The UAE regulatory agencies may also need to put heavier emphasis on sensitive information, such as "strategy" disclosure, and subject this information to close monitoring and checking. These issues go beyond the scope of the current study and therefore represent area of future research.

The study findings must be interpreted in the light of a number of limitations. First, the study measures the ACQ based on information available in each firm's corporate governance report published by end of 2010. The development of the ACQ index is based on aspects of the "best practice AC" framework suggested by Rainsbury *et al.* (2008; 2009) Yet other aspects, such as AC authority and AC resources, have not been addressed in this study (DeZoort*et al.*, 2002) This issue needs future research that addresses these missing aspects to develop a comprehensive ACQ index. Second, sample size is small. Yet, what mitigates this limitation is that the study sample represents 88% of UAE listed non-financial firms that disclose strategy related information on the internet. Third, the timeframe of the study is one year. Therefore, further studies may perform a longitudinal analysis to examine the impact of the governance mechanisms on the IRSI. Finally, the paper measures the IRSI via an un-weighted disclosure checklist that examined the website of UAE non-financial listed firms at a single point in time (December 2010) Future research may take two points of time to improve the study results.

References

Abbott, L.J., G. Peters, & Raghunandan, K. (2003) "The association between audit committee characteristics andaudit fees", *Auditing: A Journal of Practice and Theory,* vol. 22(2): 17-32

Abdelsalam, O., Bryant, S. & Street, D. (2007) "An examination of the comprehensiveness of corporate internet reporting provided by London-listed companies", *Journal of International Accounting Research,* vol. 6(2): 1-33

Adams, M. & Hossain, M. (1998) "Managerial discretion and voluntary disclosure: empirical evidence from New Zealand life insurance companies", *Journal of Accounting and Public Policy,* vol. 17(3): 245–281

Ajinkya, B., Bhojraj, S. &Sengupta, P. (2005) "The association between outside directors, institutional investors and the properties of management earnings forecasts", *Journal of Accounting Research,* vol. 43(3): 343–375

Aljifri, K. & Khasharmeh, H. (2006) "An investigation into the suitability of international accounting standards to the United Arab Emirates environment", *International Business Review,* vol. 15(1): 505-526)

Alssaeed, K. (2006) "The association between firm-specific characteristics and disclosure: the vase of Saudi Arabia", *Managerial Auditing Journal,* vol. 21(5):476-496

American Institute of Certified Public Accountants (AICPA) (1994) A Customer Focus Meeting the Information Needs of Investors and Creditors, *Special Committee on Financial Reporting,* AICPA, New York, NY.

Ashbaugh H., Johnstone K.M. &Warfield T.D. (1999) "Corporate reporting on the Internet", *Accounting Horizons,* vol. 13(2): 241–258

Bao, B. & Bao, B. (1989) "LIFO adoption: a technological diffusion analysis", *Accounting, Organization and Society,* vol. 14(4): 303-319

Barako, D., Hancock, P. & Izan, H. (2006) "Factors influencing voluntary corporate disclosure by Kenyan companies", *Corporate Governance: An International Review,* vol. 14(2): 107-125

Barua, A., Rama, D. V. & Sharma, V. (2010) "Audit committee characteristics and investment in internal auditing", *Journal of Accounting and Public Policy,* vol. 29(3): 503-513

Baxter, P. (2010) "Factors associated with the quality of audit committees", *Pacific Accounting Review,* vol. 22 (1): 57 – 74

Baydoun, N., Maguire, W., Ryan, N. & Willett, R. (2013) "Corporate governance in five Arabian Countries", *Managerial Auditing Journal,* vol. 28(1): 7-22

Beasley, M.S. (1996) "An empirical analysis of the relation between the board of director composition and financial statement fraud", *The Accounting Review*, vol. 71: 443-465

Bédard, J., Chtourou, S. M. & Courteau, L. (2004) "The effect of audit committee expertise, independence, and activity of aggressive earnings management", *Auditing: A Journal of Practice & Theory*, vol. 23(2): 13–35

BjØrnenak, T. (1997) "Diffusion and accounting: the case of Activity Based Costing in Norway", *Management accounting Research*, vol. 8: 3-17

Boubaker, S. Lakhal, F. & Nekhili, M. (2011) "The determinants of web-based corporate reporting in France", *Managerial Auditing Journal*, vol. 27(2): 126 – 155

Bushman, R., Chen, Q., Engel, E. & Smith, A. (2004) "Financial accounting information, organizational complexity and corporate governance systems", *Journal of Accounting and Economics*, vol. 37(2): 167-201

Capriotti, P. & Moreno, A. (2007) "Communicating corporate responsibility through corporate web sites in Spain", *Corporate Communication: An International Journal*, vol. 12(3): 221-237

Carcello, J. V. & Neal, T. L. (2003) "Audit committee characteristics and auditor dismissals following 'New' going-concern reports, *The Accounting Review*, vol. 78(1): 95–117

Carpenter, V. L. & Feroz, E. H. (2001) "Institutional theory and accounting rule choice: an analysis of four US state governments' decisions to adopt GAAP", *Accounting, Organizations and Society*, vol. 26 (5): 565-596

Cerbioni, F. & Parbonetti, A. (2007) "Exploring the effects of corporate governance on intellectual capital disclosure: an analysis of European Biotechnology Companies", *European Accounting Review*, vol. 16(4): 791-826

Chalmers K. & Godfrey, J. (2004) "Reputation costs: the imputes for voluntary derivative financial instruments reporting", *Accounting, Organization and Society*, vol. 29 (2): 95-125

Chen, C. J. P. & Jaggi, B. (2000) "Association between independent non-executive directors, family control and financial disclosure in Hong Kong", *Journal of Accounting and Public Policy*, vol. 19(2): 285-310

Cheng, E. C. M. & Courtenay, S. M. (2006) "Board composition, regulatory regime and voluntary disclosure", *The International Journal of Accounting*, vol. 41(2): 262–289

Clarke, P. J., Hill N. T. & Stevens, K. (1999) "Activity Based Costing in Ireland: Barriers to, and opportunities for, change", *Critical Perspectives on Accounting*, vol. 10(4): 443-468

Cormier, D., Magnan, M. &Velthoven, B. (2005) "Environmental disclosure quality in large German companies: Economic incentives, public pressures or institutional conditions", *European Accounting Review*, vol. 14(1): 3-39

Craven B.M. & Marston C.L. (1999) "Financial reporting on the internet by leading UK companies", *European Accounting Review*, vol. 8(2): 321–333

Cullen, L. & Christopher, T. (2002) "Governance disclosure and firm characteristics of listed Australian mining companies", *International Journal of Business Studies*, vol. 10(1): 37–58

DeAngelo, L. (1981) "Auditor size and audit quality", *Journal of Accounting and Economics*, vol. 3(1): 189-199

Debreceny R., Gray G.L. & Rahman A. (2002) "The determinants of Internet financial reporting", *Journal of Accounting and Public Policy*, vol. 21(3): 371–394

DeFond, M.L. & Francis, J.R. (2005) "Audit research after Sarbanes-Oxley", *Auditing: A Journal of Practice and Theory* (Supplement): 5–30

Depoers, F. (2000) "A cost-benefit study of voluntary disclosure: some empirical evidence from French listed companies", *The European Accounting Review*, vol. 9 (2): 245-263

DeZoort, F.T., Hermanson, D.R., Archambeault, D.S. & Reed, S.A. (2002) "Audit committee effectiveness: a synthesis of the empirical audit committee literature", *Journal of Accounting Literature*, vol. 21: 38-75

DFSA (2007) The DFSA in action, DFSA news publication, vol.1, December

DiMaggio, P. J. & Powell, W. W. (1983) "The iron cage revisited: institutional isomorphism and collective rationality in organizational field", *American Sociological Review*, vol. 48(1):147-160

Eng, L.L. & Mak, Y.T. (2003) "Corporate governance and voluntary disclosure", *Journal of Accounting and Public Policy*, vol. 22(3): 325-345

ES&CMA amendments (2005) Decision No (75) Year 2004 Decision No (155) Year 2005

Ettredge, M., Richardson, V.J. & Scolz, S. (2002) "Dissemination of information for investors at corporate web sites", *Journal of Accounting and Public Policy*, vol. 21(3): 57-69

Evans, T. G. (2003) *Accounting theory: contemporary accounting issues*, Thomson South Western, USA.

Ezat, A. & El-Masry, A. (2008) "The impact of corporate governance on the timeliness of corporate internet reporting by Egyptian listed companies" *Managerial Finance*, vol. 34(12): 848 – 867

Federal Act No 4 of 2000 Concerning the Emirates Securities & Commodities Authority and Market

Field, A. (2000) *Discovering Statistics: Using SPSS for Windows*, 1st ed., Sage, London.

Gallego -Alvarez, I., Garcıa-Sanchez, I.M. & Rodrıguez-Domınguez, L. (2008) "Voluntary and compulsory information disclosed online: effect of industry concentration and other explanatory factors", *Online Information Review*, vol. 32(5): 596-622

Gallego-Alvarez, I., Rodriguez-Dominguez, L. & Garcia-Sanchez, I. M. (2011) "Information disclosed online by Spanish universities: content and explanatory factors", *Online Information Review*, vol. 35 (3): 360-385

Garcia-Sanchez, I., Rodriguez-Dominguez, L. & Gallego-Alvarez, I. (2011) "Corporate governance and strategic information on the internet: A study of Spanish listed companies", *Accounting, Auditing and Accountability Journal*, vol. 24(4): 471-507

Gul, F.A. & Leung, S. (2004) "Board leadership, outside directors' expertise and voluntary corporate disclosures", *Journal of Accounting and Public Policy*, vol. 23(3): 351-379

Haniffa, R.M. & Cooke, T.E. (2002) "Culture, corporate governance and disclosure in Malaysian corporations', *Abacus*, vol. 38(3): 317–349

Haniffa, R.M. & Cooke, T.E. (2005) "The impact of culture and governance on corporate social reporting", *Journal of Accounting and Public Policy*, vol. 24(2): 391–430

Hashim, M. F., Nawawi, A. & Salin, A. (2014) "Determinants of strategic information disclosure – Malaysian evidence", *International Journal of Business and Society*, vol. 15 (3): 547- 572

Hassan, M.K. (2008) "The development of accounting regulations in Egypt: legitimating the international accounting standards", *Managerial Auditing Journal*, vol. 23(5): 467-484

Hassan, M. K. (2009) "UAE corporation-specific characteristics and level of risk disclosure", *Managerial Auditing Journal*, vol. 24(7): 668-687

Hassan, M.K. (2012) "A disclosure index to measure the extent of corporate governance reporting by UAE listed corporations", *Journal of Financial Reporting and Accounting*, vol. 10(1): 4-33.

Hassan, M., and El-Kelish, W. (2012) "The United Arab Emirates financial institutions corporate governance: Evolution, regulations, and practices in action", in Mizuno, M., Gerner-Beuerle, C., and Kostyuk, A. (Ed.): *Evolution of Corporate Governance in Banks*, Virtus Interpress, Ukraine

Hassan, M. K. (2014) "Risk narrative disclosure strategies to enhance organizational legitimacy: evidence from UAE financial institutions", *International Journal of Disclosure and Governance*, vol. 11(1): 1-17

Hasseldine, J., Salama, A.I. & Toms, J.S. (2005) "Quantity versus quality: the impact of environmental disclosures on the reputations of UK PlCs", *The British Accounting Review*, vol. 37(2): 231–248

Healy, P. & Palepu, K. (2001) "Information asymmetry, corporate disclosure, and the capital markets: a review of the empirical disclosure literature", *Journal of Accounting and Economics*, vol. 31(1-3): 405-440

Ho, S.S.M. & Wong, K.S. (2001) "A study of the relationship between corporate governance structures and the extent of voluntary disclosure", *International Journal of Accounting, Auditing and Taxation*, vol. 10(1): 139-156

Hussainey, K. & Al-Nodel, A. (2008) "Corporate governance online reporting by Saudi listed companies", *Research in Accounting in Emerging Economies*, vol. 8: 39–64

Hussein, M. E. (1981) "The innovation process in the accounting standard setting", *Accounting, Organization and Society*, vol. 6(1): 27-37

Ika, S.R. & Ghazali, N. M. (2012) "Audit committee effectiveness and timeliness of reporting: Indonesian evidence", *Managerial Auditing Journal*, vol. 27(4): 403–424

Inchausti, B.G. (1997) "The influence of company characteristics and accounting regulation on information disclosed by Spanish firms", *The European Accounting Review*, vol. 6(1): 45–68

Irvine, H. (2008) "The global institutionalization of financial reporting: the case of the UAE", *Accounting Forum*, vol. 32(2): 125-142

Jamil, N. N. & Nelson, S.P. (2011) "An investigation on the audit committees' effectiveness: the case for GLCs in Malaysia", *Gadjah Mada International Journal of Business*, vol. 13(3): 287 – 305

Jones, M.J. & Xiao, J.Z. (2003) "Internet reporting: current trends and trends by 2010", *Accounting Forum*, vol. 27(2): 132-165

Karamanou, I. & Vafeas, N. (2005) "The association between corporate boards, audit committees, and management earnings forecasts: an empirical analysis", *Journal of Accounting Research*, vol. 43(3): 453-486

Kelton, A.S. & Yang, Y.W. (2008) "The impact of corporate governance on internet financial reporting", *Journal of Accounting and Public Policy*, vol. 27(1): 62-87

Klein, A. (2002) "Audit committee, board of director characteristics, and earnings management", *Journal of Accounting and Economics*, vol. 33(3): 375–400

Li, J., Mangena, M. & Pike, R. (2012) "The effect of audit committee characteristics on intellectual capital disclosure", *The British Accounting Review*, vol. 44(1): 98-110

Lim, S., Matolcsy, Z. &Chow, D. (2007) "The association between board composition and different types of voluntary disclosure", *European Accounting Review*, vol. 16(4): 555-583

Lim, S., Matolcsy, Z., & Chow, D. (2007) "The association between board composition and different types of voluntary disclosure", *European Accounting Review*, vol. 16 (3): 555-583

Lipton, M. &Lorsch, J.W. (1992) "A modest proposal for improved corporate governance", *Business Lawyer*, vol. 59(1): 59–77

Lodhia, S.K., Allam, A. & Lymer, A. (2004) "Corporate reporting on the internet in Australia: an exploratory study", *Australian Accounting Review*, vol. 14(3): 64-71

Lopes, P. T. & Rodrigues, L. L. (2007) "Accounting for financial instruments: an analysis of the determinants of disclosure in the Portuguese stock exchange", *The International Journal of Accounting*, vol. 42(1): 25-56

Mangena, M. & Pike, R. (2005) "The effect of audit committee shareholding, financial expertise and size on interim financial disclosures", *Accounting and Business Research*, vol. 35(4): 327-349

Marston C. & Polei, A. (2004) "Corporate reporting on the Internet by German companies", *International Journal of Accounting Information Systems*, vol. 5(2): 285-311

Naiker, V.& Sharma, D.S. (2009) "Former audit partners on the audit committee and internal control deficiencies", *The Accounting Review*, vol. 84 (2): 559–587

Naser, K., Al-Hussaini, A., Al-Kwari, D. & Nuseibeh, R. (2006) "Determinants of corporate social disclosure in developing countries: the case of Qatar", *Advances in International Accounting*, vol. 19(1): 1-23

Obay, L.A. (2009) "Corporate governance and business ethics: A Dubai-based survey", *Journal of Legal, Ethical and Regulatory Issues*, vol. 12 (2): 29-47

Oyelere P., Laswad F. & Fisher R. (2003) "Determinants of internet financial reporting by New Zealand companies", *Journal of International Financial Management and Accounting*, vol. 14(1): 26-63

Oyelere, P. & Kuruppu, N. (2012) "Voluntary internet financial reporting practices of listed companies in the United Arab Emirates", *Journal of Applied Accounting Research*, vol. 13(3): 298-315

Padia, N. & Yasseen, (2011) "An examination of strategy disclosure in the annual reports of South African listed companies", *South African Journal of Business Management*, vol. 42(33): 27-35

Petersen, C. & Plenborg, T. (2006) "Voluntary disclosure and information asymmetry in Denmark", *Journal of International Accounting, Auditing and Taxation*, vol. 15(1): 127-149

Rainsbury, E. A., Bradbury M. E. &Cahan, S. F. (2008) "Firm characteristics and audit committees complying with 'best practice' membership guidelines", *Accounting and Business Research*, vol. 38(5): 393-408

Rainsbury, E. A., Bradbury, M. & Cahan, S. F. (2009) "The impact of audit committee quality on financial reporting quality and audit fees", *Journal of Contemporary Accounting and Economics*, vol. 5(1): 20-33

Santema, S. & Van de Rijt, J. (2001) "Strategy disclosure in Dutch Annual Report", *European Management Journal*, vol. 19: 101-108

Santema, S., Hoekert, M., Van de Rijt, J. & Van Oijen, A. (2005) "Strategy disclosure in annual reports across Europe: a study on differences between five countries", *European Business Review*, vol. 17: 352-366

Shehata, N., (2015) "Development of corporate governance codes in GCC: an overview", *Corporate Governance*, vol. 15 (3): 315-338

Touron, P. (2005) "The adoption of US GAAP by French firms before the creation of the International Accounting Standards Committee: an institutional explanation", *Critical Perspectives on Accounting*, vol. 16(6): 851-873

Trabelsi, S., Labelle, R. & Laurin, C. (2004) "The management of financial disclosure on corporate websites: a conceptual model", *Canadian Accounting Perspectives*, vol. 3(2): 235-259

UAE code of governance: Securities and Commodities Authority Chairperson (2007): Decision No. (R/23) on Corporate Governance Code for Joint-Stock Companies and Institutional Discipline Criteria: amended by decision 518 of 2009.

UAE ICT Fund report, 2011. Available at: http://www.ictfund.ae/ICT-Fund.html

Watts L. R. & Zimmerman J. L. (1978) "Towards a positive theory of the determination of accounting standards", *The Accounting Review*, vol. 43(1): 112-134

White, G.P. (1996) "A survey and taxonomy of strategy-related performance measures for manufacturing", *International Journal of Operations & Production Management*, vol. 16(3): pp. 42-61

World Forum (2011) 2011 Report, Available at: http:// www3. weforum.org / docs / WEF _GITR _Report 2011.pdf.

Xiao J.Z., Yang H. & Chow C.W. (2004) "The determinants and characteristics of voluntary Internet-based disclosures by listed Chinese companies", *Journal of Accounting and Public Policy*, vol. 23(1): 191-225

Xiao, J.Z., Jones, M.J. & Lymer, A. (2002) "Immediate trends in internet reporting", *European Accounting Review*, vol. 11(2): 245-275

Appendix 1 (sources of IRSI index items)

Strategic Disclosure Items	Directly address the issue of IRSI						Indirectly address the issue of IRSI				
	Garcia-Sanchez et al. (2011)	Santema et al. (2005)	Padia and Yasseen (2011)	Santema and Rijt (2001)	Hashim et al. (2014)	Lim et al. (2007)	Gallego Álvarez (2008)	Gallego Álvarez (2011)	Depoers (2000)	White, (1996)	Petersen, and Plenborg (2006)
1. Objectives, mission and company's philosophy	X	X	X	X	X	X	X	X			X
2. Strategic alliances	X				X		X	X			
3. Strategic position of company in its sector (leader, 2nd etc.)	X				X	X	X	X			
4. Company strategic planning (projects of expansion into other markets, products, regions)	X		X	X	X	X	X	X			X
5. Company annual planning/ performance against targets/graphs	X		X	X	X		X	X			X
6. Description of the competition context	X		X		X		X		X	X	X
7. Risk Control and management - Governance		X	X			X	X	X			
8. Information on risks (financial, commercial, technical)/	X				X		X		X	X	X
9. Information on production processes	X				X		X				X
10. Strategic Business Unit – deleted		X	X	X					X		
11. Weakness and Threats – deleted		X							X	X	
12. Information on quality certification - added							X		X	X	X
13. Information on cost effective strategy -added							X	X			X
14. Information on innovative approaches - added							X	X			X
15. Health, Safety and Environment Strategy - added						X	X	X			X
16. Strategy towards workforces and their benefits –added											X
17. The firm's customer groups – added		X							X	X	X

i The paper uses SPSS software in order to perform the statistical analysis

[1] The paper uses SPSS software in order to perform the statistical analysis

6

The effects of IFRS adoption and Big 4 audit firms on audit and non-audit fees

Alhassan Musah[a,1], Fred Kwasi Anokye[b] and Erasmus Dodzi Gakpetor [a,1]

[a] *Dominion University College, Ghana*
[b] *University of Ghana, Legon*

Abstract: The study was conducted to examine the effect of IFRS adoption on audit and non-audit fee and also the relationship between the big4 audit firm and audit and non-audit fees. Using a sample of financial and non-financial firms in Ghana, the results show that IFRS adoption has a positive and significant relationship with audit and non-audit fees post IFRS adoption. The results further revealed that there is positive association between the year of IFRS adoption (transition period) and audit and non-audit fees. On the big4 audit firms, the results show that the big4 charge higher audit and non-audit fees than non-big4 as there was a positive and significant relationship between Big4 and audit and non-audit fees. The results support the argument that the adoption of IFRS increased the complexities of financial reporting and audit risk resulting in a higher audit and non-audit fees charged during the transition period and post IFRS adoption. The paper extends previous studies on the subject matter by including the year of IFRS adoption and non-audit fees within the context of a developing economy with weak financial regulatory regime.

Keywords: International Financial Reporting Standards, Audit fees, Non-audit fees, Big4, Ghana National Accounting Standards

[1] *Corresponding author*: School of Business, Dominion University College; PMB CT69, Accra. email address: a.musah@duc.edu.gh

1. Introduction

Prior to the adoption of IFRS for financial reporting by public entities in Ghana, companies were using the Ghana National Accounting Standards which was issued by the Institute of Chartered Accountants – Ghana (ICAG). Osei-Afoakwa and Asare (2013) the institute was expected to ensure that Ghana's Accounting Standards were in harmony with International Accounting Standards (IAS). Unfortunately, the ICAG did not have the legal mandate to enforce compliance with its directives as there was no legal basis for its operations (Osei-Afoakwa & Asare, 2013). Rahman (2004) noted that even though these standards were supposed to be in harmony with IAS, they were never reviewed and this compelled most practitioners who got confused by the inconsistencies in the standards and the lack of guidelines to abandon them. In 2004, a report by the World Bank and the International Monetary Fund (IMF) titled Report on the Observance of Standards and Codes (ROSC) listed a number of weaknesses in the financial reporting framework of Ghana and stated that the ICAG lacked the capacity to function properly as an effective professional accounting body. A number of recommendations were made which included legal reforms as well as regulatory and structural reforms including adopting or converging with IFRS/IAS.

Ghana adopted IFRS for listed firms, government businesses, banks, insurance companies, security brokerage firms, pension funds and public utility companies in 2007 based on the recommendations of the ROSC report in 2004. The date for full compliance was set a year later even though some companies had complied by the end of 2007. The ROSC report (2004) revealed that the GNAS had significant weaknesses in regulation, compliance and enforcement of standards. This placed doubts on the quality of accounting information prepared in accordance with the GNAS. Assenso-Okofo et al. (2011) reviewed the development of accounting and reporting in Ghana and reported that IFRS adoption improved earnings quality and analyst forecast. Most importantly, previous studies on disclosure requirements under the GNAS standards reported that disclosure was generally low (Aboagye-Otchere et al., 2012; Assenso-Okofo et al., 2011; Bokpin, 2013; Tsamenyi et al., 2007). The ROSC report argued that the country must improve on its financial reporting regulatory systems and framework and to that effect recommended that the country should fully adopt IFRS and the IFRS for SMEs when they are available without any attempt to modify them. Osei-Afoakwa and Asare (2013) argue that there was a significant gap between the GNAS and the IFRS/IAS which compelled the country to fully adopt IFRS instead of issuing its own standards in harmony with IFRS/IAS.

Researchers have argued that the adoption of IFRS for listed and non-listed firms globally is the most significant regulatory change in the history of the accounting profession in most countries (Klibi & Klibi, 2016; Camaran & Perrotti, 2014;

Nulla, 2013; Daske *et al.*, 2008). The results of this major regulatory change on audit and its related cost such as audit and non-audit fees has gained the attention of researchers, practitioners and other stakeholders (Loyeung *et al.*, 2016; Choi & Yoon, 2014; Kim *et al.* 2013; Mudawaki, 2012; Choi *et al.*, 2010). The perceived benefits of instituting a single set of global accounting standards are: potential improvements in the quality of reported information to stakeholders as well as convergence benefits such as greater ease of comparing financial statements of companies across countries; increased ability to secure cross-border listing, better management of global operations and decreased cost of capital (De George *et al.*, 2013; Naoum *et al.* 2011). However, these benefits must be contrasted with the potential cost of mandatory adoption of IFRS. Vieru and Schadewitz (2010) argue that auditors view the complexity of the IFRS transition and the client's potential insufficient preparations as issues that increase the uncertainties and risks in their audit assignments. For example, Hoogendoorn (2006) further notes that companies have underestimated the complexities, effects and costs of IFRS (see also Jermakowicz & Gornik-Tomaszewski, 2006).

Auditing activity is a critical aspect of switching to the application of new accounting standards, and audit fees represent a part of the related implementation costs (Loukil, 2016; Cameran & Perroti, 2014). The mandatory adoption of IFRS has two opposing effects on audit fees: on the one hand, greater effort is required from auditors, which is likely to be reflected by higher fees; on the other hand, if IFRS improve the quality of financial reporting, expected liability costs could decrease, and lower fees may be demanded (de Feuntes & Sierra-Grau, 2015; Choi *et al.* 2010; Cameran & Perroti, 2014).

The effect of the adoption of IFRS on fees paid to auditors is at the Centre of a debate among practitioners. Cameran and Perroti (2014) documents that only a few academic works are concerned with the change in audit fees after IFRS adoption. Griffin *et al.* (2009) find an audit fee increase associated with the adoption of IFRS and the concurrent introduction of new corporate governance rules in New Zealand. Loukil (2016) found evidence of increased audit fees in the year of adoption using French companies but found no significant increase in audit fees post-adoption period. Vieru and Schadewitz (2010) examined fee determination in the transition year to the IFRS for small and medium-sized Finnish companies. Lin and Yen (2016) study on Chinese firms found that auditors with IFRS experience charged significantly higher fees in the initial years of adoption. The results of the study generally revealed an increase in fees after IFRS adoption. The sample of all the analyses is limited to developed and emerging economies even though countries like Kenya adopted IAS/IFRS in 1998. The studies in Africa on IFRS has focused on adoption and implementation and compliance with IFRS (Osei-Afoakwa & Asare, 2013; Madawaki, 2012; Atsunyo *et al.* 2017) and the impact of IFRS adoption on reporting quality (Ames, 2013; Assenso-Okofo *et al.* 2011; Klibi & Klibi, 2016). Majority of these studies have also focused on only audit fees but it is argued that the cost of the transition should also be looked at within the context of consultancy fees companies will have to incur in order to change from the local GAAP to IFRS. Moreover, a lot of work is expected to be done by way of consultancy and audit in the year of adoption like reinstatement of previous years' financial statement in compliance with IFRS which could translate into higher audit and non-audit fees

It is obvious from the forgoing arguments that evidence of the impact of IFRS adoption on audit and non-audit fees has focused on western economies particularly the developed countries with little on Africa and for that matter Ghana. Ghana was the first country in West Africa to adopt IFRS after other Africa countries in Eastern and Southern Africa had adopted it. It is argued, that the institutional environment in which a firm operates to a large extent influence the impact of the mandatory IFRS adoption on audit and non-audit fees (Wang *et al.*, 2008; Taylor and Simon, 1999). Ghana is said to have a weak financial regulatory regime (World Bank & IMF, 2004). Thus, in order to better understand audit and non-audit fee formation during IFRS transition, more insight is needed to assess whether the complexity of the transition coincides with audit and non-audit fees in the African context. Furthermore, the magnitude of the impact of IFRS adoption on audit and non-audit fees will depend largely on the difference between the local GAAP and IFRS. This study therefore addresses the knowledge gap in the literature and explores the effect of the mandatory IFRS adoption in Ghana and its association with audit and non-audit fees.

The study makes significant contribution to literature and policy. The study goes beyond current research on IFRS and audit fees by introducing variables such as the year of IFRS year of adoption, and non-audit fees into the research. These variables have received little attention in literature even in developed economies. The study is relevant because it responds to the limited literature on IFRS and audit and non-audit fees and its implication in Sub-Saharan Africa especially for countries who are considering adopting IFRS. The results have significant implications for other African countries that have not adopted IFRS yet but have plans to adopt it in the near future.

2. Literature review

2.1 Adoption of IFRS in Ghana and Africa

Adoption of IFRS in Africa started in the late 1990s with countries such as Uganda and Kenya adopting it in 1998 and 1999 respectively (Atsunyo *et al.*, 2017). This was followed by Malawi and Mauritius in 2001, Botswana in 2003, Tanzania in 2004, South Africa in 2005, Ghana in 2007, Rwanda and Zambia in 2008, Sierra Leone in 2009, Algeria and Mozambique in 2010, and finally Swaziland and

Nigeria in 2012. What is common among the African countries that have adopted IFRS is that 10 out of the 16 countries are in Southern Africa with only Ghana, Sierra Leone and Nigeria in West Africa. Algeria and Mozambique adopted IFRS with modifications to suit local content but the rest of the African countries including Ghana fully adopted IFRS as published by the International Accounting Standard Board (IASB). Nigeria delayed in adopting IFRS because the Nigerian Accounting Standards Board unlike Ghana had the legal authority, the financial support and the structural integrity to issue accounting standards and enforce same (Osei-Afoakwa & Asare, 2013).

Ghana's adoption of IFRS in 2007 was spearheaded by weaknesses in the local GAAP (ROSC, 2004) and lack of confidence by practitioners in Ghana (Rahman, 2004). Atsunyo et al. (2017) posited that the Institute of Chartered Accountants Ghana realised that there was a significant gap between the GNAS and International Accounting Standards and therefore decided to migrate to IFRS. The study further argued that the adoption of IFRS by Ghana in 2007 was also informed by the unprecedented inflow of Foreign Direct Investment (FDI) into West Africa and the increasing need for companies to raise foreign capital through the Stock Exchange. Ghana subsequently adopted IFRS for Small and Medium Scale Enterprises (SMEs) in 2009 even though effective implementation was delayed till 2012 (Aboagye-Otchere & Agbeibor, 2012). Osei-Afoakwa and Asare (2013) argues that Ghana's decision to adopt IFRS was a hasty decision born out of desperation as a result of the inability of the ICAG to provide credible reporting standards for use in Ghana.

It is important to add that despites the adoption of IFRS by some African countries, studies have not examined the effect on audit and non-audit fees which can guide other countries yet to adopt.

Ghana plays a critical role in the West African Sub-region in terms of financial accounting practices through the Association of Accountancy Bodies in West African (ABWA) where it is a founding member. Ghana has been assisting and continues to assist Anglophone countries in the sub-region on Accounting practice and regulations. Currently, ICAG professional Exams are written in Liberia. Other countries such as The Gambia and parts of Cameroun get assistance from the ICAG to develop and enhance financial reporting practices. The Anglophone countries in West Africa follow France domestic guideline in financial reporting and as such have not adopted IFRS yet.

2.2 Empirical review

Several studies have examined the impact of IFRS adoption on audit fees and to some extent on non-audit fees in different jurisdictions. Majority of the results shows a positive relationship between IFRS adoption and audit fees even in developed economies where there exist an efficient Professional Accounting regulatory body. The results are usually attributed to differences in the gap between local GAAP and IFRS in these jurisdictions as well as weaknesses in financial reporting regulations which require more effort during adoption and post-adoption of IFRS. For instance, Houque (2017) examined the effect of IFRS adoption on New Zealand firms. The study based on a sample of 141 firms found evidence to support the hypothesis that IFRS adoption has a positive effect on audit fees.

Chen and Khurana (2017) examined the impact of IFRS versus US GAAP on audit fees and going concern opinion using a sample of US foreign firms. The results of the study revealed that on average foreign IFRS firms pay more audit fees than foreign US GAAP firms. The study argues that the rigidities in IFRS as well as the judgments that preparers of financial statements exercise increase audit risk, hence higher audit fees is charged. Higgins *et al.* (2016) extended previous studies on the impact of IFRS adoption to include increases in audit fees during IFRS adoption and post-IFRS adoption and whether the increases are consistent in the post-adoption period. The results of the study revealed that post-IFRS adoption increase in audit fees is consistent and not driven by short term transitional cost. The results also showed that PwC and Deloitte experienced lower (higher) marginal pricing post- IFRS adoption meaning that they have relatively higher (lower) fixed cost and higher (lower) variable cost structure. Shan and Troshani (2016) examined the impact of mandatory eXtensible Business Reporting Language (XBRL) and IFRS adoption on audit fees using listed firms on the Shanghai Stock Exchange. The results showed that IFRS increased audit fees for all the companies sampled while XBRL was negatively associated with audit fees.

Loukil (2016) studied the impact of IFRS adoption on audit fees using a sample of large French listed companies. The results of the study showed that audit fees increased during the transition period but were not significant during the post-adoption period contrary to the findings of Higgins *et al.* (2016). De Fuentes and Sierra-Grau (2015) examined the impact of IFRS adoption on audit and non-audit fees using a sample of listed firms in Spain. The study revealed an unexpected higher audit fees associated with group accounts for the firms three consecutive years of adoption. The study revealed that the behaviour of non-audit fees was more erratic compared to the audit fees during the same period. Camaran and Perotti (2014) examined the effect of IFRS adoption on audit fees using a sample of Italian banks. The results show that the real audit cost of these banks increased by 19.29% after the adoption of IFRS. The study also revealed that the increase in audit fees is associated with the presence of financial derivatives held for hedging purposes. The study however did not find any effect of IFRS on financial reporting quality.

Choi and Yoon (2014) studied the effect of IFRS adoption, the big N factor, and IFRS-related consultancy services on auditors and audit fees using firms from

Korea. The results of the study showed that for Korean firms that are audited by the big N, there is a positive relationship between IFRS adoption and audit fees. The results also showed that IFRS-related consultancy service provided by auditors have a negative association with IFRS adoption. The study concluded that provision of consultancy service by auditor increase auditors' knowledge of the client which mitigates audit costs. De George *et al.* (2012) examined the cost of IFRS in the transition period using sampled firms from Australia. The study reported that the mean cost of IFRS adoption in the transition period increased by 23% beyond the normal yearly increase. The study also showed that firms that have a higher exposure to audit complexity have a greater cost of compliance in the transition period.

Yaacob and Che-Ahmad (2012) examined the impact of IFRS on audit fees after the adoption by Malaysian listed companies. The results of the study showed that there is a significant positive association between IFRS adoption and audit fees. Griffen *et al.* (2009) examined the relationship between overseas and New Zealand governance regulatory reforms on audit and non-audit fees. The study used IFRS indicator variables to relate the timing of the fee changes to the incidence of the overseas and New Zealand reforms. The results of the study showed an increase in audit fees after the adoption of IFRS by New Zealand firms. The study also reported a decrease in non-audit fees which could not be linked with the adoption of IFRS.

Kim *et al.* (2012) examined the effect of mandatory IFRS adoption on audit fees using a sample of firms within the European Union. The results of the study showed that the mandatory adoption of IFRS within the European Union increased audit fees. The result also showed that audit premium increased with increase in audit complexities as a result of IFRS adoption and reduces the quality of financial reporting. The results further showed that IFRS related premium fees are lower in countries with strong legal regimes. Risheh *et al.* (2014) studied the effect of IFRS adoption on audit fees using listed Jordanian firms. The results from a sample of 1274 Jordanian listed firms revealed a positive and significant association between IFRS adoption and audit fees. The study also reported a positive association between international audit firms and audit fees.

Redmayne and Laswad (2013) examined the impact of IFRS adoption on public sector audit fees and audit effort using sample firms from New Zealand. The results of the study showed a significant increase in audit fees and audit effort in the first year of IFRS adoption. With regards to sectors with the most increase in audit fees and audit effort, the study revealed that local authorities and energy sector had the most significant increase. Schadewitz and Vieru (2009) examine the fees paid to statutory auditors of the small and medium sized companies that are in the stage of using IFRS for the first time in Finland. They used the magnitude of IFRS adjustments on income before tax, net income, equity and total liabilities as the proxy of the complexity of IFRS transition. They find a positive relation between the complexity proxy and the pricing of auditing services which suggest that audit fees are related to the degree of IFRS adjustments. Hart *et al.* (2009) found that prior to the adoption of IFRS in New Zealand and in the year of the adoption, audit fees increased by 48%. Lim *et al.* (2009) examined the practical challenges in the adoption of IFRS through a survey of auditors, auditees and other important users of accounting information and found a 30% increase in audit time, audit risk and audit fees after the adoption of IFRS.

The overall conclusion from previous studies in different jurisdiction is that IFRS adoption increases audit fees. However, very few studies examined the effect of IFRS adoption on non-audit fees. Also, these studies have not examined the subject matter within an African context even though some African countries adopted IFRS even before the compulsory adoption by the European Union in 2004/2005. This study is conducted to address these discrepancies in literature by examining the effect of IFRS adoption of both audit and non-audit fees within an African context and a developing country for that matter.

3. Hypothesis development

3.1 IFRS adoption and audit fees

Prior studies document that the most important factors that affect audit premium and hence audit costs are litigation risk, audit risk and the complexity of audit assignment (Chen & Khurana, 2017; Musah, 2017; Khaled *et al.* 2014; Redmayne & Laswad, 2013; Schelleman & Knechel, 2010; Diehl, 2010; Hay *et al.* 2006). Extant literature document that the adoption of IFRS will increase the additional effort to become knowledgeable about the new standards to allow them evaluate if the firms have duly complied with the reporting standards which will add up to the audit cost (De George *et al.* 2013; Kim *et al.* 2012). Previous studies have even found evidence that IFRS financial statement prepared after first time adoption is about 60% longer than the financial statements in the pre-adoption period (Webb, 2006; Ernst and Young, 2005). Johnson (2009) reports that IFRS adoption and its transition costs ranges between 0.1 to 0.7 percent of annual revenue. Other studies have reports that the mandatory shift from local GAAP to IFRS increases audit risk at the time of the mandatory shift (Charles *et al.* 2010; Ghosh & Pawlewicz, 2009). Several other studies in Europe reports that IFRS adoption by the European Union increased the burden on private companies and the complexities in financial reporting and auditing leading to a higher audit cost (Hung & Subramanyam, 2007; Hoogendoorn, 2006; Jermakowicz & Gornik-Tomaszewski, 2006).

Based on the above review, the study posits that auditing firms will charge higher audit fees to compensate the increased litigation risk, efforts and audit cost after the adoption of IFRS in Ghana especially as it was established that the GNAS was of low quality and suffered various weaknesses. As a result, the study expect that more audit fees are required to compensate the higher level of litigation risk and the more auditing complexities after the IFRS adoption in Ghana. The study therefore hypothesis that:

H1: IFRS adoption is positively and significantly associated with audit fees in Ghana.

3.2 IFRS adoption and non-audit fees

According to Choi and Yoon (2014) audit firms the world over provide both audit and other non-audit or consultancy services to companies and their clients. The study argues that non-audit services include such themes as accounting assistance, accounting compilation, ad hoc accounting advice, due diligence, and tax consulting. The decision to engage the service of audit firms in non-audit roles is a decision that rest with management of the respective organizations. Some researchers have argued that the provision of non-audit services by auditors will affect their independence as there could be some potential self-review threats (Hay *et al.* 2006; Levitt, 2000).

As auditors are likely to prefer non-audit duties that could generate higher profitability than audit duties could, the loss leader phenomenon can occur in the audit services (Choi & Yoon, 2014; Shin & Kim, 2010). Sharma and Sidhu (2001), however, concluded that large non-audit fees to total fees undermine auditor independence when auditors have a tendency to not issue a going concern qualification to clients. Prior research has usually found a positive relationship between IFRS adoption and audit and non-audit fees whiles others did find significant association between IFRS adoption and non-audit fees. For instance, Choi and Yoon (2014) and Naoum *et al.* (2011) have all documented a positive relation between audit and non-audit fees, while no relationship is found by Griffen *et al.* (2009) and O'Keefe, *et al.* (1994). Whisenant *et al.* (2003) and Geiger and Rama (2003) also provide evidence of a positive relationship between IFRS adoption and audit and non-audit fees in a single-equation estimates. However, the relationship between the variables is not evident when simultaneous-equation analysis is employed, suggesting that audit fees and non-audit fees are jointly determined. Antle *et al.* (2006) extended the analysis to include abnormal accruals as suggested by Frankel *et al.* (2002) since the strength of the economic bond between auditors and their clients is believed to be positively associated abnormal accruals.

In practice, auditors are usually the most natural IFRS advisors and consultants for a company (Jermakowicz & Gornik-Tomaszewski, 2006). Indeed, in many annual reports it is explicitly written, among other things that part of the non-audit fees is related to IFRS transition consultation (Choi and Yoon, 2014). Research has shown that a lower audit qualification or modification incidence is associated with non-audit fees (Firth, 2002). Also, the lack of competition in the IFRS transition market for non-audit services can result in a positive relationship between audit and non-audit fees (Solomon, 1990). If there are only few IFRS specialists available, and the common understanding within companies about the IFRS transition requirements is poor (Jermakowitz & Gornik-Tomaszewski, 2006), it is tempting to charge extra fees from the clients. Accordingly, the following hypothesis is developed.

H2: IFRS adoption is positively and significantly associated with non-audit fees in Ghana

3.3 Auditor type and audit fees

Previous studies have argued that auditing firms charge differently for same or similar jobs depending on the level of audit quality (Choi & Yoon, 2014; Redmayne & Laswad, 2013). Lin and Yin (2009) argued that audit quality is enhanced by externally-connected audit firms as they get to share experiences and skills acquired in other jurisdictions. Based on the expectation that members of international accounting firms are capable of providing better auditing service than other local Ghanaian audit firms, the study expect higher incremental audit fees will be charged by member firms during the implementation. Previous studies in other jurisdiction have found a positive relationship between externally-connected audit firms (herein referred as Big4) (Campa, 2013; Choi & Yoon, 2014; Redmayne & Laswad, 2013; Choi et al., 2008). Positive effect of auditor type on audit fees was reported for firms that have not adopted IFRS in Ghana based on a study of Microfinance companies in Ghana (Yalley et al., 2013). Also Musah (2017) study on determinants of audit fees in Ghana using a sample of listed non-financial firms in Ghana reported a positive relationship between auditor type and audit fees. Very few studies have examined auditor type and non-audit fees. Choi and Yoon (2014) study reported a positive association between internationally-connected audit firms and non-audit fees. Based on these findings the following hypothesis can be deduced.

H3: Big four audit firms are associated with higher audit fees and non-audit fees.

4. Methodology

The study is based on firms sampled in Ghana. The study used sample firms in Ghana because Ghana was the first West African country to adopt IFRS in 2007 before Sierra Leone and Nigeria did same in 2012. Ghana is the second largest economy in West Africa and has a lot of influence in the sub-region because of its history as the first independent country and the beacon of democracy in Africa. Also, previous reviews by the World Bank and IMF as well as previous studies all agree that Ghana had a very weak accounting standards and regulatory environment and structures prior to the adoption of IFRS (Osei-Afoakwa & Asare, 2013; Atsunyo et al., 2017; Assenso-Okofo et al., 2011). Ghana joined the International Federation of Accountants (IFAC) in 2005 and was advised to adopt IFRS as its local standards were not up to international standards.

The study did not include Nigeria and Sierra Leon who are the other two countries to adopt IFRS and are Anglophone countries in the sub-region because of currency differences which makes it impossible to convert at a common currency. Previous studies on IFRS adoption and audit fees have focused on only audit fees to the neglect of non-audit fees. In developing countries like Ghana where accounting practice were low at the time of adoption, more effort is needed in terms of preparing and even transition costs. To perfectly capture the full effect of transition costs of IFRS adoption, the study include non-audit fees as well as the year of adoption (IFRSYR) into the model.

Also, in an attempt to increase sample size as the number of listed non-financial firms in Ghana are few, the study extended the sample to included banks and insurance companies who were all mandated to adopt IFRS. This resulted in the dropping of control variables that are unique to manufacturing and trading firms like inventory and receivable which previous studies argue influence audit fees.

The study adopted a quantitative approach relying on panel data regression analysis to achieve the objectives of the study. Previous literature indicate that several variable that influence audit fees include clients size, operational risk and complexities, the type of auditor, profitability of the clients etc. (Houqe, 2017; Camaran & Perotti, 2014; Choi & Yoon, 2014; Griffin et al., 2009; Kim et al., 2012; De George et al., 2013; Vieru & Schadewitz, 2010). The study examined the effect of these variables including IFRS adoption on both audit and non-audit fees. Based on the above, the study developed a cross-sectional regression model as follows:

$$AF_{it} = \beta_0 + \beta_1 IFRS_{it} + \beta_2 IFRSYR_{it} + \beta_3 BIG4_{it} + \beta_4 SIZE_{it} + \beta_5 LEV_{it} + \beta_6 ROA_{it} + \beta_7 LOSS_{it} + \varepsilon_{it}$$

$$NAF_{it} = \beta_0 + \beta_1 IFRS_{it} + \beta_2 IFRSYR_{it} + \beta_3 BIG4_{it} + \beta_4 SIZE_{it} + \beta_5 LEV_{it} + \beta_6 ROA_{it} + \beta_7 LOSS_{it} + \varepsilon_{it}$$

Table 1. Variable definition and their measurement

Variable	Measurement
LogAF	Natural log of the audit fees
IFRSYR	Dummy, IFRS-adoption year coded 1 for First time IFRS financial statements
IFRS	Dummy variable, coded 1 if firm adopt IFRS, 0 Otherwise
SIZE	Natural log of total assets at end of financial year to measure size
LEV	Ratio of total debts (total liabilities - deferred tax) to total assets
LogNAF	Natural log of non-audit fee
LOSS	Net loss (or negative income) reported by a company in the current year coded as 1 if company suffers loss and 0 otherwise.
ROA	Ratio of earnings before interest and tax to ending total assets.
BIG4	Auditor type=1 if the current auditor were a BIG 4 or 0 otherwise

4.1 Control variable

Previous studies have found that firm characteristics such as leverage, loss in a particular year, complexity of operations, company size, riskiness of operations, and profitability of the audited firm affect audit fees (Choi & Yoon, 2014; Shan & Troshini, 2016; Yalley, 2013). In the Ghanaian context Yalley et al. (2013) found that the size of rural banks was positively associated with audit fees whiles Musah (2017) fond a positive relationship between audit fees and firm size. The study included some of these variables as control variables.

4.2 Data

The study is based on publicly available data obtained from financial statement of the sampled firms. All public companies including banks and insurance are required to publish their financial statement online and with the relevant regulatory bodies. The data was hand-collected from the annual report of these companies. The sample consist of 530 financial statement for the audit fee model equivalent to 53 firms and 350 financial statement for the non-audit fees model representing 35 firms because some companies did not disclose non-audit fees in the note to their accounts. The sample comprise of 20 non-financial firms, 24 banks and 5 insurance companies. The sample period covers 2003 to 2013 but based on an unbalanced panel data. The effective year of IFRS adoption for all these firms is 2007 even though some complied with the directive in 2008 because of technical difficulties in complying and the need to train staff to be familiar with the new standard.

5. Analysis and discussion

Table 2 presents the descriptive analysis of the study.

Table 2. Descriptive statistics

Variable	Mean	St. Deviation	Minimum	Maximum
AF	4.811	0.466	3.398	6.799
NAF	3.526	0.341	2.664	4.558
IFRS	0.614	0.488	0.000	1.000
SIZE	8.604	0.543	7.234	9.754
LEV	0.870	0.075	0.092	0.997
IFRSYR	0.154	0.414	0.000	1.000
ROA	0.059	0.031	-0.053	0.085
LOSS	0.065	0.247	0.000	1.000
BIG4	0.622	0.487	0.000	1.000

On the adoption of IFRS, the results show that 61% of the firms' sampled financial statements have been prepared in compliance with IFRS. The results from the descriptive statistics also shows that firm in the financial sector are highly leveraged with 87% of capital being debt. The results of the Big4 suggest that majority of the firms are audited by internationally-linked audit firms.

5.1 Effect of IFRS adoption on audit fees

To examine the impact IFRS adoption have on audit and non-audit fees, a panel regression model was used to establish the relationship between the two variables. Various tests were undertaken to determine the reliability of the estimate and to decide which model (fixed effect or random effect) was best for the model. For instance the Breusch- Pagan test was conducted to test for heteroscedasticity. The results for the two models were significant at 5% suggesting that null hypothesis is rejected and that there is heteroscedasticity. The robust estimates in STATA were applied to both models to resolve issues of autocorrelation and heteroscedasticity. The study also used the variance inflation factor (VIF) to test for multicollinearity. The results show that the overall VIF for the first and second model were 1.85 and 1.35 respectively which are less than 2 and as such there is little or no problem for multicollinearity. Finally, the Haussmann test was conducted to decide which model to use. After conducting the Haussmann test, the study settled on the random effect model for the first model and fixed effect for the second model because it's provided more consistent results using the R^2 values and the outcome of the Haussmann test in line with previous studies.

The overall Adjusted R-square is 0.818 for the first model and 0.627 for the second model which suggest that the independent variables have higher explanatory power. The Wild Chi^2 which is a measure of the fitness of the model in the case of a random effect model in a Stata program also had a significant probability for both models which suggest that the model is well fit. The regression results for the first model that examined the effect of IFRS adoption on audit fees is presented in Table 3 below.

Table 3. Regression results on IFRS adoption and audit fees

Variables	Coefficient	Standard Deviation
IFRS	0.091**	1.970
IFRSYR	0.028***	4.289
BIG4	0.096***	2.845
SIZE	0.577***	13.621
LEV	0.004	0.210
ROA	0.011	0.129
LOSS	0.081**	1.966
CONST	0.120	0.314
Number of observations	530	
Wald Chi^2	39.299	
Prob > Chi^2	0.000	
Adjusted R	0.818	

(***significant at 1%, ** significant at 5%, * significant at 10% level)

The results show that IFRS adoption is positive and significantly associated with audit fees at 1% significance level. This suggests that the adoption of IFRS has increased audit fee. This result confirms the results of previous studies (Camaran & Perotti, 2014; Choi & Yoon, 2014; De George *et al.* 2012; Kim *et al.* 2012; Redmayne & Laswad, 2013; Kim *et al.* 2012; Griffin *et al.* 2009; Shan & Troshani, 2016) as well as the first hypothesis of the study which states that IFRS adoption has significant effect on audit fees in Ghana. The year of adoption (IFRSYR) however also showed a positive association with audit fees which also suggest IFRS adoption increased during the transitional period. The results is consistent with previous studies (Camaran & Perotti, 2014; Choi & Yoon, 2014).

The variable Big4 was positively associated with audit fees at a 1% significance level. The result confirms previous studies such as Hongerdoorn (2006) as well as Schadewitz and Vieru (2010) and suggests that big4 audit firms charge higher audit fees than non-big4.

On the control variables; size of the firm and loss which is a measure of risk is significantly associated with audit fees. Size was significant at 1% significance level and had a positive relationship with audit fees as expected. Firm reporting loss was also positively associated with audit fees as expected because of additional risk loss reporting brings.

Other control variables were found not to have any significant association with audit fees. Some of these control variables include; leverage and return on asset which is a measure of profitability and leverage which is a measure of risk. The expectation of these variables as per literature is that they influence audit fees positively.

5.2 Discussion of findings on IFRS and audit fees

The results of the first model as discussed above show that IFRS adoption has resulted in an increase in audit fees consistent with literature and the first hypothesis of the study. The results imply that additional effort was brought to bear on auditors with the mandatory adoption of IFRS by listed firms in Ghana. The results show that auditors in Ghana consider IFRS adoption as causing significant changes to the components which determines audit fees.

The results can be interpreted from three different perspective based on literature. First, the risk that financial statement prepared in compliance with IFRS could be materially misstated is high. Second, the fact that auditors in Ghana provided non-audit and consultancy services which could increase their knowledge of the client financial statement and result in a spill over effect from non-audit service to auditing may not exist. Third, there is less competition for audit firms in Ghana resulting in these firms translating IFRS compliance financial statements auditing into audit costs. This result is not consistent with the finding of Vieru and Schadewitz (2010) that conducted a similar study in Finland and had a positive but statistically insignificant relationship with audit fees.

The results are however consistent with most studies across the globe especially from Europe, Australia and New Zealand. From the auditor's point of view there was an increase in accounting regulation as a result of mandatory IFRS adoption, therefore, increases client related risk and potentially results in more time-consuming work for the auditor to collect evidence in support of the audit opinion (Choi & Yoon, 2014; Kim *et al.*, 2012). The results confirm the assertion in literature that IFRS adoption increases the complexities in the client's financial statements and its associated risk which auditors compensate that additional responsibility with a higher audit fees.

5.3 Big 4 audit firms and audit fees

The results from the regression also confirms the third hypothesis which is to the effect that the Big4 audit firms charge higher audit fees as compared to non-big 4. The significant positive coefficient on BIG4 suggests that a member of the Big 4 firms charge a much higher level of auditing fees than the domestic auditing firms in Ghana. The significant positive effect is not explained by the adoption of IFRS but the fact that the big4 provide high quality audit hence charge higher fees. This finding is consistent with the results of Campa (2013) and Lin and Yen (2016) but different from the findings of Jianfang *et al.* (2012). The higher audit fees charged by the Big4 is as a results of the perceived audit quality and richer expertise and experience to assist them to deal with the higher level of demand for the auditing quality under the new accounting standards.

Table 4. Effect of IFRS adoption on non-audit fees

Variables	Coefficient	Standard Deviation
IFRS	0.141***	2.988
IFRSYR	0.027***	4.336
BIG4	0.106***	2.872
SIZE	0.500***	11.411
LEV	0.002	0.010
ROA	0.080	0.869
LOSS	0.209**	2.348
CONST	0.274	0.699
Number of observations	350	
Wald Chi2	96.150	
Prob > F	0.000	
Adjusted R	0.627	

(***significant at 1%, ** significant at 5%, * significant at 10% level)

The results of the regression analysis show that IFRS adoption has a positive effect on non-audit fees just like audit fees. Also, the relationship is statistically significant at 1% significance level suggesting that IFRS adoption have significant impact on non-audit fees as it did in audit fees. The year of adoption also have significant positive relationship with non-audit fees.

The Big 4 audit firm as expected had also a positive and significant relationship with non-audit fees. The results imply that the big4 audit firms charge higher amount as non-audit fees just like audit fees in the first model.

Almost all the control variables in the model were statistically insignificant with the exception of firm size and Loss which had a positive significant relationship with non-audit fees at a 1% and 5% significance level respectively.

5.4 Discussion of findings on IFRS and non-audit fees

The results of the study revealed that IFRS adoption have a significant impact on non-audit and accounting consultancy services cost. This result is consistent with the second hypothesis which states that IFRS adoption has significant effect on non-audit fees in Ghana. The reason for this result could be attributed to the fact that there was a significant gap between the Local GAAP which is the Ghana National Accounting Standards and IFRS which required that auditors assist companies to comply with the new standards by proving consultancy services. The results suggest that IFRS adoption required technical skills which most of the listed firms did not have and had to engage these audit firms who have the expertise as a result of working in other jurisdictions where IFRS was adopted before Ghana. The result was not just significant for the post-adoption period but was significant during the transition period as IFRSYR was also positively associated with non-audit fees.

The result of the study is consistent with prior studies as more research has usually found a positive relationship between IFRS adoption and non-audit fees. Prior research (Choi & Yoon, 2014; Shin & Kim, 2010; Whisenant et al., 2003; Geiger & Rama, 2003 and Naoum et al., 2011) has documented a positive relation between IFRS adoption and non-audit fees the result is however inconsistent with the findings of O'Keefe et al. (1994) which found no significant relationship between IFRS adoption and non-audit fees.

Overall, it can be said that IFRS adoption did not require companies adopting IFRS for the first time to engage the services of professional accounting bodies in the transition period as the year of adoption was also negatively associated with non-audit fees. The overall impact was felt on the post adoption period and not the year of adoption.

5.5 Big 4 Audit firm and non-audit fees

The results of the second regression analysis in table 4 shows that firms that are audited by the big 4 audit firms or the internationally-linked audit firms charge higher audit fees than non-big 4. This result has nothing to do with IFRS adoption but simply suggest that the internationally-linked audit firms have the expertise and produce high audit quality hence they charge premium for their service. The result is consistent with the expectations of the third hypothesis and consistent with the results of Choi and Yoon (2014).

6. Conclusions

IFRS is a principled-based accounting standard that requires preparers of financial statements to establish logic and reason within the context of the framework of accounting and apply those principles consistently. The complexities that mandatory IFRS brings as well as the related audit risk requires that auditors exercise high levels of professional scepticism, more effort both as consultants to their clients and auditors. The increased burden as a result of mandatory IFRS adoption has translated into increased audit and non-audit fees in even developed economies which are supported by the findings of this study. The results of the study showed that there was a positive and significant association between mandatory IFRS adoption by firms in Ghana and audit and non-audit fees. The results emphasize the complexities of IFRS and the professional judgement needed to be exercised by preparers of financial statements required more effort and technical skills from audit firms in the form of consultancy services and audit fees. Also both the audit fees model and the non-audit fee model had a positive association with the year of adoption suggesting that IFRS cost increased in the transition period consistent with the finding of some studies in other jurisdictions.

The results also show that big 4 audit firms charge higher audit fees than non-big4. This finding means that Ghanaian affiliated Big 4 firms can offer high-quality audit services because they have invested heavily in gaining experience and in improving expertise and as such charge higher fees for their expertise.

This study has implications for African countries that are yet to adopt IFRS especially companies in Liberia and other Anglophone African countries and even the Francophone countries. Companies in those countries should anticipate the cost associated with the mandatory adoption of IFRS and compare it with the anticipated benefits. Also, future studies could expand the scope of the study to include specific IFRS requirements that increases the complexities and audit risk which results in higher audit fees. A related research question could involve the nature of the longer-term trend of fees after IFRS adoption.

References

Aboagye-Otchere, F., & Agbeibor, J. (2012) "The International Financial Reporting Standard for Small and Medium-sized Entities (IFRS for SMES) Suitability for small businesses in Ghana", *Journal of Financial Reporting and Accounting*, vol. 10, no. 2: 190-214

Aboagye-Otchere, F., Bedi, I. & Ossei Kwakye, T. (2012) "Corporate governance and disclosure practices of Ghanaian listed companies", *Journal of Accounting in Emerging Economies*, vol. 2, no. 2: 140-161

Adeyemi, S.B., Okpala, O. & Dabor, E.L., (2012). "Factors affecting audit quality in Nigeria", *International Journal of Business and Social Science*, vol. 3, no. 20:

Ames, D. (2013) "IFRS adoption and accounting quality: The case of South Africa", *Journal of Applied Economics and Business Research*, vol. 3, no. 3: 154-165

Antle, R., Griffin, P.A., Teece, D. & Williamson, O.E. (1997) "An economic analysis of auditor independence for a multi-client, multi-service public accounting firm"

Assenso-Okofo, O., Ali, M. J., & Ahmed, K. (2011) "The development of accounting and reporting in Ghana", *The International Journal of Accounting*, vol. 46, no. 4: 459-480

Atsunyo, W., Gatsi, J. G. & Frimpong-Manson, E. (2017) "The success of IFRS in Africa: Comparative evidence between Ghana and Kenya", *European Journal of Business, Economics and Accountancy,* vol. 5, no. 1: 46-56

Ball, R. (2006) "International Financial Reporting Standards (IFRS): pros and cons for investors", *Accounting and business research*, vol. 36, no. 1: 5-27

Basioudis, I.G., Geiger, M.A. & Papanastasiou, V. (2006) "Audit fees, non-audit fees, and auditor reporting on UK stressed companies", In *National Auditing Conference*, 1-24

Bokpin, G.A. (2013) "Determinants and value relevance of corporate disclosure: Evidence from the emerging capital market of Ghana", *Journal of Applied Accounting Research*, vol. 14, no. 2: 127-146

Cameran, M. & Perotti, P. (2014) "Audit fees and IAS/IFRS adoption: evidence from the banking industry", *International Journal of Auditing*, vol. 18, no. 2: 155-169

Campa, D. (2013) "Big 4 fee premium and audit quality: latest evidence from UK listed companies", *Managerial Auditing Journal*, vol. 28, no. 8: 680-707

Charles, S.L., Glover, S.M. & Sharp, N.Y. (2010) "The association between financial reporting risk and audit fees before and after the historic events surrounding SOX", *Auditing: A Journal of Practice & Theory*, vol. 29, no. 1: 15-39

Chen, L. H., & Khurana, I. K. (2017) "The Impact of IFRS versus US GAAP on Audit Fees and Going Concern Opinions: Evidence from US-Listed Foreign Firms". Unpublished paper. Accessed from m.xmu.edu.cn/uploadfile/2017/0401/20170401090320734.pd.

Choi, J.H., Kim, C., Kim, J.B. & Zang, Y. (2010) "Audit office size, audit quality, and audit pricing", *Auditing: A Journal of practice & theory*, vol. 29, no. 1: 73-97

Choi, W. & Yoon, S. (2014) "Effects of IFRS adoption, Big N factor, and the IFRS-related consulting services of auditors on audit fees: the case of Korea", *Asian Journal of Business and Accounting*, vol. 7, no. 1

Daske, H. & Gebhardt, G. (2006) "International financial reporting standards and experts' perceptions of disclosure quality", *Abacus*, vol. 42, no. 3-4: 461-498

Daske, H., Hail, L., Leuz, C. & Verdi, R., (2008) "Mandatory IFRS reporting around the world: Early evidence on the economic consequences", *Journal of accounting research*, vol. 46, no. 5: 1085-1142

de Fuentes, C., & Sierra-Grau, E. (2015) "IFRS adoption and audit and non-audit fees: empirical evidence from Spanish listed companies", *Spanish Journal of Finance and Accounting/Revista Española de Financiación y Contabilidad*, ol. 44, no. 4: 387-426

De George, E.T., Ferguson, C.B. & Spear, N.A. (2012) "How much does IFRS cost? IFRS adoption and audit fees", *The Accounting Review*, vol. 88, no. 2: 429-462

Diehl, K.A. (2010) "The real cost of IFRS: The relationship between IFRS implementation and audit, tax, and other auditor fees", *International Research Journal of Finance & Economics*, vol. 37: 96-101

Ernst & Young (2005) "The impacts of IFRS on Australian companies: A study of the financial statement disclosures by Australia's top 100 listed companies" Available at: http://www.ey.com

Firth, M. (2002) "Auditor–provided consultancy services and their associations with audit fees and audit opinions", *Journal of Business Finance & Accounting*, vol. 29, no. 5-6: 661-693

Ghosh, A. & Pawlewicz, R. (2009) "The impact of regulation on auditor fees: Evidence from the Sarbanes-Oxley Act", *Auditing: a journal of practice & theory*, vol. 28, no. 2: 171-197

Griffin, P. A., Lont, D. H., & Sun, Y. (2009) "Governance regulatory changes, International Financial Reporting Standards adoption, and New Zealand audit and non-audit fees: empirical evidence", *Accounting & Finance*, vol. 49, no. 4: 697-724

Hail, L., Leuz, C. & Wysocki, P. (2010), "Global accounting convergence and the potential adoption of IFRS by the US (Part I): Conceptual underpinnings and economic analysis", *Accounting Horizons*, vol. 24, no. 3: 355-394

Hart, C., Rainsbury, E.A. & Sharp, J. (2009) "NZ IFRS–the impact on fees paid to auditors", *Chartered Accountants Journal*, vol. 88, no. 6: 42-43

Hay, D.C., Knechel, W.R. & Wong, N. (2006) "Audit fees: A Meta-analysis of the effect of supply and demand attributes", *Contemporary accounting research*, vol. 23, no. 1: 141-191

Higgins, S., Lont, D., & Scott, T. (2016) "Longer term audit costs of IFRS and the differential impact of implied auditor cost structures", *Accounting & Finance*, vol. 56, no. 1: 165-203

Hoogendoorn, M. (2006) "International accounting regulation and IFRS implementation in Europe and beyond–experiences with first-time adoption in Europe", *Accounting in Europe*, vol. 3, no. 1: 23-26

Houqe, M. N. (2017) "IFRS adoption and audit fees-evidence from New Zealand", *International Journal of Business and Economics*, vol. 16: 1-75.

Hung, M. & Subramanyam, K.R. (2007) "Financial statement effects of adopting international accounting standards: the case of Germany", *Review of accounting studies*, vol. 12, no. 4: 623-657

Jermakowicz, E.K. & Gornik-Tomaszewski, S. (2006) "Implementing IFRS from the perspective of EU publicly traded companies", *Journal of International Accounting, Auditing and Taxation*, vol. 15, no. 2: 170-196

Johnson, M.F., Nelson, K.K. & Frankel, R.M. (2002) "The Relation Between Auditor's Fees for Non-audit Services and Earnings Quality" (No. 1696r).

Johnson, S. (2009) "Guessing the costs of IFRS conversion", *CFO Magazine*.

Kim, J.B., Chung, R. & Firth, M. (2003) "Auditor conservatism, asymmetric monitoring, and earnings management", *Contemporary Accounting Research*, vol. 20, no. 2: 323-359

Kim, J.B., Liu, X. & Zheng, L. (2010) "Does Mandatory IFRS Adoption Impact Audit Fees?: Theory and Evidence", In *Annual Conference of the Canadian Academic Accounting Association, CAAA 2010*. Canadian Academic Accounting Association Inc...

Kim, J.B., Liu, X. & Zheng, L. (2012) "The impact of mandatory IFRS adoption on audit fees: Theory and evidence", *The Accounting Review*, vol. 87, no. 6: 2061-2094

Klibi, M. F., & Klibi, M. F. (2016) "Using international standards as a complement to overcome the unachieved nature of local GAAPs: The case of a developing country", *Journal of Applied Accounting Research*, vol. 17, no. 3: 356-376

Lin, H.L. & Yen, A.R. (2016) "The effects of IFRS experience on audit fees for listed companies in China", *Asian Review of Accounting*, vol. 24, no. 1: 43-68.

Loukil, L. (2016) "The impact of IFRS on the amount of audit fees: the case of the large French listed companies", *Quarterly Journal of Finance and Accounting*, vol. 54, no. 1/2: 41

Loyeung, A., Matolcsy, Z., Weber, J., & Wells, P. (2016) "The cost of implementing new accounting standards: The case of IFRS adoption in Australia", *Australian Journal of Management*, vol. 41, no. 4: 611-632

Madawaki, A. (2012) "Adoption of international financial reporting standards in developing countries: The case of Nigeria", *International Journal of Business and management*, vol. 7, no. 3: 152.

Musah, A. (2017) "Determinants of audit fees in a developing economy: evidence from Ghana", *International Journal of Academic Research in Business and Social Sciences*, vol. 7, no. 11: 716-730

Naoum, V.C., Sykianakis, N. & Tzovas, C. (2011) "The perceptions of managers of Greek firms regarding the Costs and Benefits ensuing from the adoption of International Financial Reporting Standards in Greece", *International Journal of Economic Sciences & Applied Research*, vol. 4, no. 3:

Nulla, Y.M. (2013) "IFRS adoption in research and development companies", *Journal of Administrative Sciences and Policy Studies*, vol. 1, no. 1: 34-48

O'Keefe, T.B., Simunic, D.A. & Stein, M.T. (1994) "The production of audit services: Evidence from a major public accounting firm", *Journal of Accounting Research*, 241-261

Osei-Afoakwa, K., & Asare, M. (2013) "From accounting standard-setters to standard-takers: The Nigerian and Ghanaian standard-setting experiences in retrospect", *International Journal of Social Science Tomorrow*, vol. 2, no. 4: 1-12

Previts, G.J., Walton, P. & Wolnizer, P.W. (2010) *A Global History of Accounting, Financial Reporting and Public Policy: Europe*, Emerald Group Publishing.

Rahman, M.Z., Linde, G. & Yankey, F. (2004) "Report on the Observance of Standards and Codes (ROSC): Ghana-Accounting and Auditing. *ROSC*", *Under the initiative of the World Bank and IMF.[Online]. Available: http://www. worldbank. org/ifa/rosc-aa. html. Accessed on*, 27(12), p.12.

Redmayne, N.B. & Laswad, F. (2013) "An assessment of the impact of IFRS adoption on public sector audit fees and audit effort–some evidence of the transition costs on changes in reporting regimes", *Australian Accounting Review*, vol. 23, no. 1: 88-99

Risheh, K.E.A. (2014) "The impact of IFRS adoption on audit fees: evidence from Jordan", *Accounting and Management Information Systems*, vol. 13, no. 3: 520

Schelleman, C. & Knechel, W.R. (2010) "Short-term accruals and the pricing and production of audit services", *Auditing: A Journal of Practice & Theory*, vol. 29, no. 1: 221-250

Shan, Y.G. & Troshani, I. (2016) "The effect of mandatory XBRL and IFRS adoption on audit fees: Evidence from the Shanghai Stock Exchange", *International Journal of Managerial Finance*, vol. 12, no. 2: 109-135

Sharma, D.S. & Sidhu, J. (2001) "Professionalism vs commercialism: The association between non-audit services (NAS) and audit independence", *Journal of Business Finance & Accounting*, vol. 28, no. 5-6: 563-594

Simunic, D.A. (1980) "The pricing of audit services: Theory and evidence", *Journal of accounting research*, 161-190

Sun, Y., Lont, D.H. & Griffin, P.A. (2008) "Governance regulatory changes, IFRS adoption, and New Zealand audit and non-audit fees: Empirical evidence", working paper

Taylor, M.H. & Simon, D.T. (1999) "Determinants of audit fees: the importance of litigation, disclosure, and regulatory burdens in audit engagements in 20 countries", *The International Journal of Accounting*, vol. 34, no. 3: 375-388

Tsamenyi, M., Enninful-Adu, E. & Onumah, J. (2007) "Disclosure and corporate governance in developing countries: Evidence from Ghana", *Managerial Auditing Journal*, vol. 22, no. 3: 319-334

Vieru, M. & Schadewitz, H. (2010) "Impact of IFRS transition on audit and non-audit fees: evidence from small and medium-sized listed companies in Finland", working paper

Walker, A., & Hay, D. (2013) "Non-audit services and knowledge spillovers: An investigation of the audit report lag, *Meditari Accountancy Research*, vol. 21, no. 1: 32-51

Wang, X., Young, D. & Zhuang, Z. (2008) "The effects of mandatory adoption of International Financial Reporting Standards on information environments", *Unpublished paper, The Chinese University of Hong Kong*

Webb, R. (2006) "Brace yourselves: IFRS will be bumpy", *Financial Review*, vol. 25, no. 1: 26-34

Whisenant, S., Sankaraguruswamy, S. & Raghunandan, K. (2003) "Evidence on the joint determination of audit and non-audit fees", *Journal of Accounting Research*, vol. 41, no. 4: 721-744

World Bank & International Monetary Fund (2004) Report on the observance of Standards and Codes (ROSC), Corporate Governance Country Assessment: Ghana, Washington, DC: World Bank and IMF.

Yaacob, N.M. & Che-Ahmad, A. (2012) "Audit fees after IFRS adoption: Evidence from Malaysia", *Eurasian Business Review*, vol. 2, no. 1: 31-46

Yalley, P.M., Henry, A.A., Zhongming, T.A.N. & Yaw, N.E. (2013) "The Determinants of Audit Fees in Rural and Community Banks in Ghana: An Empirical Analysis", *International Journal of Business and Social Research*, vol. 3, no. 5: 212-218

7

Effects of Turkish Accounting Standards application on independent audit procedures

Fatih Coşkun Ertaş [a] and Atila Karkacıer [a,1]

[a] *Gaziosmanpasa University, Tokat, Turkey*

Abstract: The main purpose of this study is to determine the effects of Turkish Accounting Standards, which are compatible with International Financial Reporting Standards composed by the International Accounting Standards Board and providing to eliminate the differences among the accounting practices of the countries and to compare companies' accounting information, on independent audit procedures. Independent audits are essential to verify the accuracy and reliability of the financial statements belonging to companies. In this study, first of all, a number of examinations on the Turkish Accounting Standards applications have been carried out. Then, the information about the independent audits have been submitted. Finally, whether Turkish Accounting Standards Applications have positive or negative effects on independent audit firms and on independent auditors was searched through the questionnaire technique conducted among the independent auditing firms affiliated to the Free Market Board. Ultimately, it was concluded that the auditors consider International Accounting Standards as modern, reliable and sufficient to answer the purpose. In addition to this, Turkish Accounting Standards must be absolutely performed by companies, but it makes audit procedures difficult for audit firms and for independent auditors.

Keywords: International Accounting Standards Board, Turkish Accounting Standards, Independent Audit

[1] *Correspondence address*: Atila Karkacıer, Gaziosmanpaşa University, Research Assistant at GOÜ Faculty of Business/Accounting & Finance Division. E-mail: atila.karkacier@gop.edu.tr

1. Introduction

The investment decisions, which have become international with the globalization of capital markets, the economic conditions emerging around the world, and accounting scandals encountered have damaged the reliability level of financial statements seriously. After these incidents, it has been understood that a common accounting language and consistency in accounting practices are necessary. Therefore, the International Accounting Standards Board is the primary organization which functions to provide these requirements.

In Turkey, Public Oversight Accounting and Auditing Standards Authority carries out this duty which involves to set Turkish Accounting Standards and to publish them. As for independent audit, it is the process of checking the suitability and the accuracy of financial information obtained as a result of economic activities of firms and of financial statements according to the financial reporting standards as well as evaluating and affiliating to a report. The required independent audit techniques are performed during this checking, evaluating and reporting processes. The financial statements of firms must be reliable so that managers of firms and relevant people using those financial statements can take the right decisions and take action properly. This reliability can be provided through independent audits. When viewed from this aspect, the independent audit has a significance which interests many sectors.

The aim of this study is to determine the effect of Turkish Accounting Standards on independent audits and to evaluate it in terms of both independent audit firms and independent auditors. Within this context, the survey, which has been conducted among the audit firms getting authorization from the Capital Market Board of Turkey (CMB) in order to determine the effect of Turkish Accounting Standards (TAS/TFRS) on independent audit processes, and the findings obtained via this survey have been mentioned in this study.

Ultimately, it was concluded that the auditors consider International Accounting Standards as modern, reliable and sufficient to answer the purpose. In addition to this, Turkish Accounting Standards must be absolutely performed by companies, but it makes audit procedures difficult for audit firms and for independent auditors.

The rest of the paper is organized as follows: Section 2 examines the International/Turkish Accounting Standards. Section 3 gives information about the external audit. Section 4 discusses the merits of the relevant empirical literature. In addition, section 5 describes the sample and data and analyzes the empirical findings. Finally, section 6 presents the conclusion.

2. Applications of Accounting Standards in Turkey

In Turkey, the development of the accounting standards has become under the leadership of the government. By means of the laws taken as example, the effects of the implementations in the countries with which we have close economic and political relationships can be seen. Our standards were set under the influence of French legislation and publications at first, then of German legislation and publications. After 1950, the influence of the accounting system belonging to the USA, with which we developed a close relationship, was seen. With our application for full membership in the EU in 1987, the EU regulations and, lately, International Accounting Standards have been effective (Başpınar, 2004: 46).

In 1994, in order to meet the need for accounting standards and to generate standards compatible with the international accounting standards, the association of accounting professionals, the Union of Chambers of Certified Public Accountants Turkey (TURMOB), was founded, which made a significant contribution to establish the Turkish Accounting and Auditing Standards Board. But these standards were underutilized due to the absence of compulsory enforcement. Therefore, the Turkish Accounting Standards Board (TASB) was founded on the purposes of filling the deficiency of standardization in accounting, generating accounting standards which are internationally valid, providing the use of these standards and meeting the need for an organization which has sanction power before the goverment (Bostancı, 2002: 77).

The main purpose of the TASB, which was founded in 1999, is to determine and publish the national accounting standards to be used for the public weal and to provide the development as well as the adoption of the national accounting principles so that the financial statements can fit the bill and be accurate, reliable, balanced, comparable, also understandable in the presentation of audited financial staments. The board decided to adopt International Accounting Standards in order to be integrated into the modern world applications and to accord with the European Union and the acquis commonautaire (Seviğ, 2006: 1).

In 2011, the Public Oversight Accounting and Auditing Standards Authority was founded in order to constitute and publish Turkish Accounting Standards compatible with the international standards, to provide the application union in independent audits as well as required reliance and quality, to determine the audit standards, to authorize independent auditors and independent audit firms, also to audit their activities and to conduct public oversights in the field of the independent audit (Arıkan, 2011: 7).

Thus, the TASB ended up and was transfered to the Public Oversight Accounting and Auditing Standards Authority. From that date on, the Public Oversight

Accounting and Auditing Standards Authority has maintained the duty to set and publish Turkish Accounting Standards compatible with International Accounting Standards.

3. Independent audit

Today, economic activities has become more complicated with the fast change and development of these activities. Hence, fulfilling these activities is getting more and more difficult. On this occasion, the need for auditing which is essential for the business world is rising day by day. Also, auditing is considered as a significant matter by both society and the business world (Güredin, 2007: 3).

Policy makers have to take various precautions for these explained information which are not reliable enough, in case of errors, mistakes and irregularity in the information derived from different reasons both within and beyond control such as carelessness, negligence, intention, etc., varying depending on knowledge and skill levels of the employees working in any positions, from the lowest to the highest, in an institution and an organization. The most common method used concerning the reliability of the information is the auditing activity which unbiased, objective and surely experienced person or persons carry out by checking information under some certain standards and by approving their truth (Aksoy, 2006: 46).

As for independent audit, it can be defined as a process during which an independent auditor examines the fidelity of the relevant firms' financial statements to the principles and criteria, which have been set before, objectively through collecting evidence and evaluating methods by acting according to the audit standards and s/he reports the obtained results to the users and the relevant persons in those firms (Dönmez & Ersoy, 2006: 71). The reports prepared as a result of the independent audit indicate the financal status of a firm clearly, impartially and objectively (Ulusoy, 2005: 278). Independent auditing is highly signifiant in terms of both providing reliable information and being directive about determining the prospective predictions concerning some matters such as financial statements, analysis, audit and report preparation (Çelen, 2001: 185).

4. Literature review

Turkish Accounting Standards (TAS/TFRS), which is completely compatible with IAS/IFRS and has a translation, and accounting audit have been discussed in a good number of studies. Accordingly, some studies about these subjects can be organized as follows.

Aksoy (2005) discussed the harmonization in financial accounting and in reporting standards as well as the parallel developments in the context of the orientation tendency to the global accounting standards in his study. He stated that working with IFRS, as a set of global standards, had not only advantages but also drawbacks to take into consideration.

In their study, Alkan and Doğan (2012) aimed to identify the differences between ratio analyses that was made with financial statements of companies traded in Istanbul Stock Exchange between 2000 and 2009 in accordance with International Financial Reporting Standards and prior to International Financial Reporting Standards. First, averages of the companies for each ratio was calculated both for prior to standards and after the standards and the results were compared. Significant differences were reached between the results obtained in the 2004-2005 compliance period and the findings obtained in 10 years.

Barth, Landsman and Lang (2008), compared characteristics of accounting amounts for firms that apply International Accounting Standards (IAS) to a matched sample of firms that do not to investigate whether applying IAS is associated with higher accounting quality and lower equity cost of capital. They found that firms applying IAS evidence less earnings management, more timely loss recognition, and more value relevance of accounting amounts than do those applying domestic GAAP.

Beke (2012), examined the impact of the adoption of accounting standards on company performance. The results indicated that the internal efficiency measured by accounting indicators depended on financial situations, capitalizations after standards adoption

In their study, Çankaya and Dinç (2012) seek to identify factors affecting the success of financial reporting standards application. The survey that was carried out on the independent auditors in Turkey has been analyzed and was assessed through structural equation model. They have concluded that education factor and economic factor has effect on the successs of TAS/ TFRS application.

Çelen (2001) indicated that every business needed to subject their business to Independent Accounting Audit, because the reliable information which was generated by accounting and audited was required while taking managerial decisions. He remarked that accounting information had to be reliable and what provided this was auditing. As for Damant (2003), he analyzed the recent developments in financial reporting and pointed out its inevitable complicacy. He argued that if financial reporting rules were written accurately as in the framework, the results of reports would be more complicated; therefore, professional analysis would be required to comprehend and explain these reports.

In another study, Dönmez and Ersoy (2006) evaluated the independent auditing system in Turkey from the view of the independent audit firms which were charged with making independent audits by the Capital Market Board (CMB). They concluded that the regulations, in Turkey, regarding independent audits were inadequate. Besides, they found that the most significant problems which firms encountered during an audit process were "legislation complexity", "inadequacy in regulations regarding auditing" and audited firms' disapplying International Accounting Standards.

In their study, Elitaş, Karakoç and Özdemir (2011) aimed to analyze Turkish Accounting Standards from the perspective of accountant professionals. For this purpose, a survey was applied to accountant professionals in Afyon, Denizli, Uşak provinces and results were analyzed. According to this, 80% of professionals stated that they have sufficient information about Turkish Accounting Standards (TAS). However, 81% think that there is a need for a systematic training on TAS.

George, Ferguson and Spear (2013) provided evidence of a directly measurable and significant cost of International Financial Reporting Standards (IFRS) adoption, by examining the fees incurred by firms for the statutory audit of their financial statements at the time of transition. They found that firms with greater exposure to audit complexity exhibit greater increases in compliance costs for the transition to IFRS. Güler (2006) explained the legal legislation about accounting control and its applications in Turkey and in the world. Also, he conducted an emprical study to determine whether independent audit firms had effects on crises during a time of crisis. As a result, he concluded that independent audits did not have any profound effects on a crisis and on a bank bankruptcy, but it had new requirements to be more effective.

Jeanjean and Stolowy (2008), examined the effects of the international accounting standards on earnings management. In the study, they focused on Australia, France and England, first countries to comply with IFRS. As a result of the study carried out, it was seen that there was not a decline in the proliferation of earnings management after the compliance with IFRS. Actually, in France, it increased more. It was understood that the compliance with the standards did not provide a recovery in earnings management.

Kandemir and Akbulut (2013) aimed to fill the information gap in this field by emphasizing the significance of audit comittee in the application of an independent audit effectively. They carried out an emprical study to explain the contributions which the independent audit firms functioning in Turkey received from the comittees responsible for auditing. They concluded that committees responsible for the audits strengthened the independence of independent auditors and increases the effectiveness of independent audits.

Morril and Morrill (2003) examined the changes observed in the applications and the internal auditor dimension which needed to participate in independent audits. They tried to clarify this argument by using the concepts about transaction costs economics to define the conditions lying behind the organizations which promoted the participation in internal audits within independent audits.

Morris *et al.* (2013) analyzed preparers' sensations of the costs of the implementation process and the likely benefits arising for their companies. Their results showed a very negative tone among respondents reflecting concerns about the problems of IFRS implementation and the low level of expected benefits.

Türk (2008) aimed to determine the effects belonging to the fidelity of auditing service to the accepted standards on perceived quality of auditing service and on customer satisfaction. The questionnaire technique was applied on the firms registered to ISE. According to the research and the data analysis results, it was determined that perceived quality and customer satisfaction were considerably affected by the conformity to the accepted standards.

Yavaşoğlu (2001) handled independent audits in terms of the procedure and principles. He evaluated the subject with the legislation and practice dimensions. In addition, he suggested his personal opinions by making comments and explanations on the cases, which he mentioned, about the legislation.

5. Research on determining the effects of Turkish Accounting Standards on independent audit procedures

In this section, the analysis and results of the questionnaire study, which has been conducted to research the effects of the Turkish Accounting Standards applications on independent audit procedures, are mentioned.

5.1 Research objectives

The main aim of the research is to investigate the effects of Turkish Accounting Standards on independent audit procedures. Accordingly, the viewpoints of independent auditors about Turkish Accounting Standards and their opinions about the effects of the Turkish Accounting Standards applications on independent audit procedures have been researched. Also, this research tries to clarify whether the audit of the financial statements which are prepared in conformity with Turkish Accounting Standards and the other audit operations have negative or positive effects on audit firms and on independent auditors.

5.2 Scope of research

The scope of the research is composed of the organizations authorized with the independent audit in the capital market. The greatest factor in the selection of the independent audit firms in the Capital Market Board (CMB) is that the business affiliated to the CMB practise Turkish Accounting Standards. By the date of December 2008, 95 audit firms affiliated to the CMB existed. These firms compose our population. The data source in the research is the auditors in different positions. A questionnaire was applied to all these 95 firms, which were authorized by the CMB and were the universe of the research, via e-mails. The firms were leaded to the questionnaire form via a web link given in the e-mails. Since the responses were recorded in the database at that moment, the firms did not need to send another e-mail to convey their responses. 52 firms responded to it. But 3 of them were not convenient for the analysis; therefore, the responses of the 49 firms were used as data.

5.3 Method of research

Primary data is defined as the data which a researcher needs and collects on her/his own through different instruments (Altunışık, *et al.*, 2004: 68). In this study, tyhe questionannaire technique was used as the method of collecting primary data. This questionnaire was composed of 30 questions. 5 of them were prepared with the aim of determining the features of the auditors responding this questionnaire. The other 25 questions were prepared to determine their knowledge levels about Turkish Accounting Standards, the levels of the accouting standards applications in the firms they audited and the changes for the auditors in the audit procedures after Turkish Accounting Standards had started to be practised. Also, they were closed-end questions and were prepared according to the 5 point Likert scale. The questionnaires were conveyed to all the 95 firms authorized by the CMB, but the 49 questionnaires which were convenient returned. That is, the return rate was 51.6%.

5.4 Data analysis

The data obtained in the survey were analyzed by using SPSS Statistics. In the study, firstly, frequency analysis and then T test for the independent samples and one-way analysis of variance (One Way Anova) were applied. And alpha method (cronbach alpha coefficient) was employed for the reliability analysis. Cronbach Alpha Coefficient analyzes whether the questions in the scale form an integrity so as to explain a homogeneous structure. As a result of the reliability analysis, Cronbach Alpha Coefficient was found as 0.8835. This figure indicates the reliability level of the questionnaire is quite high.

5.5 Findings

The demographic features of the independent auditors in these 49 firms, which participated the questionnaire and the frequency distributions of their opinions are presented below collectively.

5.5.1 Frequency distribution of variables

Table 1. The demographic features of the independent auditors

Demographic Features		Frequency	Percentage	Cumulative Percentage
Gender	Male	42	85.7	85.7
	Female	7	14.3	100
	Total	49	100	
Age	25-35	21	42.9	42.9
	36-45	15	30.6	73.5
	46 and over	13	26.5	100
	Total	49	100	
Title	Responsible Partner Lead Auditor	11	22.4	22.4
	Lead Auditor	13	26.6	49.0
	Senior Auditor	11	22.4	71.4
	Auditor	10	20.4	91.8
	Assistant Auditor	4	8.2	100
	Total	49	100	
Occupational Experience	Less than 1 year	1	2.0	2.0
	1-5 years and more	9	18.4	20.4
	6-10 years and more	14	28.6	49.0
	11-15 years and more	13	26.5	75.5
	16-20 years and more	2	4.1	79.6
	21 years and more	10	20.4	100
	Total	49	100	
Educational Background	Bachelor's Degree	43	87.8	87.8
	Master's Degree	6	12.2	100
	Total	49	100	

85.7% of the independent auditors responding the questionnaire were male and 14.3% were female. The age range of 73.5% was 25-42 and 26.5% of them were 46 and over. 22.4% of the independent auditors were responsible partner lead auditors. 26.6% ofage range them were lead auditors. 22.4% were senior auditors. 20.4% were auditors and 8.2%. the lowest percentage. were assistant auditors. 49% of the independent auditors had 1-10 years job experience. 36.6% had 11-20 years and 20.4% had job experience more than 21 years. 87.8% of the independent auditors had Bachelor's degree while 12.2% of them had MA.

Table 2. The knowledge levels of the respondents about Turkish Accounting Standards (TAS/TFRS)

	Frequency	Percentage
Yes	36	73.5
No	0	0.
Partly	13	26.5
Total	49	100.0

While 73.5% of the respondents havd enough konwledge about TAS/TFRS, 26.5% of them had partial knowledge. These independent auditors had knowledge because they were inclined to the continuing training subjects.

Table 3. The applications of the accounting standards in the firms where the audit operations were carried out

	Frequency	Percentage
Yes	27	55.1
No	5	10.2
Partly	17	34.7
	49	100.0

While 55.1% of the respondents stated that the applications of the accounting standards were practised in the firms where they carred out audit operations, 34.7% of them stated they were partially practised and 10.2% state that they did not have any accounting standards applications. That the firms affiliated to the CMB practise Turkish Accounting Standards was effective in this result.

Table 4. The independent auditor satisfaction level of the financial statements preparation of the audited firms according to TAS/TFRS

	Frequency	Percentage
Yes	9	18.4
No	13	26.5
Partly	27	55.1
	49	100.0

As for the satisfaction with the financial statements which had been prepared according to TAS/TFRS, 18.4% of the independent auditors responding the questionnaire stated the firms they audited were entirely satisfied with those financial statements, 55.1% stated they were partly satisfied while 26.5% stated they were not satisfied at all. Thus, it was concluded that the independent auditors participating in our survey thought the financial statements which the firms had been prepared according to TAS/TFRS had not been composed at the required level properly.

In the rest of our research, T test and one way analysis of variance (One Way Anova) were used for examining the differences between the groups and for the independent samples. In the questionnaire form, 22 questions which were prepared according to 5 point Likert scale were divided into 4 groups. First seven questions were gathered in the "convenience" group because they were composed with the thought that the audited firms provide convenience for the auditors after the applications of Turkish Accounting Standards. Secondly, the questions 8-14 were gathered in the "benefit" group with the thought of that TAS/TFRS provide benefits for the audit procedure. Thirdly, the questions 15-18 were gathered in the "difficulty" group with the thought of the difficulties encountered in the audit procedure after the applications of Turkish Accounting Standards. Finally, the questions 19-22 were gathered in the "drawback" group with the thought of that TAS/TFRS cause a number of troubles. The division of the auditors in these 4 groups and the arithmetic avarage of the responses given to the statements in these groups are shown in Table 5. Scoring of the statements prepared according to 5 point Likert scale is as follows: (1) Strongly Disagree, (2) Disagree, (3) Neither agree or disagree, (4) Agree, (5) Strongly Agree

Table 5.The arithmetic average of the statements divided in 4 groups

Statements	Average (n=49)	Standard Deviation
Convenience	**2.676**	**0.758**
01. Convenience in audit operations has been provided after TAS/TFRS.	2.632	1.093
02. After TAS/TFRS, Customer Selection and Taking the Job processes have become easier.	2.285	1.000
03. After TAS/TFRS, audit planning has become easier.	3.000	1.060
04. After TAS/TFRS, conducting audit program has become easier.	3.020	1.089
05. After TAS/TFRS, reporting findings has become easier.	3.102	1.278
06. After TAS/TFRS, there has been a decrese in time required for audit.	2.163	0.920
07. I use the statistical methods including analytical review procedures.	2.530	0.892
Benefit	**2.900**	**0.681**
08. After TAS/TFRS, internal controls in the firms are performed more efficiently.	2.653	1.164
09. After TAS/TFRS, efficiency and quality in audit have been enhanced.	3.061	1.087

Statements	Average (n=49)	Standard Deviation
10. After TAS/TFRS, we collect adequate and required amount of audit evidence faster.	2.612	1.057
11. After TAS/TFRS, the rate of filing reports involving positive views has increased.	2.571	0.889
12. After TAS/TFRS, the possibility of financial statements' containing error has decreased.	2.795	1.060
13. I am of the opinion that TAS/TFRS are modern, reliable and satisfactory.	3.673	0.774
14. Audit risks have decreased in the firms practising TAS/TFRS.	2.938	1.068
Difficulty	**3.811**	**0.738**
15. After TAS/TFRS, we constantly need training about auditing.	4.000	0.935
16. Raising awareness of the auditors and company accountants about TAS/TFRS has a remarkable effect on the audit quality.	4.000	1.154
17. After TAS/TFRS, the need for the techniques of computer assisted audit has risen.	3.816	1.148
18. It is difficult to perform the solution suggestions to the problems involving TAS/TFRS, which we encounter during an audit process.	3.428	0.978
Drawback	**2.683**	**0.645**
19. After TAS/TFRS, the other services which the firms can get from the audit firms have become limited.	2.122	0.904
20. After TAS/TFRS, there has been an increase in the fees received in return for audit services.	2.163	0.986
21. After TAS/TFRS, there has been an increase in the cost of audit operations.	3.551	1.042
22. After TAS/TFRS, there has been an increase in firms' changing their audit firms.	2.898	0.984

*(1) Strongly Disagree, ……. (5) Strongly Agree

5.5.2 Differences in terms of TAS/TFRS' convenience, difficulty, benefits and drawbacks concerning audit procedures

H_0: *There are not significant differences in the avarages of TAS/TFRS' convenience, difficulty, benefits and drawbacks.*

H_1: *There are significant differences in the avarages of TAS/TFRS' convenience, difficulty, benefits and drawbacks.*

One-way variance analysis was used in testing the hypotheses created. The differences between the averages of the responses the auditors gave to these four factors (convenience, benefit, difficulty, drawback) were analyzed. Below is the table which shows the analysis results.

Table 6. The differences between Convenience, Benefit, Difficulty, Drawback Factors

	Sum of Squares	Degree of Freedom	Mean Squares	F	Significance
Between-groups	3.776	3	1.259	6.794	.003
Within-group	3.335	18	.185		
Total	7.111	21			

majority * α = 0.01

In terms of the general averages of the auditors' responses to these four factors, it was found that there was a significant difference between them, statistically at 0.01 significance level. H$_0$ hypothesis was rejected (p=0.003). See Table 7 for the results of one way analysis of variance/ One Way Anova (Scheffe) test, which was conducted to determine which group was different from the other / the others.

Table 7. The difference level between the convenience, benefit, difficulty and drawback factors

	Average Difference	Standard Error	Significance
Convenience Benefit	-.2240	.23007	.814
Drawback	-.0073	.26978	1.000
Difficult	-1.1326*	.26978	.006
Benefit Convenience	.2240	.23007	.814
Drawback	.2167	.26978	.885
Difficulty	-.9086*	.26978	.029
Drawback Convenience	.0073	.26978	1.000
Benefit	-.2167	.26978	.885
Difficulty	-1.1253*	.30435	.015
Difficulty Conveniency	1.1326*	.26978	.006
Benefit	.9086*	.26978	.029
Drawback	1.1253*	.30435	.015

* α = 0.05

The results of Scheffe test are as follow: It was determined that there was a statistically significant difference between conveniency and difficulty of TAS/TFRS during the audit procedure (p=0.006). According to the results, it was seen that the participant auditors stated TAS/TFRS did not ease, conversely, made it difficult. The average difference between conveniency and difficulty factors was 1.1326 and the significance level was below 0.05.

It was determined that there was a statistically significant difference between the benefits and challenges of TAS/TFRS towards audit procedures (p=0.029). According to the results, it was seen that the participant auditors neither agreed nor disagreed to the benefits of TAS/TFRS while they confirmed their challenges. The average difference between the benefit and difficulty factors was 0.9086 and the significance level was below 0.05.

It was determined that there was a statistically significant difference between the drawback and difficulty of TAS/TFRS in audit procedures (p=0.015). According to the results, it was seen that the participant auditors indicated TAS/TFRS did not have any drawbacks for audit procedures, but they made it diffucult. The average difference between the drawback and difficulty factors was 1.1253 and the significance level was below 0.05.

5.5.3 Views of the auditors to the difficulty of TAS/TFRS in terms of their genders

H_0: In terms of the auditors' genders, there are not any significant differences between the averages of the statements regarding the difficulty of TAS/TFRS.
H_1: In terms of the auditors' genders, there are significant differences between the averages of the statements regarding the difficulty of TAS/TFRS.

T test was used for the independent samples to examine the hypotheses created. The differences between the averages of the responses to the difficulty factor in terms of the auditors' genders were examined. The table showing the result is as follows.

Table 8. The differences between the genders of the auditors in terms of the difficulty factor

	N	Average	T test	p
Male	42	3.76	-1.149	.257
Female	7	4.10		

* $\alpha = 0.05$

In terms of the general average of the difficulty factor, a significant difference at 0.05 significance level could not be found between the auditors' genders. H_0 hypothesis could not be rejected (p=0.257). Although the average of the female auditors was a bit higher in comparison to the males' in that TAS/TFRS made audit procedures difficult, it did not make a sense statistically. The auditors divided according to their genders pointed out that TAS/TFRS make the audit procedure difficult by agreeing to the statements in the difficulty factor equally.

5.5.4 Views of the auditors to the difficulty of TAS/TFRS in terms of their ages

H_0: *In terms of auditors'ages, there are not any significant differences between the averages of the statements regarding the difficulty of TAS/TFRS.*
H_1: *In terms of auditors'ages, there are significant differences between the averages of the statements regarding the difficulty of TAS/TFRS.*

One-way variance analysis was used in the examination of the hypotheses created. The differences between the averages of the auditors' responses to the difficulty factor were examined in terms of their ages. See the table below for the analysis result.

Table 9. The differences between the age ranges in terms of the difficulty factor

	Sum of squares	Degree of freedom	Mean squares	F	Significance
Between-groups	.834	2	.417	.756	.475
Within-group	25.358	46	.551		
Total	26.191	48			

* $\alpha = 0.05$

Between the auditors' ages, in terms of the general average of difficulty factor, a significant difference at 0.05 significance level could not be found. H_0 hypothesis could not be rejected (p=0.475). Although the auditors in the age range of 36-45 agreed with the statement that TAS/TFRS made the audit procedure difficulty more than the auditors in the other age ranges, it did not make a sense statistically. The auditors divided according to their age ranges pointed out that TAS/TFRS made the audit procedure difficult by agreeing to the statements in the difficulty factor equally.

5.5.5 Views of the auditors to the difficulty of TAS/TFRS in terms of their titles

H_0: *In terms of the auditors' titles, there are not any significant differences between the averages of the statements regarding the difficulty of TAS/TFRS.*

H_1: *In terms of the auditors' titles, there are significant differences between the averages of the statements regarding the difficulty of TAS/TFRS.*

One-way variance analysis was used in the examination of the hypotheses created. The differences between the averages of the auditors' responses to the difficulty factor were examined in terms of their titles. See the table below for the analysis result.

Table 10. The differences between the auditors' titles in terms of the difficulty factor

	Sum of squares	Degree of freedom	Mean squares	F	Significance
Between-groups	1.756	4	.439	.790	.538
Within-group	24.435	44	.555		
Total	26.191	48			

* α = 0.05

Between the auditors' titles, in terms of the general average of the difficulty factor, a significant difference at 0.05 significance level could not be found. H_0 hypothesis could not be rejected (p=0.538). The senior auditors' average, concerning TAS/TFRS made audit procedures difficult, was a bit higher than the other auditors'. However, it did not make a sense statistically. The auditors divided according to their titles stated that TAS/TFRS made audit procedures difficult by agreeing to the statements in the difficulty factor equally.

5.5.6 Views of the auditors to the difficulty of TAS/TFRS in terms of their service periods

H_0: In terms of auditors' service periods, there are not any significant differences between the averages of the statements regarding the difficulty of TAS/TFRS.

H_1: In terms of the auditors service periods, there are significant differences between the averages of the statements regarding the difficulty of TAS/TFRS.

One-way variance analysis was used in the examination of the hypotheses created. The differences between the averages of the auditors' responses to difficulty factor were examined in terms of their service periods. Below is the table showing the analysis result.

Table 11. The differences between the auditors' service periods in terms of the difficulty factor

	Sum of squares	Degree of freedom	Mean squares	F	Significance
Between-gropus	1.173	2	.586	1.078	.349
Within-group	25.018	46	.544		
Total	26.191	48			

* α = 0.05

A significant difference at 0.05 significance level could not be found between the auditors' service periods in terms of the general average of the difficulty factor. H_0 hypothesis could not be rejected (p=0.349). The auditors divided according to their service periods point out that TAS/TFRS make audit procedure difficult by agreeing to the statements in difficulty factor equally.

5.5.7 Views of the auditors to the difficulty of TAS/TFRS in terms
*   of their educational status*

H_0: *There are not any significant differences between the averages of the statements regarding the difficulty of TAS/TFRS in terms of the auditors' educational status.*

H_1: *There are significant differences between the averages of the statements regarding the difficulty of TAS/TFRS in terms of the auditors' educational status.*

T test was used for the independent samples to examine the hypotheses created. The differences between the averages of the auditors' responses to the difficulty factor were examined in terms of their educational status. See the table below for the analysis result.

Table 12. The differences between the auditors' educational status in terms of the difficulty factor

	Sum of squares	Degree of freedom	Mean Squares	F	Significance
Between-groups	.076	1	.076	.137	.713
Within-group	26.115	47	.556		
Total	26.191	48			

* α = 0.05

A significant difference at 0.05 significance level between the auditors' educational status in terms of the general average of difficulty factor could not be found. H_0 hypothesis could not be rejected (p=0.713). The auditors divided according to their educational status stated that TAS/TFRS made the audit procedure difficult by agreeing to the statements in difficulty factor equally.

6. Conclusion

Accounting information is important for the individuals in a business as much as for the relevant individuals out of the business and for some other organizations. Accounting standards are required so that the finance markets, in many different regions around the world, can function as a single market which has the similar rules and regulations. Also, they are essential for the investors who will make investments, in that they can make worldwide comparisons and evaluations. Besides, they provide accurate and quality information to be produced. The comparison of the financial statements composed without accounting standards is not reliable; moreover, it causes to take wrong decisions. Thanks to the accounting standards, it becomes easy for the investors to make international investments in foreign capital markets. Since the financial reports are composed according to the certain standards, they become understandable and comparable. As a result of this, misunderstandings are eliminated and firm managers, relevant individuals and organizations can take sound decisions. In addition, the individuals who practise the standards must know the standards very well and perform them properly.

Accounting information must be understandable enough to reflect the current state clearly, impartially and comparably. The accounting information presented needs to be evaluated by the third parties according to the certain standards in the sense that whether it reflects the facts, which provides the reliability of the information, as well. At this point, independent audits are required. Because these evaluations are carried out by this way. What lies under independent audits is the necessity of the public disclosure. In addition to this, independent audits also play an instructive role in that they give insight into the future decisions to be taken by reflecting a business' real state.

According to the findings obtained at the end of the questionnaire study, which was conducted in accordance with the main purpose of the study to measure the effects of Turkish Accounting Standards on independent audit procedures and was applied to the audit firms affiliated to the CMB in Turkey, it is seen that the independent auditors need continuing training even if they have enough information about Turkish Accounting Standards. Also, it is concluded that the vast majority of the independent auditors want to improve themselves much more, because they are inclined to the training subjects. The audited firms, however, are not able to practise the acounting standards in their financial statements and in the accounting applications at the required level. Accordingly, the firm acountants need to be trained continually. That auditors and firm accountants are trained about TAS/TFRS will enhance the audit quality.

Turkish Accounting Standards offer various options in reflecting financial events to the information system and in the evaluation of them. And business can choose the option which is suitable for their structure. That these options are known by the auditors increases the quality and the efficacy of the audit.

According to the findings, the auditors consider Turkish Accounting Standards as modern, reliable and sufficient to answer the purpose. That the independent auditors' think in this way is also a positive situatiton in that IAS/IFRS have been adopted and applied in many countries around the world and in the EU. This situation affects our country's integration with the world markets and the EU accession process positively, as well.

The computer assisted auditing techniques provide an auditor to work faster and more effectively. Within the frame of the findings, the need for the computer assisted auditing techniques has increased after TAS/TFRS. This case indicates that the work load of auditors has increased more after TAS/TFRS.

In addition, the findings point out that there has not been any increase in the fees received in return for auditing services after TAS/TFRS applications. But there has been an increase in the cost of audit operations. That there has been an increse in the cost of audit operations, although there has not been an increase in fees taken in return for audit services, is a negative statement for the audit firms and for their auditors. This increase in the cost of the audit operations, also, indicates that an increase in the work load of the auditors may happen.

Finally, when we evaluate the findings obtained from this study, it is concluded that Turkish Accounting Standards applications make audit procedures difficult; however, Turkish Accounting Standards applications must be absolutely carried out properly.

References

Akgül, A. & Çevik, O. (2003) *İstatistiksel Analiz Teknikleri: SPSS'te İşletme Yönetimi Uygulamaları [Statistical Analysis Techniques: Management Applications in SPSS]*, Emek Ofset Ltd. Şti.,Ankara.

Aksoy, T. (2005) "Finansal Muhasebe ve Raporlama Standartlarında Uyumlaştırma ve UMS/UFRS Bazında Küresel Muhasebe Standartları Setine Yöneliş Eğilimi *[Harmonization in Financial Accounting and Reporting Standards and Trend for Tending to Global Accounting Standards Set on IAS / IFRS Basis]*", *Mali Çözüm Dergisi*, vol. 71: 182-199

Aksoy, T. (2006) *Tüm Yönleriyle Denetim: AB ile Müzakere ve Uyum Sürecinde Denetimde Yeni Bir Paradigma [Audit with all Aspects: A New Paradigm in Audit in Negotiation and Compliance Process with EU]*, Cilt 1, Genişletilmiş 2. Baskı, Yetkin Yayınları, Ankara.

Alkan, G. İ. & Doğan, O. (2012) "Uluslararası Finansal Raporlama Standartları'nın Finansal Rasyolara Kısa ve Uzun Dönemli Etkileri: İMKB'de Bir Araştırma [Short and Long Term Effects of International Financial Reporting Standards on Financial Ratios: A Research in İMKB]", *Muhasebe ve Finansman Dergisi*, vol. 54: 87-100.

Altunışık, R., Coşkun, R., Bayraktaroğlu, S. & Yıldırım, E. (2004) *Sosyal Bilimlerde Araştırma Yöntemleri SPSS Uygulamalı[Research Methods in Social Sciences with SPSS Practical]*, Genişletilmiş 3. Baskı, Sakarya Kitabevi, Sakarya.

Arıkan, Y. (2011) "Kamu Gözetimi, Muhasebe ve Denetim Standartları Kurumu *[Public Oversight, Accounting and Auditing Standards Authority]*", *Mali Çözüm Dergisi*, vol. 107: 7-18.

Barth, M. E., Landsman, W. R. & Lang, M. H. (2008) "International accounting standards and accounting quality", *Journal of Accounting Research*, vol. 46(3): 467-498.

Başpınar, A. (2004) "Türkiye'de ve Dünya'da Muhasebe Standartlarının Oluşumuna Genel Bir Bakış *[A General Outlook on Formation of Accounting Standards in Turkey and in the World]*" *Maliye Dergisi*, vol. 146: 42-57.

Beke, J. (2012) "Effects of the Application of Accounting Standards on Company Performance: A Review", *International Journal of Management*, vol. 29(3): 110-124.

Bostancı, S. (2002) "Küreselleşen Muhasebede Standartlaşma ve Türkiye Muhasebe Standartları Kurulu *[Standardization in Globalizing Accounting and Turkish Accounting Standards Board]*", *Mali Çözüm Dergisi*, vol. 59: 71-81.

Chiapello, E. & Medjad, K. (2009) "An unprecedented privatisation of mandatory standard-setting: The case of European accounting policy", *Critical Perspectives on Accounting*, vol. 20: 448-468.

Çankaya, F. & Dinç, E. (2012) "Türkiye Finansal Raporlama Standartlarının Uygulama Başarısını Etkileyen Faktörler: Bağımsız Denetçiler Üzerine Bir Araştırma [Factors Affecting Application Success of Turkish Financial Reporting Standards: A Research on Independent Auditors]", *Süleyman Demirel Üniversitesi İktisadi ve İdari Bilimler Fakültesi Dergisi*, vol. 17(1): 81-102.

Çelen, E. (2001) " Bağımsız Denetimin Önemi, Yararları ve Kamuyu Aydınlatma İlkesi *[Importance, Benefits of Audit and Principle of Public Disclosure]*", *Mali Çözüm Dergisi,* vol. 55: 185-191.

Çiftci, Y. & Erserim, A. (2008*) Muhasebe Standartlarında Uluslararası Uyumlaştırma Çalışmaları ve Türkiye'deki Durumun İncelenmesi [International Harmonization Studies in Accounting Standards and Examining the Situation in Turkey]*, Uluslararası Sermaye Hareketleri ve Gelişmekte Olan Piyasalar Uluslararası Sempozyumu Bildirileri Kitabı, Balıkesir Üniversitesi, Bandırma İİBF, vol. 233-242, Bandırma.

Damant, D. (2003) "Accounting Standards-A New Area", *Journal of Balance Sheet*, vol. 11(1): 9-20.

Dönmez, A. & Ersoy, A. (2006) "Bağımsız Denetim Firmaları Bakış Açısıyla Türkiye Bağımsız Dış Denetim Sisteminin Değerlendirilmesi *[Evaluation of Turkey's Independent External Auditing System with Perspective of Independent Auditing Firms]*", *Türk Dünyası Sosyal Bilimler Dergisi (bilig)*, vol. 36: 69-91.

Dunn, L. J. (2002) "Harmonization of Financial Reporting and Auditing Across Cultural Boundaries: An Examination of 201 Company Financial Reports", *International Journal of Auditing,* vol. 6: 265-275.

Elitaş, C., Karakoç, M. & Özdemir, S. (2011) "Muhasebe Meslek Mensupları Perspektifinden Türkiye Muhasebe Standartları [Turkish Accounting Standards from the Perspective of Accountant Professionals]", *World Of IFRS-UFRS Dünyası Dergisi*, vol. 5: 1-14

George, E. T., Ferguson, C. B. & Spear, N. A. (2013) "How Much Does IFRS Cost? IFRS Adoption and Audit Fees", *The Accounting Review*, vol. 88(2): 429-462.

Güler, E. (2006) *Bağımsız Dış Denetim Süreci Kurumsal-Sosyal Sorumluluk İlişkisi Bankacılık Sektörü Uygulaması [Independent External Auditing Process Corporate-Social Responsibility Relation Banking Sector Application],* unpublished PhD thesis, Marmara Üniversitesi Bankacılık ve Sigortacılık Enstitüsü, İstanbul.

Güredin, E. (2007) *Denetim ve Güvence Hizmetleri: SMMM ve YMM'lere Yönelik İlkeler ve Teknikler[Audit and Assurance Services: Principles and Techniques for CPAs (Certified Public Accountant) and CAs (Chartered Accountants)],* 11. Bası, Arıkan Basım Yayım Dağıtım Ltd. Şti., İstanbul.

İbiş, C. & Akarçay, A. (2003) "IOSCO Deklarasyonu ve Menkul Kıymet Borsalarında IAS'ın Uygulanması Süreci [IOSCO Declaration and Implementation Process of IAS in Stock Exchanges]", *6. Muhasebe Denetimi Sempozyumu*, 16-19 April 2003, İstanbul.

Jeanjean, T. & Stolowy, H. (2008) "Do accounting standards matter? An exploratory analysis of earnings management before and after IFRS adoption", *Journal of Accounting and Public Policy*, vol. 6: 480-494.

Kandemir, T. & Akbulut, H. (2013) "Bağımsız Denetimin Etkinliğinde Denetimden Sorumlu Komitenin Rolü: Türkiye'deki Bağımsız Denetim Firmalarına Yönelik Bir Araştırma [Role of the Audit Committee in Effectiveness of Independent Audit: A Research on Independent Audit Companies in Turkey]", *Uluslararası Yönetim İktisat ve İşletme Dergisi,* vol. 20: 37-55.

Morril, C. & Morrill, J. (2003) "Internal Auditors and the External Audit: A Transaction Cost Perspective", *Managerial Auditing Journal,* vol. 18(6/7): 490 – 504.

Morris, R. D., Gray, S. J., Pickering, J. & Aisbitt, S. (2013) "Preparers' perceptions of the costs and benefits of IFRS: Evidence from Australia's implementation experience" *Accounting Horizons*, vol. 28(1): 143-173.

Oksay, S. & Acar, O. (2005) *Sigorta Sektöründe Uluslararası Finansal Raporlama Standartları: Kurumlar ve Standartların Özetleri [International Financial Reporting Standards in Insurance Sector: Summary of Institutions and Standards],* Sigorta Araştırma ve İnceleme Yayınları – 3., İstanbul.

Önçü, S., Taner, B., Karasioğlu, F. & Arıcı, H. (1997) "Bağımsız Denetçilerin Yetki ve Sorumlulukları *[]*", *III. Türkiye Muhasebe Denetimi Sempozyumu*, 30 April- 4 May 1997, Antalya.

Seviğ V. (2006, Mayıs 1) Türkiye Muhasebe Standartları *[*Turkish Accounting Standards*]*, Dünya Gazetesi.

Ulusan, H. (2005) "Menkul Kıymet Borsalarına Kayıtlı Şirketlerde IAS/IFRS' nin Kabulü veya IAS/IFRS' ye Uyum *[*IAS / IFRS Adoption or IAS / IFRS Compliance in Companies Registered to Stock Exchanges*]*", *Muhasebe ve Denetime Bakış Dergisi,* vol. 5(15): 9-30.

Türk, Z. (2008) "Denetim Firmalarının Sundukları Bağımsız Denetim Hizmetinin Kalitesi ve Müşteri Tatmini *[*Quality of Independent Audit Service of Audit Firms and Customer Satisfaction*]*", *T.C Selçuk Üniversitesi İktisadi ve İdari Bilimler Fakültesi Dergisi*, vol. 15: 35-52.

Ulusoy, Y. (2005) "Halka Açık Anonim Ortaklıklarda Bağımsız Dış Denetimin Fonksiyonları ve Denetçi Bağımsızlığı *[*Functions of Independent External Audit and Auditor Independence in Publicly-Held Corporations*]*", *Dokuz Eylül Üniversitesi Hukuk Fakültesi Dergisi*, vol. 7(2): 265-300.

Türkiye Muhasebe Standartları Kurulu Faaliyet Raporu *[*Activity Report of the Turkish Accounting Standards Board*]* 2006, http://kgk.gov.tr/contents/files/rapor_2006.pdf., 28 March 2016.

Türkiye Muhasebe Standartları Kurulu Faaliyet Raporu *[*Activity Report of the Turkish Accounting Standards Board*]* 2007, http://kgk.gov.tr/contents/files/2007_Faaliyet_Raporu.pdf., 28 March 2016.

Yavaşoğlu, M. (2001) *Sermaye Piyasası Mevzuatında Bağımsız Denetim Yorum Uygulama ve Açıklamalar [Independent Auditing in Capital Market Legislation Comment Application and Remarks]*, Seçkin Yayıncılık, Ankara.

8

The impacts of introduction of VAT on the audit profession and economy in the UAE: Auditors' perspective

Aisha Saderuddin[a] and Yasser Barghathi[a,1]

[a]*Heriot-Watt University Dubai, UAE.*

Abstract: Commencing 1st January 2018, Value Added Tax (VAT) was made effective in the UAE. The decision was made in light of the fall in oil prices and with the aim of diversifying the country's revenue to non-hydrocarbon sectors. This paper examines the impacts of introducing VAT on the audit profession and the economy in the UAE. Unlike previous studies which have viewed this topic from a business or consumer perspective, this paper examines it from an auditor's perspective. Given that this topic relates to a new policy and there isn't much literature available on it, this study explores the auditors' perceptions about the implications of this new policy on both; audit profession and the economy. This paper employs semi-structured interviews with auditors from both Big-Four as well as Non-Big-Four audit firms in order to collect data. This research, apart from being a timely and trending topic, may be useful to academicians, tax specialists, auditors, businesses and regulatory bodies. The findings of the study suggest that auditors are optimistic about VAT implementation in the UAE with respect to the growth in the economy in the long run. However, they have mixed perceptions regarding the audit profession and believe that there is no material impact on it due to VAT implementation.

Keywords: VAT, auditors, UAE, perceptions, economy, qualitative, Big 4 and non-Big 4.

---

[1] *Corresponding author*: Social of Science School, Department of Accountancy, Economics and Finance, Heriot-Watt University Dubai, UAE.
Email addresses: y.barghathi@hw.ac.uk

1. Introduction

Value added tax is a vital source of revenue for nations all over the world. Apart from its significant impacts on the GDP, it is one of the most widely accepted means of indirect taxation. VAT can help the UAE government diversify its revenues so that it may reduce its dependency on the oil sector. From 1st January 2018, the United Arab Emirates (UAE) Government has imposed a VAT of 5% (Ministry of Finance, 2017). This paper aims to understand the impacts of introduction of VAT on the audit profession in the UAE as well as the economy as a whole. VAT is the first form of taxation being adopted by UAE and thus makes it an interesting research topic.

The International Monetary Fund (IMF) played an important role in influencing UAE to adopt a VAT. Though the issues of implementation, compliance and general increase of standard of living will be present, VAT will bring about new employment opportunities and foster economic growth of the nation. Research is silent on the auditor's perspective of impacts of introduction of VAT on the economy and this will be the dimension adopted by this paper.

The six member-nations of the Organization of the Petroleum Exporting Countries (OPEC) also realized that there was a pressing need to resort to renewable sources of energy instead of oil as there is a rising awareness globally about environmental issues such as pollution. Moreover, since oil reserves will run out in a few years, the nations need to identify means to cope with this depletion, as seen in Figure 1:

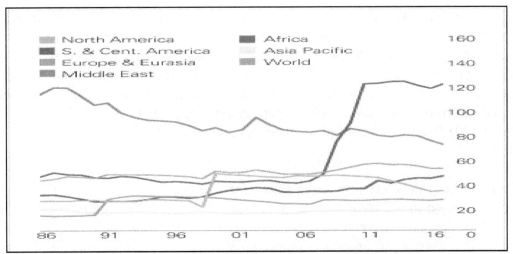

Figure 1. Reserves to Production (R/P) Ratios History (Years)
(Source: BP, 2017)

In 2008, an initiative called Gulf Common Market was approved for launch by the GCC in order to improve trade and investment through the provision of a single market (Al Murad, 2017). To make this initiative a smoother process, the GCC decided to introduce a single rate of VAT applicable to all goods and services with the exception of basic necessities such as food, healthcare and education (PwC, 2017).

The UAE follows a system of fees rather than taxes such as sponsorship fee of employees, license fee etc. There is no income or corporate tax which adds on to the willingness of organizations to startup businesses in the UAE. Moreover, 'Free Zone Areas' have been set up which are characterized by a tax-free environment and confer free customs duty benefits (PwC, 2015). Taxation aims to, among other things, support the economic growth. According to economic theory the economic system of any country will be affected by its tax policy (Gober & Burns, 1997; Stoilova, 2017).

This paper seeks to investigate the implication of VAT policy on UAE, in particular, the paper tries to answer the following questions:
   a) What potential implications does the introduction of VAT have on the audit profession in the UAE?
   b) What are the likely impacts of introduction of VAT on the UAE economy?

A country's economy is affected by the taxation system of the country and therefore it is crucially important for regulators to assess the implication of any taxes adopted by the country (Gober & Burns, 1997). According to Stoilova (2017), conventional economic theory holds that taxation may create distortion may adversely affect the economic growth.

To the best of our knowledge, this paper is different as it may be the first empirical one after the implementation of VAT in the UAE. Literature has been silent with regards to the impact of VAT on the audit profession and practices as well as the impacts on the economy from an auditor's perspective. This study aims to tackle this gap in the literature. Previous studies on VAT in relation to the UAE have been carried out from a business or consumer perspective such as Gilder (2017) and Al Murad (2017) and those cited in them such as Al Mehrazi (2014) and Mears (2016).

The findings of the current research suggest that auditors are optimistic about VAT implementation in the UAE with respect to the growth in the economy in the long run. However, they have mixed perceptions regarding the audit profession and believe that there is no material impact on it due to VAT implementation. Such finding may be of interest to some stakeholders. For example, regulators whose concern would be the consequences of any new economic policy.

The papers is structured as follows: the following section, Section 2, reports on the literature review about VAT. Section 3, discusses research methodology and methods while Section 4 analyses and discuss the findings. Section 5 concludes the study and limitation and further research recommendations are reported in Section 6.

2. Literature Review

2.1 VAT- Origin and Definition

In 1918, a German businessman by the name of Dr. Wilhelm von Siemens originated the idea of VAT while Maurice Laure who was the Joint Director of the French Tax Authority, was the first to implement it in 1954 (Charlet & Owens, 2010: 943). France was identified as the first country to adopt VAT (Shenk & Oldman, 2007). VAT was rarely heard of beyond France till around fifty years ago (Keen & Lockwood, 2007). More than 150 countries have implemented VAT and it is an extensively recognized indirect taxation system globally (Brown & Gale, 2012) which accounts for at least 20% of the entire tax revenue (Grinberg, 2009).

Basic and special rates for certain goods and services along with exemption for some economic activities, good and services is the structure of many VAT systems (Kamruddin, 2012). The definition of VAT has been scrutinized by many academics (Bird, 2005; Charlet & Buydens, 2012; Keen, 2013; Onwuchekwa & Aruwa, 2014) which advocates that it is an indirect tax which is charged on goods and services consumption; levied on the value of imports; and the value added on goods and services provided by one entity to another whilst it reaches its ultimate customer (Xing & Whalley, 2014). In a multistage production, businesses engage in upstream and downstream transactions in order to produce the final product. Indirect taxes are levied by the government on the production or sale of goods at every stage. In order to prevent double taxation, VAT is devised to tax the "value-added" in each step (Xing & Whalley, 2014).

Timing is critical with VAT. The time of supply will decide if a supply will be subject to VAT as well as determine the rate which is chargeable. This is commonly referred to as the 'tax point'. In the context of the UK and in particular VAT on land, a tax point is formed for a contract on sale of land in the sole instance of the deposit being taken as agent for the seller and not as a stakeholder. In such a scenario, only the deposit can be charged for. Since the land was barren at the contract stage, VAT was exempted on the deposit. A noteworthy point is that the final use of land was immaterial in this scenario (Harper, 1995).

The greatest drawback of VAT is substantial administrative burden which implies that the cost of tax administration as well as taxation are high. However, the benefits include neutral effect of taxation, deterrence of tax evasion and greater transparency (Hajdúchová et al., 2015).

2.2 Impacts of VAT on the economy

Limitations of government expenditure, ineffective tax collection and international tax competition may pose a constraint on policymakers. This may lead to implementation of more consumption taxes such as VAT. Such taxes are frequently recommended to improve compliance (Weller & Rao, 2010). Studies on VAT stress on the significance of the circumstances under which VAT is completely optimal wherein an efficient tax structure necessitates the advancement of VAT and income taxes in the case of Romania (Keen, 2008; Zee, 2008; Pantazi & Straoanu, 2011).

Taxes are a vital portion of state budget revenues and VAT accounts for majority of the income from taxation in Slovak Republic. As per a study conducted, it is seen that regardless of the gradual rise of tax revenue to state budget, the portion of VAT on total tax revenues did not increase even though the rate was increased by one percentage point. On analysis of the effectiveness of VAT, it is comprehended that the tax revenues are multiple times greater than the expenditures for tax collection, and tax collection can be concluded as effective (Hajdúchová et al., 2015). VAT has significantly contributed to fiscal revenue in developing countries such as China as compared to developed countries (Xing & Whalley, 2014). In developing countries, where tax revenue is much-needed, VAT is expected to improve efforts to assemble it through efficiency in tax compliance and administration. However, the opponents to this school of thought contrast this view by saying that there is no proof regarding how the government uses this revenue (Keen & Lockwood, 2007). This view is the true in the context of the United States (only OECD country without VAT) where the presidential panel was unsure of whether to adopt VAT or not: "Some panelists were.... concerned that introducing a VAT would lead to higher total tax collections over time and facilitate the development of a larger federal government—in other words, that the VAT would be a 'money machine'" (President's Advisory Panel, 2006. 192).

Only two studies have considered the effect of VAT on the efficiency of and the income generated by the entire tax system. A primary evaluation of the impact on revenue of a few VAT implementations was done through case study by Nellor (1987). In the most recent past, Ebrill et al. (2001) have observed the same, however, using a single cross-section of data. Moreover, all the papers cited above consider the existence or absence or a VAT as exogenous which may result in a biased conclusion.

An empirical study involving an uneven panel of 143 countries over 26 years showed that VAT adoption is linked with a long-term rise in the overall revenue-to-GDP ratio of around 4.5% (Keen & Lockwood, 2007). Several researchers have claimed that VAT can be progressive when basic consumption items have the provision to be excluded (Munoz and Sang-Wook 2003; Decoster, 2005; Jenkins, Jenkins & Kuo, 2006). With respect to CEE-5 countries, for the period 1995-2005, a rise in VAT rate positively affects economic growth in the long run. On the short run, however, this rise will cause consumption tax collection difficulties which will decrease the GDP rate (Simionescu & Albu, 2016).

2.3 VAT in the UAE

VAT has been the flagship of tax reform in many emerging nations apart from extensive implementation in sub-Saharan Africa. In the recent decades, the ascent of VAT has been the most crucial growth in tax policy and administration. This has influenced Libya, Syria and several Caribbean countries, apart from UAE which is our point of interest, to consider adoption of VAT in the near future (Keen & Lockwood, 2007). VAT has been found to be a good means to increase resources and modernize the tax system in totality (Ebrill *et al.*, 2001).

The role of IMF is also quite significant in the spread of VAT. The prospect of embracing VAT substantially increases with partaking in a non-crisis IMF program. Moreover, if a large percentage of other nations in the region have already implemented VAT, this may act as an additional influence. Fascinatingly, results strongly suggest that VAT implementation is less likely in more open economies (Keen & Lockwood, 2007).

Value Added Tax is deemed to be the most stable source of revenue which has the least negative consequences on investments. UAE, which is a macro-fiscal environment, a rate such as 5% which is minimal could be considered. Revenue can be raised at low efficiency costs by means of broad-based consumption taxes such as VAT (IMF, 2015).

Simultaneously, there would be comparatively insignificant equity consequences as the taxes are minimal and the expenditures by government are backed by oil revenue. Tax administration would receive a substantial and positive lift. VAT yield is estimated to be 2.7% of non-hydrocarbon GDP (IMF, 2013). VAT collection in other regions include 1.5% of GDP in Algeria to around 8% in Chile and Norway from oil exporters, as seen in Figure 2 below (IMF, 2015).

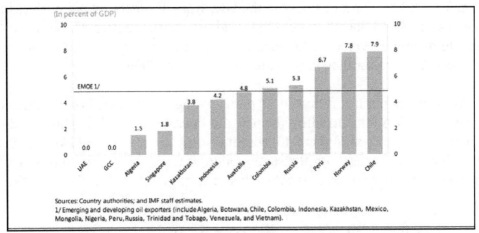

Figure 2. VAT Revenue (2014)
(Source: IMF, 2015)

Commencing 1st January 2018, VAT has been introduced across UAE at a nominal rate of 5% (Ministry of Finance, 2017). Debates on whether a uniform or differentiated rate of VAT are extensive since there is constant progress in the optimal tax theory (Ramsey, 1927; Atkinson & Stiglitz, 1972; Sadka, 1977; Keen, 2007). Public services such as schools, roads, waste management etc. are rendered by the UAE Federal and Emirate governments which are financed by the government budgets (Ministry of Finance, 2017). Empirical evidence doesn't support the notion that public expenditure effectively serves the requirements of target groups (Filmer & Pritchett, 1999; Gauthier & Wane, 2008).

UAE needs to harmonize its VAT implementation with other GCC countries as it is a part of "The Economic Agreement between the GCC States" and "The GCC Customs Union". Historically, these countries have worked together to propose and adopt new public policies which they identify as working in the best interest of the region (Ministry of Finance, 2017). According to IMF, the government will be able to diversify its sources of revenue as well as reduce reliance on oil and other hydrocarbons which marks a growing economy. Around two-thirds of the GDP is attributed to non-hydrocarbon undertakings. The volatility of these exports which is 68% of entire exports of goods which is facilitating the growth drive even with the dip of oil prices post June 2014 and appreciation of the local currency owing to the fixed peg to the US dollar (Al Mansoori, 2017).

Non-hydrocarbon exports increased by 3.4% in 2015, and 4% in 2016 which gave a lift to the progress of export-oriented trades. In terms of GDP growth, it slowed down in 2015 to 3.2% and 2.7% in 2016. However, it is expected to recoup to 3.1% in 2017 and 3.4% in 2018 due to improved oil prices and a spike in growth globally (Al Mansoori, 2017). The Gulf-wide VAT scheme will omit VAT on key food items, education and healthcare according to Younis Haji Al Khoori who is the under-secretary of the UAE's Ministry of Finance. A zero rate will be applied to the education and healthcare sector. Tax is exempted from around 94 foodstuffs (Kundnaney, 2017). For a business in the UK, from an international business point of view, paying VAT locally would make administration easier. However, if there is scope to handle it overseas, the business may strategically base itself in a nation where the VAT is lesser than that of the UK (Newark, 2006).

The UAE government has followed its policy along these lines. Foreign businesses can recover the VAT incurred by them while operating in UAE. This has a dual-goal wherein it motivates them to continue operations in the UAE as well as provides local businesses with the same opportunity of being able to recover VAT when operating in other nations who charge a higher rate (Ministry of Finance, 2017).

Government entities will be subject to VAT for their supplies which safeguards that they are not unfairly advantaged in comparison to private entities. However, certain supplies produced by government entities for which they are sole suppliers or there is no private competition, will be exempted from the scope of VAT (Ministry of Finance, 2017). Standard rate of VAT will be applicable to commercial property (leases and sales). Residential property (leases and sales) will be exempted from the standard rate except for the first sale of a new property, in which case, the zero rate of VAT will apply. VAT is exempted for bare land and residential rents. However, this exemption to rent applies only when the lease exceeds six months (Nair, 2017).

However, studies on the implications of VAT on cross-border trade suggest that other than high-income nations, export performance and openness are both inversely related to the existence of VAT as well as the degree of revenue dependence on it (Desai & Hines Jr., 2005). However, the above study considers the presence or absence or a VAT as external which may result in a biased conclusion. Newark (2006), in his study, suggests that VAT isn't confined to the accounts division only. It has extended its reach to the boardroom where its repercussions on any new business deals or undertakings are considered. Initial checks include whether or not the good/service is subject to VAT (Newark, 2006). When VAT wasn't even due and the customer can't reclaim it, it becomes quite relevant.

An unnecessary VAT charge may impact the product's competitive positioning which is crucial for retail businesses (Newark, 2006). The aim of businesses in the UAE should be to address VAT implications at the boardroom level instead of limiting it to the accounts department which can help minimize losses.

There are various technical and administrative hardship for authorities. These include drafting detailed regulations, registering tax paying companies and creating bureaucracies to supervise the system. Some specialists also expect VAT to slow down economic growth which deepens the current economic situation (Khaleej Times, 2017)[1].

The consumption pattern of women is different which may lead to a gender bias due to VAT. Apart from nutrition, education and health, women are likely to purchase more goods and services than men. These include luxury items, entertainment and items of daily use. In addition to "pink tax", which already renders products of girls and women more expensive as compared to men, VAT would aggravate this inequality. Thus, the impact of VAT may be weighted towards women despite exemptions and zero ratings (Kundnaney, 2017).

Gender-specific expenditures include beauty services, cosmetics and sanitary products. Sanitary product taxation has been a debated topic in various nations in the past. As of now, there is no information regarding this in relation to UAE.

Despite these drawbacks, VAT will serve as a new source of employment with the creation of employment opportunities for men and women in VAT consultancies, thus generating a new industry of employment for oil-based economies (Kundnaney, 2017).

3. Research methodology and methods

This paper falls under the case study design which includes a detailed and rigorous analysis of a single case (Bryman & Bell, 2011). It is a very popular approach adopted in business research (Eisenhardt & Graebner, 2007). Researchers who adopt a case study design tend to favour qualitative approaches involving participant observation and interviews. If a qualitative approach is adopted, it may result in an inductive approach between theory and research. Lee *et al.* (2007) believe that particularization rather than generalization is one of the key strengths of case studies. Thus, the aim of case study analysis is to emphasize on the individuality of the case as well as develop a deep understanding of its complexity (Bryman & Bell, 2011).

Qualitative methods focus on context and provide a more holistic account of the reality (Liamputtong, 2013). This means that the outcomes will differ from person to person which results in a wide range of answers, thus enabling the researcher to look at the larger picture (Holloway, 1997). The key advantage of qualitative method is that it discloses the "natural, interactive and personal" side of human attitude.

The above discussion shows that an inductive approach facilitated through a qualitative methodology is most appropriate. The inductive approach moves from particular observations to broader theories and generalizations (Saunders *et al.*, 2012). The method of data collection adopted under the qualitative methodology is interviews. Interviews are one of the most frequently used methods for collecting data in qualitative researches (Symon & Cassell, 2012). The interview questions for this study can be found in Appendix 1.

The advantage of semi-structured interviews is that it has a certain degree of flexibility which allows the questions to be modified according to the respondents so that the quality of the data can be enhanced. A total of sixteen interviews have been conducted using both traditional as well as modern techniques of interviewing which are face-to-face (9) and telephone (1) and Google Forms (6) respectively. Majority of the interviews were conducted face-to-face. However, to suit the convenience of some of the interviewees, telephone interviews and electronic interviews via Google Forms have also been used. Since the interviews have been conducted during the demanding season for auditors (year-end audits), many found the electronic interviews easier. The time frame for conducting all the interviews is one month. Telephone interviews are considered convenient, speedy and cost-effective (Saunders *et al.*, 2012). As per Morgan and Symon (2004), electronic interviews fall into two categories which are synchronous (in real time) and asynchronous (offline), as seen in the next page:

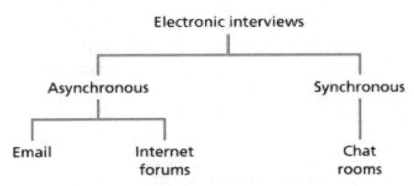

Figure 3. Types of electronic interviews
(Source: Saunder *et al.*, 2012)

This study has adopted asynchronous electronic interviews via internet forums (Google Forms). The first section of the form requires some inputs regarding personal details. The following section has all the interview questions. Once all the interviews are completed, Google Forms transcribes the responses into spreadsheets which is used for data analysis.

The first five questions of the interview are related to the audit profession and the remaining four relate to the economy. For the face-to-face and telephone interviews, each one would last between 15-20 minutes as mentioned in the information sheet provided to each interviewee. The consent of the interviewees will be obtained before the interviews so that the sample size remains unaffected. The interviews will be recorded to provide supporting evidence to the written summaries.

Overall, the number of male interviewees were slightly higher than female interviewees. Similarly, the number of non-big-four interviewees were marginally more than the big-four interviewees. The qualifications held by most of the auditors were ICAI, followed by the ACCA. Majority of the interviewees have 2-5 years of experience in the audit profession. The auditors with more than six years of experience held senior posts such as Director, CEO, Partner etc. Table 1 summarised the interviewees' demographic information.

Table 1. Interviewees' demographic information

Respondents				
Non-Big 4	**Code**	**Gender**	**Experience**	**Qualification**
MM	N1	Male	6-10 years	ICAI
RR	N2	Female	6-10 years	ICAI

Respondents				
Non-Big 4	**Code**	**Gender**	**Experience**	**Qualification**
RE	N3	Female	2-5 years	ICAI
MS	N4	Male	2-5 years	ICAI
JM	N5	Female	2-5 years	ACCA
VS	N6	Male	2-5 years	ICAI
KG	N7	Male	2-5 years	Others: CMA, CS
AK	N8	Male	More than 10 years	ICAI
MN	N9	Male	More than 10 years	ICAI
Big 4				
AP	B1	Female	Less than 2 years	ACCA
MD	B2	Male	2-5 years	ACCA
PC	B3	Female	6-10 years	ICAI
AI	B4	Female	2-5 years	ICAI
PS	B5	Female	More than 10 years	ICAI
AV	B6	Male	More than 10 years	ICAI
NN	B7	Male	More than 10 years	ICAI

Before the interviews were done, a pilot study was conducted with three senior audit managers. They provided ideas regarding additional areas that could be studied and this was incorporated into the final set of interview questions. Pilot study is an important step to ensure that the questionnaire is properly devised so as to obtain the most valuable answers from the selected sample (Denscombe, 2014).

4. Data analysis and findings

The data analysis technique that will be employed in this paper is thematic analysis. Thematic analysis is a "method for identifying, analyzing, and reporting patterns (themes) within data" (Braun & Clarke, 2006).

For the face-to-face interviews, the voice recordings were transcribed first. For every interview question, the data was read multiple times and responses with similar traits were grouped together to form sub-themes. These were further grouped together to arrive at the themes which presented a broader picture. Once the themes had been identified, the most relevant and valuable quotes relating to each theme/sub-theme were gathered and subsequently evaluated and the relevant concepts and findings as per previous studies in the literature review was taken into account while analyzing the responses of the interviewees.

The main themes associated with audit are the audit plan, audit quality and audit job market, which form Section 4.2.1- 4.2.3 respectively. Section 4.2.4 provides the overall outlook of the auditors with respect to the audit profession. Section 4.3 analyzes the responses related to the economy with an emphasis on relocation of businesses, relocation of people and impacts on start-ups/new businesses (Section 4.3.1- 4.3.3 respectively). Lastly, the overall perception of the interviewees regarding VAT implementation on the economy as a whole is discussed in Section 4.3.4. These themes will initially discuss the responses provided by the participants, and then trace it back to the literature review as mentioned earlier.

An essential note while progressing through the current research is that the names of the interviewees will be kept confidential throughout this study. References to the Big-Four interviewees will be done using codes beginning with 'B' while 'N' will be used for the Non-Big-Four interviewees throughout this paper. A diagram comprising the sub-themes and a respective noteworthy quote from the interviewees has been presented at the beginning of each theme.

Audit

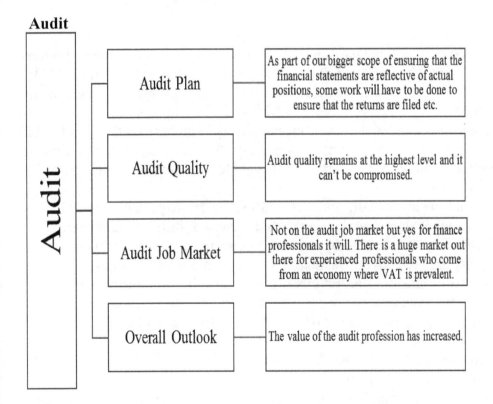

The first theme in this study is audit which will be studied through three sub-themes, namely: audit plan, audit quality and audit job market. These sub-themes were formulated to ensure that all the important aspects pertaining to impacts of VAT implementation on the audit profession were covered.

Audit Plan

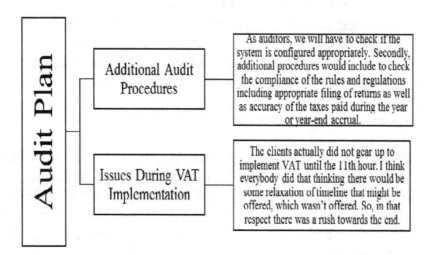

This theme is drawn based on Question 1 of the interview which asked the auditors if the audit plan would be impacted due to the implementation of VAT in the UAE. It also questioned, for instance, whether it would result in any additional audit procedures. 50% of the interviewees believed that the implementation of VAT would definitely affect the audit plan. Interviewee B5 emphasized that VAT falls within the scope of an auditor's work. Additionally, she points out that even though it falls within the scope of audit, they cannot provide complete assurance, as is the case with any other line item:

> "...typically, as an auditor, under the ISAS, we are expected to audit these as well if they are significant and have a significant financial implication ... as part of our bigger scope of ensuring that the financial statements are reflective of actual positions, some work will have to be done to ensure that the returns are filed etc. We obviously don't give a 100% assurance but we'll have to do some sampling and see whether the way they're accounting for VAT is IFRS compliant."

Moreover, Interviewee N6 said that VAT being the first tax in this region would significantly impact the audit plan as:

> "VAT is a new terminology for this market where there are no taxes. So definitely there needs to be a lot of focus emphasized in the audit plan. Once it becomes a routine practice for everyone, the quantum of risk might reduce but initially since the law isn't very clear, there isn't much to rely upon unlike India where there is GST for example, which can be related to VAT. Due to this there is a lot of confusion

going on. All in all, there is a significant increase in the audit plan due to this as well as more procedures."

On the other hand, Interviewee N4 says that it will not impact the audit plan. It is just an additional area to be considered by the auditors:

"...VAT is just a new step which we need to consider, just as other type of steps such as debtors, expenses etc."

Furthermore, Interviewee N7 gave an insight into the changes that VAT will bring to standard practices:

"Earlier customs value was different from our value but now it is the same. So as part of the audit, we need to check if the purchase value is same as that of Customs."

Four out of the sixteen interviewees were unsure about the impact of VAT implementation on the audit plan. Interviewee N5 said that it wouldn't necessarily impact the audit plan since a specialized VAT team is present to handle VAT matters. However, it would result in an increased timeline since a new area has to be taken into consideration:

"It would honestly depend as most of the VAT work is done by the VAT team. However, we need to verify if the VAT has been calculated correctly and as far as the accounting entries are concerned, whether they have been accounted for properly in the books of accounts. This is how they will make payment to the authorities and we would have to report for any mismatches. So, on a normal basis we would just check up on purchases and sales but then now we'll have to make an additional timeline for calculating VAT on those sales and purchases that have been made. It will be an increased timeline definitely."

Overall, the responses pertaining to impact on the audit plan are mixed. The most common response was that rather than a significant impact on the audit plan, it would only result in additional audit procedures. This aspect has been covered in the following section.

Additional Audit Procedures

All of the respondents unanimously agreed that it would result in additional audit procedures to ensure that VAT is computed correctly and VAT laws are being complied with. Interviewee B4 says that:

"The additional audit procedures would start from the test of the IT system where the configuration has to be changed by the clients, for e.g. invoicing (including VAT amount). As auditors, we will have to check if the system is configured appropriately. Secondly, additional procedures would include to check the compliance of the rules and regulations including appropriate filing of returns as well as accuracy of the taxes paid during the year or year-end accrual."

Interviewee B5 said that the quantum of additional procedures depends on the types of transactions the businesses deals with:

"I think it becomes a bit more challenging when you have import-export, transfers within free trade zones and certain specific items such as free samples."

The opinions of Big-Four and Non-Big-Four auditors were similar. They all believed that implementation of VAT would definitely result in added responsibility, additional work and increased timeline.

Issues Regarding VAT Implementation

This theme refers to Question 3 wherein the interviewees were asked if they faced any issues regarding VAT implementation for their clients. 50% of the interviewees said that they faced challenges while implementing VAT. It is worth noting that of these, seven out of eight interviewees belong to the Non-Big-Four category.

The general consensus among Non-Big-Four auditors is that they did face some hurdles while most of the Big-Four auditors (five out of seven) did not face issues with respect to the implementation process. As mention by Interviewee B7, this is because the Big-Four usually takes on larger clients as compared to the Non-Big-four:

"We don't usually do the implementation for the client, the clients would do it themselves and then hire consultants to help them... The big clients started preparing almost 6-9 months before the implementation date... It depended on the nature of the client, their size, complexity and confidence regarding implementation."

Specific to the airline industry, Interviewee N5 said that there was confusion of which VAT category it falls under:

"If you see for an airline company, you don't know if you need a VAT return, or if it's completely exempt, or its zero-rated VAT. It is a service entity but an airline is a zero-rated VAT entity. They don't have "costs", only revenue and expenses, so the difficulty of accounting for VAT arises."

Interviewee N6 gave some insight into the VAT implementation challenges for banks and how the Government has been lenient to ease the process. The interviewee also mentioned the issues faced by the hospitality sector:

"The banks which were earlier given return filings for one month, have now shifted to quarterly... FTA says charge VAT but the other party says the banks can't increase the rates. In the end, money is going from the banker's pockets. With regards to hospitality industry, there was a confusion on whether VAT is applicable to 'Municipal and tourism fee'. There was no clarity and then the Tourism Authority came up with a clarification."

With respect to the insurance industry, Interviewee N7 gave some shocking statistics which show that even though VAT is just 5%, at a large scale it has a huge impact on businesses. The interviewee also said that the businesses in the construction industry, predominantly transacting through post-dated cheques, have to carefully plan their cash flows so that they can correctly account for VAT:

"...the tax and internal documents are different. Thus, a lot of industry complications have been taking place. One of the big hits for the insurance sector is that if they have collected the advances for the policy falling in this year. The client is paying around AED 8 million for VAT. With regards to the construction industry, earlier they used to give and collect PDC's. Now they have to capture and pay VAT. So now they have to plan their cash flows."

The main issue faced by SMEs according to Interviewee N8 was that they may not be technically equipped to ensure a smooth transition:

"...there were some issues with the softwares. With SAP for example, if the IT guys are tech-savvy then it isn't a big task but in other cases they find it difficult to map in the integration. Usually only revenues are linked to tax but now advances are also linked to taxes."

On a slightly different angle, Interviewee N9, through the example of a transport company, said that some of the transactions that may be allowed legally, might not fulfil the VAT criteria:

"A driver may approach such a company and take a vehicle in the name of the company but paid by the driver. It will be the responsibility of the driver and they will make monthly payments but the legal responsibility lies with the company. The issue with this is that the company doesn't know where it is running, how much revenue is being generated etc. The drivers won't make tax invoices. Thus, such sort of issues exist wherein they are legally permitted to work but it doesn't satisfy the VAT requirements."

In such a case, businesses may have to rethink how to accommodate such transactions (e.g. by making sure drivers issue invoices) or may have to put an end to such dealings.

Contrasting the issues mentioned above by the Non-Big-Four auditors, most Big-Four auditors were of the opinion that the main issue faced was that the regulation came out very late and since the law is generic, there was some confusion regarding its interpretation. Moreover, Interviewee B6 said that part of the challenges faced may be attributed to the procrastination and complacency of the businesses:

> "Considering that the Government has been talking about VAT implementation for quite some time, there were a number of news articles that came on VAT but the clients actually did not gear up to implement VAT until the 11th hour. I think everybody did that thinking there would be some relaxation of timeline that might be offered, which wasn't offered. So, in that respect there was a rush towards the end."

All in all, there seems to be some industry-specific issues but the initial panic and confusion has subsided as indicated in the responses. The auditors believe that within a year's time, VAT will become a part of routine. The perspective of auditors with more than 10 years of experience was directed towards issues faced by businesses in general while those with 2-5 years of experience were able to give industry-specific examples. This may be because the latter group has hands-on experience with the clients as compared to those with more than 10 years of experience who hold positions such as directors, CEOs etc.

Audit Quality

This theme relates to Question 2 of the interview which examined whether implementation of VAT would impact the audit quality according to the auditors. The responses were very conflicting. All of the Big-Four auditors said that it would not affect the audit quality. Their underlying reason was that the audit quality can't be compromised and additional procedures are done to ensure that a correct audit opinion may be given. Interviewee B4 said that:

> "On a quantitative basis, there may be few longer audits based on the complexity and additional procedures required on a client."

In addition, Interviewee B6 conveyed that it is well within the scope of the auditor's work:

> "I think not really as it's a part and parcel of change in the economy. New things get implemented, audit quality remains at the highest level and it can't be compromised. We will have to do additional procedures to achieve and maintain that audit quality which is required for us to give an opinion on the financial statements."

Interviewee B7 believes that rather than the audit quality, it will improve the quality of records from the business point of view:

> "It will however, make companies start maintaining proper records and they'll have to formalize a lot of things. So, it will help improve documentation from the company's side. So, it will help the companies more than the auditors."

Among the Non-Big-Four auditors, five out of nine interviewees believe that it will impact the audit quality and another said that it may impact the audit quality depending on the situation. It is worth noting that the Non-Big-Four interviewees who said that it resulted in improved audit quality, said so as a consequence of increased responsibility and work. Thus, the very definition of audit quality is unclear among many of the auditors even though they are professionally qualified.

For instance, Interviewee N4 said that: "Yes, because of the VAT, auditor's responsibility will increase and he will work with more efficiency." Interviewee N7 said that businesses disclose more information now, which in turn improves the audit quality:

> "Earlier the clients wouldn't provide much information saying that it is internal information but now they are ready to give all information due to compliance requirement. So, it will definitely increase the audit quality."

On the other hand, Interviewee N9 and two other interviewees said that the audit quality would be unaffected even if the audit isn't mandatory: "Quality of the audit can't be compromised whether there is a legal requirement or not." Thus, ten out of sixteen interviewees don't believe that implementation of VAT will impact the audit quality in any manner. It will simply result in additional procedures, time and effort. The Non-Big-Four auditors who believe that it would impact the quality did not provide justifications which reconciles with the audit quality definition, as is evident from their responses. Moreover, they mainly belong to the category who have 2-5 years of experience which may suggest that their limited experience may cause their statements to be less credible.

Audit job market

Pertaining to Question 4 in the interview, this theme questions how introduction of VAT in the UAE would impact the audit job market. Similar to the previous question, the responses were varied. Eight out of nine Non-Big-Four interviewees said that the audit job market would improve. On the other hand, six out of seven Big-Four interviewees said that there would be no impact. Their rationale was that rather than the audit job market, job creation would focus on tax specialists and other finance professionals.

Interviewee N9 also goes on to highlight the rise in significance of internal audit:

> "Yes, the opportunities will be more. Importance for accounts is larger now which increases their scope. Tax audits are not required so

auditors aren't directly issuing any report for tax purposes. However, at the same time, accounts have to be maintained properly and need to be checked so audit is required. In that way, more companies are proposing for auditing to make sure everything is in line. In specific, rather than statutory audit, internal audit has got more scope. So that's the biggest change in the audit field. Sometimes, in SMEs, they aren't able to employ full time accountants so they'll approach audit firms to do part-time book-keeping."

Contrary to such views, the interviewees said that the job market would cater to finance professionals and tax specialists as mentioned earlier. Interviewee B3 says that the impact would:

"Not on the audit job market but yes for finance professionals it will. There is a huge market out there for experienced professionals who come from an economy where VAT is prevalent. They can use their expertise and guide, and in particular has opened up jobs for people with an interest/expertise in tax matters. The inflow is mainly from any developed economy which has VAT."

Some of the auditors said that it is quite similar to the Goods and Services Tax (GST) which has been implemented in India. Thus, a lot of professionals are being brought in from India and other places with strong taxation background such as European nations. For example, Interviewee N2 said:

"Since India has already implemented GST and the basic underlying concepts are same, people are brought in from India. Indian market is definitely looked up to over here."

In addition, Interviewee B5 adds that: "They are coming in from jurisdictions that already had VAT type regime, such as the UK, India, many European countries, Greece etc." The justification for getting people from Europe was provided by Interviewee B6:

"The VAT Law is designed more in line with the European law so it was very useful to have someone from the European team come down and work with us. Some of them worked in the Revenue department as well so there was a dual benefit of getting them to work with us. This provided a lot of insights as the Law will not provide every detail and it is subject to interpretation."

Thus, with respect to job creation, the auditors have opposing views. This may be explained by the type of clients they deal with. The Non-Big-Four firms mostly deal with small and medium clients, who may require additional assistance from auditors as compared to the larger clientele dealt by the Big-Four. Moreover, in the Big-Four firms, a separate tax wing is in place to assist the taxation related matters. Thus, it does not impact the auditors. It is also clear that apart from training the existing staff, for the initial implementation phase, professionals have been recruited from countries with strong taxation settings such as India, UK, and Singapore etc. The findings from the interviews which expect job creation to occur are in line with the literature which says that VAT would create a new set of employment opportunities in oil-based economies (Khaleej Times, 2017).

Overall outlook on the audit profession

This theme relates to Question 5 of the interview which concludes the audit theme by asking what was the overall perception of the auditors regarding impact of introduction of VAT on the audit profession. Eleven of the sixteen interviewees said that the audit profession would be impacted positively, increase credibility and recognition due to VAT implementation. Businesses may value auditors and their work more out of fear of incurring penalties, as mentioned by Interviewee N7:

> "Earlier audits were important to avail bank loans or revise overdraft limits. Now the clients themselves want us to check everything thoroughly. Clients are scared of the penalties. For example, for an insurance client, the authority gave a fine of AED 75,000 for not recording it in the right format. So, the value of the audit profession has increased."

Though the audit isn't mandatory for taxation, businesses will still undertake it so as to avoid the aforementioned penalties. Interviewee N9 said that: "...companies will approach audit firms to do a tax audit before giving it to the FTA." Interviewee N6 said that if VAT isn't implemented and reviewed correctly, the entire business is impacted:

> "Right from sales to procurement, everyone is now getting affected. So, it brings everyone to a common platform. If I do something wrong, everyone in the chain goes wrong."

However, Interviewee N5 feels that the recognition would be higher for tax professionals rather than auditors:

> "I think tax consultants would be more valued than auditors because what clients want is knowledge and know-how of how to go about making entries and determining the VAT amount. Auditors will be recognized for checking how the VAT is calculated, the basis for calculation, whether it has been correctly calculated. However, to understand the entire concept, a tax consultant would be more recognized."

Interviewee N8 feels that for auditors to be more recognized, audits have to become mandatory or the FTA has to recognize the audits performed by the auditors. Contrastingly, Interviewee B5 said that VAT implementation wouldn't impact the audit profession much and that the impacts are limited to the first year:

"I don't think it would have any specific implication to the audit profession. It's not going to dramatically change the way we do work. In the first year, it's going to be an added effort to make sure it's all right. The first return will be quite important because if they don't get that right, it could be a problem. Going forward, it shouldn't have too much of an impact on the audit profession per se."

Though the responses are mixed, majority of the interviewees said that they expect the audit profession to be positively impacted and that the clients give them more recognition. Four of the sixteen interviewees said that there would not be any implications due to VAT implementation, primarily in the long-run.

Economy

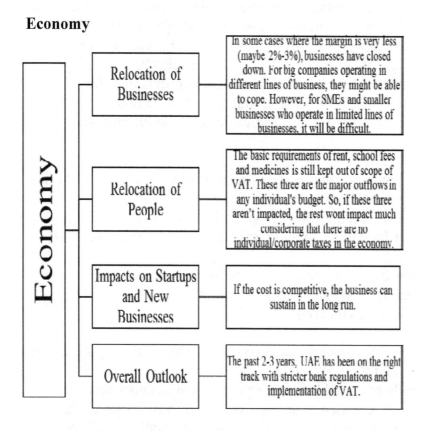

This theme analyzes how implementation of VAT will affect UAE's economy. Since it is a macro-level concept, three sub-themes were considered. The sub-themes are: relocation of businesses, relocation of people and impact on start-ups/new businesses. Finally, the overall perception of the auditors regarding impacts of introduction of VAT on the UAE economy is discussed.

Relocation of businesses

Relocation of businesses refers to the likelihood of businesses moving out of the UAE and pursuing trade in non-VAT nations, which forms Question 6 of the interview. Ten of the sixteen interviewees said that introduction of VAT would not cause businesses to move out of the UAE.

Six of the seven Big-Four auditors were of the view that it would not result in any relocation attributable to VAT. The underlying reasoning is that a VAT of 5% is very minimal as compared to other developed countries. Moreover, the tax burden ultimately falls on the consumer and businesses are simply the middlemen. However, Interviewee B7 gives an insight into the impacts on small businesses and free-zones saying:

> "To an extent that's true because we've seen a lot of small businesses have already started shutting down and they've already started moving out of UAE. Only time will tell how significant it is and how far this trend continues. However, initial evidence is that small businesses have started moving out. Free-zones may not be impacted significantly as they have VAT exempt. They just have to be careful with business with onshore companies where they have to levy VAT and claim the credit just as any other company."

Among the Non-Big-Four interviewees, there were diverse views on this matter. Interviewee N5 said that it would definitely impact businesses as:

> "They will need to get more experienced labour as well which is an additional cost. So already there isn't much revenues coming into the companies, adding in that additional cost would worsen it. They will have to implement new softwares, will have to do a whole bunch of changes in their accounting systems. Some cases where people are just working on loans or trade on a small scale, it would have an impact. At a macro level, it may have a high impact later or else people may get used to it since its just 5% or maybe the Government may increase VAT. At this point of time, it's a moderate situation. Since consumers don't want to buy due to higher prices, the sales are going down."

Specific to the jewellery and diamond industry, Interviewee N9 said that: "From the Gold and Diamonds Parks itself there was a news prior to VAT becoming effective, that a lot of companies started moving to Hong Kong." Interviewee N8 mentioned some of the possible segments which may be impacted negatively due to introduction of VAT in the UAE:

> "In some cases where the margin is very less (maybe 2%-3%), businesses have closed down. For big companies operating in different lines of business, they might be able to cope. However, for SMEs and smaller businesses who operate in limited lines of businesses, it will be difficult. There are chances of UAE not being chosen as a re-export hub. Mainly procurement business has taken a hit. Some businesses may not want to be transparent so they may also think twice."

On the other hand, the concept of fees has been prevalent in the UAE which is not very different from tax. Interviewee N6 said that:

> "In the case of the hospitality industry, we assume there are no taxes but they have other forms such as tourism and municipal fees. So, they are already dealing with it. So, for some industries it is quite easy and they can adapt to their existing practices while some industries such as the real estate where only a system of contracts existed without the use of invoices, may face challenges. Even for banks, issuance of invoices is not a practice till now but going forward they will have to do it. Adaptation to these things might be complex but it doesn't mean businesses will move out of the economy."

Similar to the opinion of Big-Four interviewees, some of the Non-Big-Four interviewees also said that 5% is a very small rate as compared to other nations. However, if the Government plans to introduce corporate taxes, it may impact the economy and businesses may decide to relocate to their home country.

Thus, the general agreement is that VAT is unlikely to drive businesses out of the UAE with the exception of small businesses. As mentioned in the literature, if businesses have the means to handle overseas trade, they would base their business in places with low VAT (Newark, 2006). UAE has the lowest rate of VAT globally so it would continue to be a business hub. Corporate tax, however, may have a significant role in relocation of businesses, which will impact the economy at large as well.

Relocation of people

This theme refers to Question 7 of the interview which asked whether the interviewees thought that introduction of VAT would cause people to quit their jobs and relocate to other countries, under the premise that salaries have not increased commensurately. Nine of the sixteen respondents said that they do not expect people to leave their jobs and move to another country, solely because of VAT. It may be the case that they were considering moving out and VAT just gave them the necessary push.

Moreover, as mentioned in the previous theme, VAT in the UAE stands at the lowest rate globally. Most nations have a tax of 20%-30% and may even have corporate and income taxes. In light of these factors, it is highly unlikely for people to shift due to a VAT of 5%. Interviewee N2 said that:

> "...the basic requirements of rent, school fees and medicines is still kept out of scope of VAT. These three are the major outflows in any individual's budget. So, if these three aren't impacted, the rest wont impact much considering that there are no individual/corporate taxes in the economy."

Interviewee N8 said that currently only around one-third of an individual budget is subject to a 5% increase. However, if the VAT rate increases to around 10% for instance, people may move out of the UAE. The likely impact on the economy would be in the form of cautious spending by the public as stated by Interviewee N9:

> "Before 2008, no one bothered about the costs as the potential of the city was quite high. After the financial crisis, everyone was at risk of losing their job, so people started thinking of their costs. Now when VAT came into the picture, people are even more cautious about costs."

On the other hand, Interviewee N5 said that majority of the population consists of expats who come to the UAE to earn money and make savings. This perspective may also be explained by the gender bias caused by VAT (Khaleej Times, 2017) as female products are generally more expensive than that of men. If they don't receive any benefits in return, people may consider moving out of the country as it is simply an added cost for them. She said that:

> "At a macro level, I feel it'll work only till Expo 2020, but after that it's all going to go downhill."

Countering this point, Interviewee N6 mentions that the general public do benefit in the form of public services and improved standards of living. This is in agreement with the literature which points out that the funds will be used for improving public services such as schools, roads and waste management (Ministry of Finance, 2017).

Overall, the respondents don't expect people to move out of the UAE due to introduction of VAT. As mentioned by Interviewee N2, the literature also highlights that education, healthcare and key food items will not fall under the scope of VAT. It may be the case only when income tax or corporate tax comes into the picture. However, people have become more cautious when it comes to spending, which will in turn impact the economy negatively. It is worth noting that most of the female respondents looked at this question from an individual budget perspective while the male respondents looked at it through a macro lens wherein they compared the VAT rate in the UAE to that of other nations.

Impact on start-ups and new businesses

Pertaining to Question 8 of the interview, this theme evaluates whether VAT will be a deterrent to start-ups and new businesses in the UAE, from the perspective of auditors. Overall, nine out of sixteen interviewees said that introduction of VAT would not be a deterrent to start-ups or new businesses in the UAE. It is worth noting that among the Big-Four respondents, six of the seven interviewees agreed with the aforementioned opinion. The Non-Big-Four interviewees had an equally mixed opinion.

The rationale behind the consensus is that the ultimate burden falls on the consumer in most cases. The business hardly incurs any costs due to VAT. Moreover, start-ups will imbibe VAT into their costing right from the beginning, so it is easier for them rather than existing businesses. Interviewee N9 said that:

> "Until they reach a turnover of AED 375,000 they need not register for VAT. Secondly, since they are new, they will comply with the regulations from the beginning itself."

Interviewee B7 said that start-ups wouldn't be impacted but it would also depend on the industry within which they operate. He said: "FMCG sector will continue to perform well but luxury goods such as jewellery, automotive retailers are getting impacted big time." Adding onto this, Interviewee N5 said that even though restaurants and food industries come under the taxable category, they will continue to grow as people will continue to eat out. Interviewee N8 also had a viewpoint similar to that of Interviewee B7 and said that:

> "...those who are into designing or structuring, the Government is promoting digital world, artificial intelligence etc. So, they can do well and it won't affect their returns. However, for trading companies and those with thin margins, it will be quite difficult to start. Businesses may be able to roll the costs onto the customer but they have to always check international pricing. If the cost is competitive, the business can sustain in the long run."

Citing the example of free-zones, Interviewee N6 said that free-zones expected that VAT would not be applicable to them. However, in reality, there are only few designated areas and within those, only few transactions which are VAT exempt. Interviewee N7 added to this saying that:

> "Free-zones will only be impacted if they transact with the mainland. Around 30%-40% of free-zones are Saudi based entities etc. So, they may choose to retain operations in their own country. In the Jebel Ali Free-zone, around 20%-30% are expected to be vacated in the next 2-3 months."

Thus, majority of the interviewees are of the opinion that VAT will not be a deterrent to start-ups/new businesses in the UAE, especially if they belong to the FMCG industry. However, it depends on the business model, scale of operation and margins. Possibly the free-zone entities may be negatively impacted to an extent.

Overall outlook on the economy
Lastly, Question 9 of the interview attempts to gauge the overall perception of the interviewees regarding implications of VAT implementation on the UAE economy. Nine of the sixteen interviewees said that VAT would have a positive impact on the economy. They said that it was the need of the hour and a measure which UAE had

to take to ensure sustainable growth. None of the Big-Four interviewees felt that there would be any negative impact on the economy.

From a business perspective, majority of the interviewees were of the opinion that VAT would result in greater transparency. Another reasoning provided was that the UAE implemented VAT to exit from the tax-haven countries list. Interviewee N8 said that:

> "If they want to achieve something similar to Singapore, for example, greater transparency is required. The past 2-3 years, UAE has been on the right track with stricter bank regulations and implementation of VAT. Moreover, the financial profession will also get due recognition which wasn't present earlier."

Contrasting the majority, Interviewee N5 said that:

> "People come here for a vacations/tourism and this is what Dubai is based on. Other countries where VAT is implemented, VAT return can be filed after you leave the country. No such regulation is there in the UAE. In the long run, it may be a negative outcome."

Some of the respondents said that the main challenge businesses faced was that the VAT Law was released quite late (just one month before it was made effective). Moreover, the Law is subject to various interpretations. Interviewee N6 said that:

> "...designated zones list got released only in the first week of January. So that one week people are not aware what is to be done."

Thus, majority of the auditors are of the opinion that VAT will have a positive impact on the UAE economy and that it will lead to sustainable growth. The findings are in line with the literature review which identified international tax competition as one of the reasons for implementation of VAT (Weller and Rao, 2010). Moreover, Keen and Lockwood (2007) found that VAT results in GDP growth which is similar to the opinion held by the auditors.

Though at a personal level their cost of living is slightly higher, they recognize that VAT is a need of the hour which is once again in agreement with the literature which pointed to the role of IMF in encouraging VAT implementation. Contrasting opinions were also noted especially with respect to the possible decline in the tourism industry which is one of the main revenue generators for the UAE.

5. Conclusion

This paper aimed to analyze the perceptions of the auditors about impacts of VAT implementation on the audit profession as well as the economy in the UAE. The overall perception of the first theme (audit) was that there isn't a material impact on the profession. However, audit as a whole is being valued more, particularly by small enterprises. Most of the respondents agreed to the fact that VAT would not result in an increase or decrease in audit quality as the quality is something which cannot be compromised. VAT is just an additional area of work which increases the auditors' responsibilities and timeline. The role of the auditor is to ensure that the VAT amounts are computed correctly and that the VAT requirements are complied with.

The analysis was able to identify various issues faced by the auditors during the implementation stage. The nature of the issue and its significance depended on the industry as well as type of business, cash flow management etc. The Non-Big-Four auditors were able to give more insight on this sub-theme as they deal with a lot of SME clients who faced relatively more issues than the bigger companies.

The auditors however were of the general view that VAT on its own would not cause businesses to shut down their operations in the UAE and pursue trade in other countries. It may impact the start-ups if they work on low margins or in luxury goods sectors such as diamond and jewellery. The auditors are quite optimistic that people will accept the VAT as part of their normal lives and that there is no major outflow from their budget as basic necessities lie outside the chargeable category. However, if and when corporate taxes come into the picture, people may reconsider living in the UAE. In other words, VAT is perceived to be supportive the UAE's economy. Overall, most auditors appreciate that VAT was a need of the hour for the UAE Government and that it will lead to a sustainable growth in the GDP, however, its impact on inflation remains a crucial factor which only time will tell.

The overall conclusion that can be drawn from this research is that VAT does not materially impact the audit profession. There are contrasting views concerning the impacts on the audit plan. However, an undisputed opinion regarding additional audit procedures existed wherein all auditors acknowledged that VAT implementation would definitely result in added procedures. Furthermore, rather than the audit job market, job creation is larger for tax specialists and accounting/finance professionals. For the implementation of VAT, tax specialists are being recruited from countries with a strong taxation background such as India, UK, Singapore etc.

Most auditors are optimistic about VAT implementation in the UAE and believe that it will lead to sustainable economic growth in the long run. For small and medium clients, VAT has resulted in the proper upkeep of books of accounts and more transparent dealings. Furthermore, they value the auditors to a greater extent. The general consensus was that VAT on its own is highly unlikely to drive out businesses and people from the UAE, barring some exceptions such as low-margin businesses. They also believed that VAT isn't necessarily a deterrent to start-ups and new businesses in the UAE.

6. Limitations and further research

One of the limitations faced while conducting this research is the shortage of literature regarding impact of VAT on the audit profession. Even with respect to the UAE, previous studies have looked at it from a consumer/ business perspective. Secondly, the sample size was limited to only sixteen auditors due to the time constraints. Purposive sampling requires the researcher to use his/her judgment which may lead to bias.

Furthermore, qualitative research is quite subjective as well as prone to error and bias. In specific, the electronic interviews lack non-verbal aspects. Most of the respondents who used Google Forms gave short responses which affect the depth of the study. Since VAT has just been implemented, some of the insights given may be short-term which may lead to misleading conclusions. If the same study is conducted after the first cycle of VAT filings, it may give a better picture.

Further studies can look at the same research topic from the perspective of regulatory bodies such as the Federal Tax Authority (FTA). By the end of this year, a quantitative study can be done on the level of compliance of VAT by businesses. An attention-grabbing research may take the form of impacts of introduction of VAT in the UAE on the inflation rate. At the macro level, another research topic could be to evaluate the extent to which the funds collected by VAT are employed in improving public facilities and infrastructures. Research can evaluate the revenue pie of the UAE before and after VAT implementation. A comparative study can be done on the impacts of VAT implementation in the UAE and the Kingdom of Saudi Arabia.

Industry-specific researches may also be undertaken such as in the jewellery and real-estate sectors which have been significantly impacted at the implementation stage. Lastly, research can also evaluate the implications of VAT implementation on the tourism industry as UAE is predominantly a tourist destination.

References

Al Murad, M. (2017) *VAT systems in the United Arab Emirates, thoughts of the implementation from the general public and organizations perspective*, Heriot-Watt University, Dissertation.

Atkinson, A. & Stiglitz, J. (1972) "The structure of indirect taxation and economic efficiency", *Journal of Public Economics*, 1(1): 97-119

Bird, R.M. (2005) *Value added taxes in developing and transitional countries: Lessons and questions*, First Global International Tax Dialogue Conference on VAT, Rome: International Tax Dialogue.

BP (2017) *BP Statistical Review of World Energy* [online] BP. Available at: https://www.bp.com/content/dam/bp/en/corporate/pdf/energy-economics/statistical-review-2017/bp-statistical-review-of-world-energy-2017-full-report.pdf [Accessed 14 Mar. 2018].

Braun, V. & Clarke, V. (2006) "Using thematic analysis in psychology", *Qualitative Research in Psychology*, 3 (2): 77-101

Bryman, A. & Bell, E. (2011) *Business research methods*, 3rd ed. Oxford: Oxford University Press

Charlet, A., & Buydens, S. (2012) "The OECD international VAT/GST Guidelines: Past and Future Developments", *World Journal of VAT/GST Law*, 1 (2):175-184

Charlet, A., & Owens, J. (2010) "An international perspective on VAT", *Tax Notes International*, 59 (12): 943-954

Dawson, C. (2006) *A practical guide to research methods*, 2nd ed. Oxford: How to Books

Decoster, A. (2005) "How progressive are indirect taxes in Russia?", *The Economics of Transition*, 13 (4): 705-729

Denscombe, M. (2014) *The good research guide*. McGraw-Hill Education (UK)

Denzin, N. & Lincoln, Y. (2005) *The Sage Handbook of Qualitative Research*, 3rd ed. London: Sage

Desai, M. & Hines Jr., J. (2005) "Value-added taxes and international trade: The evidence", working paper, The University of Michigan Law School

Dewhurst, F. (2002) *Quantitative Methods for Business and Management*, Berkshire: McGraw-Hill Education.

Ebrill, L., Keen, M., Bodin, J. & Summers, V. (2001) *The Modern VAT*, International Monetary Fund

Eisenhardt, K. & Graebner, M. (2007) "Theory building from cases: Opportunities and challenges", *Academy of Management Journal*, 50 (1): 25-32

Filmer, D. & Pritchett, L. (1999) "The effect of household wealth on educational attainment: Evidence from 35 countries", *Population and Development Review*, 25 (1): 85-120

Finn, M., Elliot-White, M. & Walton, M. (2000) *Tourism & Leisure Research Methods: data collection, analysis and interpretation*, Essex: Pearson Education Limited

Gauthier, B. & Wane, W. (2008) "Leakage of public resources in the health sector: An empirical investigation of Chad", *Journal of African Economies*, 18(1): 52-83

Gilder, B. (2017) "Effects of value added taxation on consumers and businesses in the United Arab Emirates, Heriot-Watt University

Gober, J.R. & Burns, J.O. (1997) "The relationship between tax structures and economic indicators, *Journal of International Accounting, Auditing and Taxation*, 6 (1): 1-24

Greeff, W. (2015) "Organizational diversity: making the case for contextual interpretivism", *Equality, Diversity and Inclusion: An International Journal*, 34 (6): 496-509

Grimsley, R. (1973) "Management control of VAT", *Retail and Distribution Management*, [online] 1 (1): 32-34 [Accessed 12 Oct. 2017]

Grinberg, I. (2009) "Where credit is due? Advantages of the credit-invoice method for a partial replacement VAT", Washington D.C.: American Tax Policy Institute Conference, pp. 309-358

Hajdúchová, I., Sedliačiková, M. & Viszlai, I. (2015) "Value-added tax impact on the state budget expenditures and incomes". *Procedia Economics and Finance,* 34: 676-681

Harper, J. (1995) "VAT on the transfer of a business as a going concern", P*roperty Management*, [online] 13 (3): 16-20 [Accessed 15 Oct. 2017]

Holloway, I. (1997) *Basic Concepts for Qualitative Research*, Oxford: Blackwell Science Ltd

ICAI (2017) *Background Material on UAE VAT - Federal Decree Law (No.8) 2017*, 1st ed. New Delhi: The Institute of Chartered Accountants of India, 1-10

IMF (2013) Regional Economic Outlook: Middle East and Central Asia. [online] Washington. [Accessed 20 Oct. 2017]

IMF (2015) United Arab Emirates - Selected Issues [online] 5-12 [Accessed 14 Oct. 2017]

Jenkins, G., Jenkins, H. & Kuo, C. (2006) "Is the value added tax naturally progressive?", *SSRN Electronic Journal* [Accessed 16 Oct. 2017]

Kalas, B. & Milenkovic, N. (2017) "The role of value added tax in the economy of Serbia", *Ekonomika*, 63 (2): 69-78

Kamrudin, M. (2012) "Effect of vat and tax on economy: An analysis in the context of Bangladesh", *Research Journal of Finance and Accounting*, 3 (7): 64-70

Keen, M. (2007) VAT Attacks! IMF Working Papers, 07(142)

Keen, M. (2008) "VAT, tariffs and withholding: Border taxes and informality in developing countries", *Journal of Public Economics*, 92 (10-11): 1892-1906

Keen, M. (2013) The Anatomy of the VAT, International Monetary Fund, IMF Working Paper 13/111, Washington, D.C. retrieved at: https://www.imf.org /external/pubs/ft/wp/2013/wp13111.pdf

Keen, M. & Lockwood, B. (2007) "The value-added tax: Its causes and consequences", *IMF Working Papers*, 07 (183): 1

Khaleej Times (2017) IMF highlights uncertainty over simultaneous introduction of VAT across GCC. [online] Available at: https://www.khaleejtimes.com/ region/mena/imf-highlights-uncertainty-over-simultaneous-introduction-of-vat-across-gcc [Accessed 31 Oct. 2017]

Kim, J., Choi, B., Shin, H. & Kim, H. (2007) "A methodology for constructing of philosophy ontology based on philosophical texts", *Computer Standards & Interfaces*, 29 (3): 302-315

Kundnaney, C. (2017) "Is VAT more of a burden for women than men?" Khaleej Times. [online] Available at: https://www.khaleejtimes.com/business/vat-in-uae/is-vat-more-of-a-burden-for-women-than-men- [Accessed 30 Oct. 2017]

Lee, B., Collier, P. & Cullen, J. (2007) "Reflections on the use of case studies in the accounting, management and organizational disciplines", *Qualitative Research in Organizations and Management: An International Journal,* 2 (3): 169-178

Liamputtong, P. (2013) *Qualitative Research Methods*, 4th ed. Victoria: Oxford University Press

Ministry of Finance (2017) VAT [online] [Accessed 13 Nov. 2017].

Morgan, S.J. & Symon, G. (2004) "Electronic interviews in organizational research", in C. Cassell and G. Symon (eds), *Essential Guide to Qualitative Methods in Organizational Research*, London: Sage, n/a (n/a):3-33.

Munoz, S. & Cho, S.W. (2003) "Social impact of tax reform: The case of Ethiopia", IMF Working Paper No. 03/232, Washington, D.C.: International Monetary Fund

Nair, D. (2017) "Time for a VAT realty check", Khaleej Times [online] Available at: https://www.khaleejtimes.com/business/vat-in-uae/time-for-a-vat-realty-check [Accessed 17 Oct. 2017]

Neher, W. (1997) *Organizational communication*, 1st ed. Boston: Allyn and Bacon

Nellor, D. (1987) "The effect of the value-added tax on the tax ratio", *IMF Working Paper*, 87 (47): 1-28

Neuman, W. (2005) *Social Research Methods*, 6th ed. London: Pearson

Niglas, K., Tashakkori, A. & Teddlie, C. (2010) *Sage handbook of mixed methods in social & behavioral research*, 1st ed. Los Angeles, Calif.: SAGE Publications, pp. : 215-236

Onwuchekwa, J.C. & Aruwa, S.A.S. (2014) "Value added tax and economic growth in Nigeria", *European Journal of Accounting Auditing and Finance Research*, 2 (8): 62-69

Pantazi, F., & Strǎoanu, B.M. (2011) "Fiscal and social-economic coordinates in the analysis of the salary policy in Romania", *Procedia – Social and Behavioral Science,* 15: 806-811

President's Advisory Panel on Federal Tax Reform (2006) President's Advisory Panel on Federal Tax Reform [online] [Accessed 14 Oct. 2017].

Pwc (2015) *Doing Business in the UAE: A tax and legal guide*, Available at: https://www.pwc.com/m1/en/tax/documents/doing-business-guides/doing-business-guide-uae.pdf [Accessed 8 Jan. 2018].

Pwc (2017) *An introduction to value added tax in the GCC*, Available at: https://www.pwc.com/m1/en/tax/documents/what-is-vat-faq-on-vat-in-the-gcc.pdf [Accessed 8 Jan. 2018]

Ramsey, F. (1927) "A contribution to the theory of taxation", *The Economic Journal,* 37 (145): 47

Sadka, E. (1977) "A theorem on uniform taxation", *Journal of Public Economics,* 7 (3): 387-391

Saunders, M., Lewis, P. & Thornhill, A. (2012) *Research Methods for Business Students*, 6th ed. Pearson.

Shenk, A. & Oldman, O. (2007) *Value added tax: A comparative approach*, New York: Cambridge University Press

Silverman, D. (2005) *Doing qualitative research*, 2nd ed. London: SAGE Publications Ltd

Simionescu, M. & Albu, L. (2016) "The impact of standard value added tax on economic growth in CEE-5 countries: econometric analysis and simulations", *Technological and Economic Development of Economy*, 22 (6): 850-866

Statement by the Hon. Mubarak Rashed Al Mansoori, Governor of the Fund for the United Arab Emirates (2017) [ebook] IMF [Accessed 18 Oct. 2017]

Stoilova, D. (2017) "Tax structure and economic growth: Evidence from the European Union", *Contaduríay Administración*, 62 (3): 1041-1057

Symon, G. & Cassell, C. (2012) *Qualitative Organizational Research*, London: SAGE

Weller, C. & Rao, M. (2010) "Progressive Tax Policy and Economic Stability", *Journal of Economic Issues*, 44 (3): 629-659

Xing, W. & Whalley, J. (2014) "The Golden Tax Project, value-added tax statistics, and the analysis of internal trade in China", *China Economic Review*, 30: 448-458

Yanow, D. & Ybema, S. (2009) "Interpretivism in organizational research: on elephants and blind researchers", in Buchanan D.A. & Bryman, A. (Eds), *The Sage Handbook of Organizational Research Methods*, Sage, Thousand Oaks, CA, pp. 39-60.

Zee, H., (2008) "Aspects of interjurisdictional sharing of the value-added tax", *Public Finance Review*, 36 (2): 147-168

Permissions

List of Contributors

Volkan Demir and Oğuzhan Bahadir
Galatasaray University, Istanbul, Turkey

Slobodan Kacanski
Roskilde University, Denmark

Peter Ellis
University of Queensland, Australia

Costel Istrate
Alexandru Ioan Cuza University of Iaşi, România

Ömer Faruk Güleç
Hacettepe University, Turkey

Mostafa Kamal Hassan
University of Sharjah and on leave from Alexandria University, Egypt

Alhassan Musah and Erasmus Dodzi Gakpetor
Dominion University College, Ghana

Fred Kwasi Anokye
University of Ghana, Legon

Fatih Coşkun Ertaş and Atila Karkacıer
Gaziosmanpasa University, Tokat, Turkey

Aisha Saderuddin and Yasser Barghathi
Heriot-Watt University Dubai, UAE

Index

CPSIA information can be obtained
at www.ICGtesting.com
Printed in the USA
BVHW051706180820
586707BV00004B/129